Meech Lake and Canada
Perspectives from the West

MEECH LAKE
AND CANADA

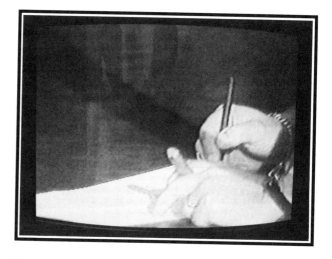

Perspectives from
THE WEST

EDITED BY
Roger Gibbins
WITH
Howard Palmer
Brian Rusted
David Taras

Published by **Academic Printing & Publishing**, Edmonton, Alberta, Canada

Canadian Cataloguing in Publication Data

Main entry under title:
Meech Lake and Canada

Includes bibliographical references.
  ISBN 0-920980-40-6 (bound).
  ISBN 0-920980-41-4 (pbk.).

  1. Canada. Constitution Act, 1982. 2. Federal-provincial relations -
Canada. 3. Canada - Constitutional law - Amendments. 4. Federal
government - Canada. I. Gibbins, Roger, 1947-
KE4184.M43 1988   342.71'03   C88-091455-6

©1988 Academic Printing & Publishing
Cover design by Ottilie Sanderson
Printed by Art Design Printing Inc., Edmonton, Alberta, Canada

TABLE OF CONTENTS

VII The Road Ahead

PREFACE

This project began in August of 1987 at a summer social gathering to welcome Roger Gibbins and his family back from their sabbatical leave in Australia. Throughout that evening, the subject of Meech Lake came up again and again. Those present discussed the magnitude of the changes that were occurring in the constitutional realm, and expressed frustration over the lack of public debate in Alberta concerning the Meech Lake Accord. The provincial Conservative government's decision not to hold public hearings, and the Alberta media's seeming lack of interest in the subject appeared to effectively choke off public debate. It was decided that a debate on the merits of the 1987 Constitutional Accord be held at the University of Calgary sometime during the fall term. It was soon realized that one debate was hardly enough to deal with the scope, complexity, and possible consequences of the new constitutional changes. After considerable planning and support gained from across the University of Calgary, a full day conference entitled Second Thoughts On Meech Lake: A Conference on Political Process was held in November 1987. Brian Rusted (Director of the pilot centre for Canadian Studies and Communications, Faculty of General Studies), Roger Gibbins (Political Science), Howard Palmer (History) and David Taras (Canadian Studies) were the members of the organizing committee. Janice Hillmo of the pilot centre did a magnificent job ensuring that abstract thoughts became concrete realities. She was indispensable in preparing and planning the conference. David Robinson worked effectively as a research assistant supplying not only needed background material but helpful advice. Sponsors included the Departments of History and Political Science, the Faculties of Continuing Education, General Studies and Social Science, the Master's programme in Communication Studies, and the University of Calgary's Special Projects Fund. Special thanks should go in particular to Deans Marsha Hanen and Anthony Rasporich for their useful advice and enthusiastic participation.

This book is largely the result of the Second Thoughts Conference in which an attempt was made to strike a balance between supporters and opponents of the Accord. Unfortunately, repeated efforts to get provincial and federal government spokespersons to defend the Accord were largely unsuccessful, although we were fortunate that Norman Riddell and Claude Rocan of the Saskatchewan government agreed to speak at the conference. As a consequence we have supplemented the conference proceedings with commissioned papers on important aspects of the debate which were not fully addressed at the conference.

The book's aim, then, is to reveal more fully and poignantly the responses in Western Canada to the 1987 Constitutional Accord – perspectives that may have been lost in the rush of governments and politicians to close the Meech Lake deal. The book is also intended to stir thoughts and consciences and to pose critical questions to all Canadians. The hope first raised on a late summer's night in Calgary was for just such an examination.

Introduction to Constitutional Politics

> *Tonight Canada is whole again, the Canadian family is together again, and the nation is one again.*
> Brian Mulroney.[1]

> *In seeking this agreement with the full and essential participation of all the provinces, we all carried out the national will. We were not struggling against one another, we were struggling together to obtain something for our mutual benefit. There were no losers. The nation, with its strengthened constitutional fabric, is clearly the winner.* Ray Hnatyshyn.[2]

> *The Accord is a seamless web and an integrated whole.* Lowell Murray.[3]

INTRODUCTION TO CONSTITUTIONAL POLITICS

The Meech Lake Accord represents the second major set of revisions to Canada's constitutional structure to have taken place during the 1980s. Although one might argue that the Constitution Act of 1982, and more specifically the Charter of Rights and Freedoms embedded with the Act, will have a greater impact on the daily lives of Canadian citizens, the Meech Lake Accord has the potential to transform the shape of government in Canada. Whereas the Constitution Act primarily addressed the relationship between citizens and their governments, the Accord attempts to redefine the relationship among governments in the Canadian federal state. In the long run, changes to that relationship could have a profound impact on the character of Canadian political life, and thus on the lives of Canadians.

The Meech Lake Accord merits close examination as much for the process of constitutional change that it embodies as it does for its written text. In the analysis which follows, the political process surrounding the origins and ratification of the Accord receives as much attention as the Accord's formal content. In part this reflects a growing unease with the emerging style and form of constitutional politics in Canada; in part it reflects an unease with the impact of the Accord on the Canadian political process in the years ahead. It may also reflect the famous observation by Marshall McLuhan that 'the medium is the message.' For many of the contributors to this collection, the message to be drawn from the Meech Lake medium is as unsettling as anything contained within the Accord itself. That message, the vision of the Canadian political community projected by the Accord, is a troublesome one for many western Canadians reflecting upon their region, their country, and the interplay between the two.

Constitutional Politics in the 1980s

The Meech Lake Accord is the product of a long, even tortuous process of constitutional change that finds its roots in the 1960s. At that
time a constellation of factors opened up the Canadian constitution
to intensive scrutiny and emotional political debate. An increasingly
assertive nationalist movement in Quebec, resurgent regional unrest
in western Canada, a growing concern with the protection of individual
rights associated in part with the American civil rights movement, the
nationalism associated with Canada's centennial celebrations in 1967,
dramatic legislative initiatives to redefine and restructure the linguistic character of Canada and Quebec, regionally unbalanced federal
governments, and incessant intergovernmental conflict across a broad
front were just some of the factors which led Canadians to question
existing constitutional arrangements.

Thus for close to twenty years Canadians both inside and outside
government were involved in a wide-ranging and frequently acrimonious constitutional debate that touched virtually all aspects of Canadian political life. That debate was finally brought to a head by the 1980
sovereignty-association referendum in Quebec, and by the commitment
of the federal Liberal government to pursue a 'renewed federalism'
should Quebec voters defeat the referendum. When the federalist option prevailed, Ottawa and the ten provincial governments were
plunged into an intensive set of constitutional negotiations which ultimately culminated in the Constitution Act, proclaimed by Queen
Elizabeth on April 17, 1982. However, on that rainy day in Ottawa,
only ten of the country's eleven first ministers were on hand to sign
the Act. Quebec's Premier René Levesque refused to sign and, in this
symbolic gesture, left the constitutional settlement incomplete. Although the Constitution Act was legally binding on the Quebec government and public, its legitimacy within Quebec had not been secured.

By entrenching language rights which had first been expressed in
the Official Languages Act of 1969, the Constitution Act shored up the
rights of francophone minorities outside Quebec and the anglophone
minority inside Quebec in a way consistent with the liberal, individualistic tenor of the Charter of Rights and Freedoms. However, the Constitution Act did not address the constitutional position of Quebec
within the Canadian federal state, and for that matter said very little
about intergovernmental relations and the constitutional division of
powers among governments. In this sense, and in its failure to define
the Aboriginal rights which it entrenched, the Constitution Act was
incomplete. Although one could argue that the Act's silence on Quebec was in itself a constitutional statement reflecting Pierre Trudeau's
stress on individual rights and his consistent opposition to any spe-

cial constitutional status for Quebec, the fact remains that the major source of political instability within the Canadian federal state since the mid 1960s — the constitutional status of Quebec — had not been addressed.

It was this loose end that was taken up by the governments of Canada after the retirements of Pierre Trudeau and René Levesque, and after the defeat of the federal Liberals in 1984 and the Parti Québécois in 1985. Brian Mulroney's election in 1984 brought a leader to the federal government who had not been a central or even active player in the prolonged constitutional debate leading up to the Constitution Act, and who was not committed to the national and political vision upon which the Act had been constructed. Robert Bourassa's election in 1985 brought to the Quebec government a premier committed to federalism, but also one determined to achieve nationalist objectives for Quebec which his predecessor had not achieved in the negotiations leading up to the Constitution Act.

While these changes in leadership put in place the preconditions for the Meech Lake Accord, the eleven First Ministers were brought back to the negotiating table by a number of more pragmatic considerations. Quebec's refusal to participate in constitutional conferences made any future fine-tuning of the constitution very difficult to accomplish, a matter of some considerable concern to those interested in, for example, the further constitutional entrenchment of Aboriginal rights or the reform of federal institutions such as the Senate. Quebec's blanket use of the section 33 notwithstanding clause threatened to undermine the political legitimacy of the Charter in Quebec, while the Act's amending formula coupled with Quebec's refusal to participate gave Ontario in effect a veto on constitutional change. There is also little question that Prime Minister Mulroney was determined to show that he could deliver in Quebec where Trudeau had failed, that he could bring Quebec into the constitutional family and, in doing so, cement his party's newly found electoral grip on Quebec. For his part, Premier Robert Bourassa was determined to prove to nationalist forces in Quebec that a federalist premier could deliver, that he could secure a place for Quebec in Canada while at the same time projecting and enhancing the political autonomy of Quebec. Thus with the First Ministers of Canada and Quebec ready to deal, the other premiers were lured back to constitutional negotiations, albeit rather low-keyed negotiations kept well away from public light until success was assured.

In June 1985, the Bourassa government set out five conditions which, if met, would enable Quebec to sign the Constitution Act. The conditions were the recognition of Quebec as a distinct society, a restriction on the federal government's spending power in areas of exclusive provincial jurisdiction, a Quebec veto on constitutional change,

Quebec's participation in appointments to the Supreme Court of Canada, and constitutional entrenchment of Quebec's existing role in immigration. In August, 1986, the ten provincial premiers stated in the Edmonton Declaration that their first constitutional priority was to commence negotiations on the five conditions set out by Quebec. These negotiations, which were conducted with little public knowledge much less fanfare, led to a meeting of the First Ministers at Meech Lake, Quebec, on April 30, 1987.

At that time the basics of the constitutional agreement were put in place and, at the conclusion of the meeting, the Meech Lake Accord was announced to the public. After limited public discussion and parliamentary debate, the First Ministers met in Ottawa on June 2nd and 3rd to consider a number of modifications to the initial text. In an all-night session in the Langevin Block, and after a number of amendments to the initial Accord were hammered out, an agreement was reached and signed by Prime Minister Mulroney and the ten provincial premiers. As this volume goes to press, that agreement has now been ratified by Parliament, over the objections of the Senate, and by the legislative assemblies of Alberta, Nova Scotia, Prince Edward Island, Saskatchewan and Quebec. The Accord will become part of the constitutional fabric of the Canadian federal state if it is ratified by the remaining five provinces by June, 1990.

In one sense, the Accord can be seen as the endpoint in a long and often tortuous constitutional journey, one that ties up a number of 'loose ends' left hanging by the Constitution Act. In another sense, however, the Meech Lake Accord should be seen as a waystation on a longer constitutional journey that stretches back to Confederation and, in all likelihood, forward into the next century. While the Accord will, if ratified, settle several constitutional issues, it will also open up a new constitutional agenda with its provisions for annual constitutional conferences dealing with, among other things, Senate reform and 'the roles and responsibilities in relation to fisheries.' From this perspective, then, the Accord is part of the evolving constitutional framework for the Canadian federal state, a constitutional journey without end but not without form and structure.

While there might be some concern about presenting an analysis of the Accord before it has even been ratified, we would argue that the Accord is too important a development to wait. As many of the essays in this collection point out, much of what is important about the Accord is the process through which it was created and through which it is being ratified, an importance which will persist no matter what the eventual fate of the Accord might be. It should also be stressed that the Accord is important for what it says about Canada, about the nature of both the national community and the provincial communities which are embedded within it. Regardless of its eventual fate, the Accord demands examination for the vision of Canada which it embodies, a vision that invites debate.

In a fundamental way, the Meech Lake Accord challenges the vision of Canada expounded by Pierre Elliott Trudeau, a vision that not only guided Trudeau's political career but which also found partial embodiment in the 1982 Constitution Act. Not surprisingly, Trudeau was drawn out of political retirement to defend his vision and to attack the Accord, first in his article in *La Presse* and *The Toronto Star*, then in his August 1987 testimony before the Parliamentary hearings on the Accord, and finally in his March 1988 testimony before the Senate hearings on the Accord in which he argued that if the Accord was not 'put out in the dustbin,' then 'in vain we would have dreamt the dream of one Canada.'⁴ Mr. Trudeau's outspoken opposition played an important role in galvanizing those groups – women, ethnic and linguistic minorities, natives and some Liberals – who had doubts about the Accord but were hesitant to break with the governmental consensus on Meech Lake.

While Trudeau's attack on the Accord is thus worthy of note in its own right, it has also played a role in shaping regional perceptions of the Accord in Western Canada. Note, for example, an Edmonton speech by Alberta Premier Don Getty to the annual convention of the provincial Progressive Conservative party. 'While I knew the accord was good,' Getty told approximately 2,400 convention delegates, 'after Mr. Trudeau's intervention I'm certain it's one hell of a deal.'⁵ In this sense, Trudeau's participation in the debate over the Meech Lake Accord has done little to promote rationale discourse on the Accord in western Canada.

However, Mr. Getty's conclusion that whatever Mr. Trudeau dislikes must be 'one hell of a deal' for the West has not been universally shared across western Canada. For some observers in the West, the Accord suffers from significant blemishes although the broad outlines of the Accord, and ratification, are still supported for a variety of reasons. Other observers in the West see the Accord as more fundamentally flawed, and thus not only question its ratification but express serious concern over the potential impact of the Accord on Canadian political life. In short, there is considerable regional dissensus on the Accord, dissensus that this volume hopes to explore.

Constitutional documents are more than sets of procedural rules and institutional formalities. They are also important as political symbols, as statements which expound and codify the political essence of national communities. Constitutions in this sense are a distillation of a nation's political culture. We might ask, then, what the Meech Lake Accord says about Canada, and to Canadians. More specifically, we might ask what the Accord says about the place of the West within the Canadian federal state, and what the Accord says to western Canadians about the nature of their regional and national communities. Do western Canadians find their vision of Canada reflected in Meech Lake? Or is the reflection distorted, pulled out of shape by currents somewhat at odds with western interests and aspirations? It is these questions which are addressed in this collection.

Yet in addressing these questions, we must never lose sight of the fact that the Meech Lake Accord is a national constitutional statement, and that western Canadians are very much a part of the national political community. To examine the Accord from a western Canadian perspective means that we must also examine it from a national perspective; a perspective too narrowly circumscribed by regional self-interest would fail to capture the ongoing effort of western Canadians to participate fully within the national community, to use that community rather than the region alone as the primary vehicle for western aspirations. Thus while our analysis begins in Section II with an examination of Meech Lake and the West, Section III examines the Accord from a Quebec perspective. Section IV extends the analysis further by exploring the constitutional process through which the First Ministers reached the Meech Lake Accord, and through which it may or may not be ratified. Section V examines the possible impact of the Accord on human rights, and Section VI examines media coverage of the Accord. The very scope of this analysis demonstrates not only the importance of the Meech Lake Accord, but also its potential impact on Canadian political life.

Notes

1 Prime Minister of Canada announcing that Canada's eleven First Ministers had signed the Meech Lake Accord.

2 Minister of Justice and Attorney General of Canada. House of Commons Debates, May 11, 1987, p. 5943.

3 Minister of State for Federal-Provincial Relations. Minutes of Proceedings and Evidence of The Special Joint Committee on the 1987 Constitutional Accord, August 4, 1987, 2:10.

4 *Globe and Mail*, March 31, 1988, p. A1.

5 Kathy Kerr, 'Getty rallies Tory troops on strong keynote speech,' *Calgary Herald*, April 10, 1988, p. A2.

Meech Lake and The West

[A]ll provinces being equal builds a stronger Canada, not a weaker Canada, and we were able to get Quebec in, I might say, based on the principle of equality and that stronger Canada. We were not prepared to sell out Alberta in order to get Quebec in, nor was it necessary, nor should it have been necessary, and Quebec understood that. Don Getty.[1]

I think it should not be lost on those of us who come from regions of Canada other than Quebec or Ontario that this Accord is probably the most important step forward in the recognition of regions like western Canada that has been passed in any constitutional amendment since confederation....It recognizes now that we are equals in confederation. Ray Hnatyshyn.[2]

The Meech Lake resolution proposals are, in my view, the political equivalent of an AIDS virus: an ailment whose symptoms are initially innocuous but build progressively to a debilitating, incurable, and inevitably fatal condition. David Elton.[3]

INTRODUCTION:
MEECH LAKE AND THE WEST

On both the political and economic fronts, the last decade has been a dramatic, even tumultuous one for western Canadians. In February, 1980, the short-lived Progressive Conservative government of Joe Clark, within which western Canadian MPs had enjoyed a strong voice, went down to defeat at the hands of the Liberal party led by Pierre Trudeau. Thus as the decade opened, western Canadians again found themselves facing a federal government virtually devoid of elected western Canadian representation, with only two Liberal MPs elected west of the Ontario border. In the fall of 1980 Ottawa first launched its unilateral attempt to patriate the Canadian constitution, and then introduced the National Energy Program which touched off a bitter confrontation between the oil-producing provinces in the West and the federal government. When an agreement between Ottawa and the energy-producing provinces was finally reached in 1981, it was followed almost immediately by a collapse in the international price of oil, and the subsequent collapse of a western Canadian economy already facing the effects of low prices and shrinking markets across a wide range of renewable and nonrenewable natural resources. Regardless of the commodity — oil, natural gas, grain, potash, lumber, metals, coal — the regional economy was severely depressed.

However, while the early 1980s offered political confrontation and economic hard times, the region began to turn around in 1984. The landslide election of Brian Mulroney's Progressive Conservative government in September of that year resulted in a national government within which the West enjoyed strong and effective regional representation. Financial relief for the region's grain farmers came quickly in the wake of Mulroney's election. The Western Accord, signed in 1985 between Ottawa and the energy-producing provinces, dismantled both the NEP and continental marketing restrictions on the sale of oil and natural gas. Although the grain economy remained on rather precarious footings, world oil prices began to climb and the western Canadian economy began to recover. Then, in the fall of 1987, the federal government completed the negotiations for a comprehensive free trade agreement with the United States, a policy initiative which enjoyed broad public and governmental support across the West, with the exception of Premier Pawley's NDP administration in Manitoba. Good times, it appeared, were here again.

This roller-coaster ride across the 1980s had a great impact on constitutional politics in the region. In the negotiations leading up to the Constitution Act of 1982, the provincial governments in the West faced a national government which seemed at best unsympathetic and at worst hostile to the regional aspirations of western Canadians. Small wonder, then, that the four premiers went into the constitutional negotiations in a very defensive stance, determined at all costs to protect provincial ownership of natural resources. To a degree they were successful in that respect; the Constitution Act did provide some additional constitutional support for provincial ownership and control of natural resources, and the amending formula adopted was largely an Alberta creation. At the same time, however, the western premiers did not achieve significant institutional reform which might have addressed long-standing western Canadian concerns about effective regional representation in the parliamentary institutions of the national government.[4] Thus while the 1982 Act did not adversely affect western Canadian interests, neither did it reflect longstanding western Canadian constitutional aspirations.

The constitutional climate, and indeed the more general political climate, changed dramatically after the 1984 federal election. A new and more accommodating national government was now in place, one more closely attuned to the regional aspirations of the West and, not inconsequentially, one more closely aligned with the dominant partisan sentiment in Saskatchewan, Alberta, and British Columbia. The four premiers who had led the early constitutional struggle had all either retired or had been defeated, and the western Canadian economy appeared to be steadily improving. With the bitter energy confrontations behind them, with the Western Accord and grain assistance on record, provincial governments in the West were in a much more receptive mood to the constitutional initiatives of Premier Robert Bourassa and Prime Minister Brian Mulroney than they had been to the constitutional initiatives of Pierre Trudeau. While the new western Canadian premiers were not prepared to abandon their own constitutional agenda, they were prepared to consider Quebec's concerns first, and to endorse the Meech Lake Accord.

The western Canadian reaction to the Meech Lake Accord has been decidedly mixed. The Accord was quickly ratified in Saskatchewan, with little public debate or legislative criticism. The Accord has also been ratified by the Alberta Legislative Assembly, although as the chapter by Howard Palmer points out, ratification did not come before public hearings sponsored by the opposition New Democrats had uncovered widespread public unease with the agreement. (All but one of the 150 individual and group presentations to the hearings were critical of the Accord.) In Manitoba, the April 1988 election of a minority Progressive Conservative government has thrown the Accord's ratification into question, a matter explored in some depth by Gerald Friesen's chapter in this section. At the time of writing, the British Columbia Legislative Assembly has yet to act on the Accord although the B.C. government remains committed in principle to the Accord.

Many of the criticisms of the Accord that have arisen in the West have gone beyond traditional regional interests and grievances to embrace concern about the Accord's impact on Aboriginal rights, the Northern territories, women, linguistic minorities and ethnic communities, concerns that are addressed in Section V. Considerable concern has also been expressed about the impact of the Accord on the national government and national political community, matters discussed at length in Section IV. However, the authors in this section primarily address the impact of the Accord on regional representation within national political institutions, a matter of longstanding and central constitutional concern in the West. David Elton and Peter McCormick both address what has become the litmus test for the Accord in the West — its impact on the prospects for Senate reform.

This issue more than any other will determine the extent to which the Accord meets the regional aspirations of western Canadians; it has become **the** regional optic through which the Accord is viewed. At the same time, however, David Bercuson's contribution demonstrates that western Canadians are also employing a number of other, non-regional optics in assessing the Accord, that western Canadian reactions to the Accord have not been shaped solely by regional aspirations, grievances, interests and mythologies. The western Canadian debate over the Accord, as expressed both by the articles in this collection and by the debate in the wider political arena, demonstrates the growing heterogeneity of political opinion in the region. No longer is the West a homogeneous region, bound together by a pervasive sense of regional alienation from the national government. Provincial governments are no longer speaking with a united voice, vocal Liberal voices are now heard among opposition parties in the West, and numerous groups have expressed a variety of concerns with the Accord which have little to do with regional interests and aspirations per se. Thus perhaps the debate over the Accord in western Canada reflects a new political maturity in which regional self-interest provides only one of many optics through which national political developments are assessed.

Notes

1 Premier of Alberta. Alberta Hansard, May 4, 1987, p. 983.

2 Minister of Justice and Attorney General of Canada. House of Commons Debates, May 11, 1987, p. 5944.

3 President, Canada West Foundation. Minutes of Proceedings and Evidence of the Special Joint Committee on the 1987 Constitutional Accord, August 6, 1987, 4:101.

4 For an extended discussion of the West's constitutional strategy and accomplishments in 1981/82, see Roger Gibbins, 'Constitutional Politics and the West,' in Keith Banting and Richard Simeon, eds., *And No One Cheered: Federalism, Democracy & the Constitution Act* (Toronto: Methuen 1983) 119-132.

Meech Lake:
The Peace of the Graveyard

David Bercuson

When Prime Minister Brian Mulroney came to power in 1984 he was determined to end the almost constant federal-provincial wrangling that had marked the Trudeau years. That was, at one level, a commendable objective because since the 1967 Confederation of Tomorrow Conference, hosted by Ontario Premier John Robarts, constitutional change has been front and centre on the national agenda. The Confederation of Tomorrow Conference was an important milestone on the road to the 1982 Constitution Act. But it did not by any means initiate this most recent period of federal-provincial constitutional wrangling. In fact, it was a response to the onset of the quiet revolution in Quebec, and to the attempts of the Pearson Liberals to accommodate themselves to that change. These events grew directly out of the centralization of powers that occurred during and after World War II — a centralization bitterly resisted by Ontario Premier George Drew and Quebec Premier Maurice Duplessis among others — and the rise of a modern welfare state in Canada. These changes of course were themselves linked to events in prior decades, and those to events even earlier.

Human events and the affairs of states and governments are dynamic and produce conflict. Conflict is the by-product of the clash between the desire to change and the desire to preserve. It is inevitable, it is necessary, and properly channelled within the traditions and social and legal boundaries of a modern democratic state, it is good. It is for this reason that Prime Minister Brian Mulroney's attempts to end conflict in federal-provincial relations are, at best, truly pathetic: such conflict cannot, will not, must not, end.

In his quest for that elusive world of reason and harmony in relations between Ottawa and the provinces, Brian Mulroney has surrendered. This might bring peace between Ottawa and the provinces for a time because surrender of one party to a conflict generally does. But he will buy that tranquility at a high cost to Canada and in the end that peace will be the peace of the graveyard.

There is a tremendous national debate which is now being raised in this country over the issue of free trade. It will be very important to Canada and may cause substantial changes in certain sections of the economy, but this passionate and continual debate over free trade has all but drowned out discussion over Meech Lake. That is ironic because Meech Lake will have a far greater impact on this society than free trade ever could. It will change Canada in almost revolutionary ways and make it a much worse place to live in.

Meech Lake is based on a dichotomy. It is at once one of the most cynically conceived documents that Canadians will ever have to deal with, but at the same time, it clearly reflects a Pollyanna-like assumption that all people who head governments are people of good will and that federal and provincial governments will always find a way to agree on the basic future direction of Canada. There are so many loose ends in Meech Lake that one shudders to think what will happen when another era of acute federal-provincial conflict occurs in Canada. Meech Lake simply fails to take care of worse case situations that may arise in the future. And the fact is, another era of acute federal-provincial conflict is always just around the corner in this country.

The architects of Meech Lake are very optimistic people. Their view of the future is a view of harmony and cooperation on the political and social level underwritten by constant economic expansion. There will be no recessions, things will always be good, the economy of the country will always expand, life will always get better for the people of Canada. But, the 'harmony' we enjoy in Canada today is really a fluke. We've had three years of relative peace in federal-provincial relations, but that has simply not been the case for most of the last hundred years. From the Interprovincial Conference of 1887 to the federal election of 1984, what we have had is constant conflict between federal and provincial governments. That conflict was good, it was vital, it contributed to the growth and development of Canada and to the maturation of Canadian society. It reflected then and reflects now a **live** people, working out real problems on a daily basis. It shows that Canada is a vital society, that it is this very vitality which produces problems and that Canadians attempt to solve those problems politically, on an ongoing basis. Meech Lake is based on the notion that this fluky, shaky peace we have today in the area of federal-provincial relations we will always have.

Meech Lake makes virtually no provision for occasionally ruthless politicians achieving power, especially in provincial governments. We have had such men in Canada before — politicians who did not hesitate to abuse the power which was placed in their hands. This has been especially true of provincial governments — Mitchell Hepburn in Ontario, William Aberhart in Alberta, Maurice Duplessis in Quebec are but a few examples. Meech Lake will give people such as this greater power and leeway than they have ever had before. No rein is to be placed on them in their own jurisdictional areas and, worse, they will be able to hold the country for ransom over a broad range of issues and programs.

Meech Lake tries to buy off Quebec nationalism by watering down the federalist nature of this country and loosening Canada's already loose federalist ties. But Quebec nationalism is part and parcel of Quebec politics and Quebec society. Quebec nationalism is something that all major elements of Quebec society have in common and all agree on; whether they are independentists, or provincialists, or federalists, they are all nationalists. Nationalism is as much a part of Quebec politics as capitalism or free enterprise is a part of North American politics. 'Quebec nationalism' cannot be bought off, nor should it be since it is one of the vital creative forces of Confederation. One of the reasons this country is so different from the United States has been the working out of an accommodation between the nationalism of Quebec and the desire of the rest of Canada to find a place for itself in the world that is at once North American but uniquely Canadian. That, of course, must be an ongoing process as long as both are still alive!

The Parti Québécois under Jacques Parizeau is probably rubbing its hands with glee at the prospect of the powers it will have when it reachieves office with Meech Lake in place. And, of course, it will likely achieve office some day because most opposition parties eventually do. The powers which Meech Lake gives to the government of Quebec will allow a nationalist government such as the Parti Québécois to basically create the kind of sovereignty-association which Rene Levesque aimed at for all of those years — and no referendum will be necessary!

In addition, far more of the laws of this land will be judge-made under Meech Lake than they are now. This is not a totally bad thing; some judge-made law is good and there's no question that under the Constitutional Act of 1982, Canada is bound to have a greater degree of judge-made law in the future than in the past. But Meech Lake's fuzziness — and it is incredibly badly drafted with many important loose ends — will make it imperative for the courts to mold large parts of Canadian law. If they don't, there is going to be either paralysis, or on-going confrontation between the federal government and the provincial governments. This is something the Meech Lake peace makers were supposed to be avoiding.

Meech Lake is going to undermine our efforts to build a humane society with minimum standards of care and maintenance for all of our people. The proponents of Meech Lake claim that all it does is stop the federal government from interfering further with respect to shared cost programs in the area of provincial powers. What those people don't mention is that by the Constitution Act of 1867, virtually **all** social legislation falls within provincial jurisdiction. There can be virtually no social legislation in Canada unless it is shared-cost legislation or unless the federal government takes part in some way because of the old dilemma: the federal government raises the bulk of the tax monies under the Constitution and the provincial governments have most of the responsibilities for spending them. Meech Lake could, therefore, bring about a paralysis in the planning of social legislation for Canada. Short of a Great Depression — and short of a popular national demand for the federal government to take the reins as occurred in the late 1930's — Canada can forget, for example, about future medicare-type schemes. The Canada Health Act of 1984, which saved Medicare in Canada, would have been impossible under Meech Lake.

Under the Meech Lake Accord, Canada is going to be far more decentralized than it has been in the past. The provincial premiers will be co-equal to the Prime Minister in many important areas of domestic policy-making. The federal government will become slowly paralyzed as the molder of the Canadian state and the shaper of the national agenda which it has been almost constantly from 1867 until now. Canada is not supposed to have eleven equal governments in this country: the federal government is supposed to be the preeminent government, deciding the basic future direction of Canada. Yes, it has to work that future out in conjunction with the provinces because they do have the important responsibilities in the areas of social legislation and education, among others. But in almost every area of governmental operation, from labour legislation to economic development to social legislation, the federal government has charted Canada's course. What Meech Lake threatens to do is take that preeminence away from the federal government and establish a new situation where eleven governments will sit at the table and try to reach some consensus on Canada's future. That is too much to expect.

There are, of course, other problems with Meech Lake. There will be no significant senate reform under Meech Lake. There will be no true self-government for native people. In guaranteeing the rights of the two charter groups of Canadian society — the so-called English and French — Meech Lake grants those two groups a superior status in this country for all time regardless of how much the demographic and ethnic composition of Canada changes in future. Meech Lake attempts to freeze the *status quo* now, before further immigration changes the ethnic and religious makeup of Canada. Meech Lake is also going to freeze out the non-charter groups from full, equal status in Canadian society for a long time to come.

Meech Lake is an attempt to make permanent peace in a system where such peace is not desirable. Canadians have made the society they enjoy today through creative dissonance. This process reflects a real 'live' people trying to work out their political problems on a daily basis: people making up new solutions as new problems evolve, as technology changes, and as the ethnic composition of the country changes. What Meech Lake tries to do is to freeze the process now; to take today's status quo and impose it on future generations of Canadians. Meech Lake is a far greater danger to Canada than free trade. But all three parties in the House of Commons have sold their souls over the issue. Tories, New Democrats and Liberals have decided that a handful of Quebec seats are more important than the future of Canada. Unless the people of Canada can de-rail this cozy little deal done by eleven men in a closed room in the dead of the night, Canada as we know it is lost.

The Enigma of Meech Lake for Senate Reform

David Elton

Two very different views have emerged about the probability of meaningful reform of Canada's Senate given the Meech Lake Accord. For many advocates of Senate reform Meech Lake has effectively killed any chance for reform of the Canadian Senate.[1] These people feel Canada's First Ministers have given them a Sisyphean task; Meech Lake condemns them to an eternal task of rolling a huge stone up a hill which, once reaching the top will always roll back down. Two items in the Accord are seen to perpetrate this purgatory: the requirement that all provinces and federal government formally approve constitutional changes regarding Canada's national political institutions and the development of an interim nomination and appointment procedure that requires premiers to provide a list of nominees to the Senate from which the Prime Minister will then appoint a senator.

For another group of Senate reform advocates, Meech Lake provides the first real step along the road to Senate reform taken since Confederation.[2] They point out that prior to the Accord, Senate reform wasn't even on the national agenda, whereas as soon as Meech Lake becomes a reality Senate reform obtains first priority on the constitutional agenda. In addition, proponents of Meech Lake point out that from a practical point of view, Senate reform could not take place without unanimous consent regardless of the formal amendment provisions. They also argue that the interim appointment procedure provides provinces with a tool which can be used to ensure there is a minimum of footdragging in realizing Senate reform.

This essay examines the assumptions underlying both points of view. The implications of the Accord's requirement that all provinces approve changes to the Senate are discussed, as are the possible ramifications of the newly established selection procedure for Senate appointments. Finally, two alternate approaches to dealing with Senate reform are discussed, alternatives which are outgrowths of the Meech Lake initiative. One approach requires a simple amendment to the Meech Lake Accord. The second approach outlines a plan of action available to committed Senate reformers regardless of the fate of the Meech Lake Accord initiative.

The Amending Process

From the outset of the debates on constitutional change it has been recognized that one of the primary obstacles to reform of the Senate lies in Canada's restrictive constitutional change process. Unlike other federations which provide for considerable public input into the initiation and ratification of constitutional changes, Canada's amending process severely restricts non-government participants. When it comes to changing the governing process, the very people with the greatest vested interest in maintaining the status quo, the eleven First Ministers, are the same people responsible for both initiating and ratifying changes in Canada's constitutional order. Canada's amending process is far more restrictive, far less open to public input than is the amending process in Australia, Switzerland or the United States. Substantiation of this observation was attained by developing a numeric index which rank ordered the degree of participation in the amending process in the four federations with regards to the initiation, amendment, and ratification of constitutional changes.[3] Australia and the United States turned out to be twice as open to influence by legislators and/or the public as did Canada, while Switzerland was three times as open.

Canada's existing government-controlled amending process (which requires the concurrence of the Parliament of Canada and 7 provinces representing at least 50 percent of the population) creates a near insurmountable obstacle for those advocating changes to institutional structures. That Meech Lake moves the constitutional high jump bar from 2.4 metres (a height no Canadian has yet cleared) to 2.5 metres (a height that no one has ever cleared) seems quite academic. Because Senate reform seeks to modify the political powers of the very people charged with initiating and ratifying the necessary constitutional changes, First Ministers should not be expected to be overly anxious to see any significant reform initiative through to fruition. Indeed, it is to be expected that First Ministers and their advisors (who in a real sense have just as much to gain or lose as their ministers) will dwell on problems at the expense of an overall solution.

Not surprisingly, Senate reform serves up a number of very thorny problems. For example, finding agreement on the role and functions of the Senate will require First Ministers to voluntarily relinquish some of their existing powers. Second, to create a Senate capable of providing a balanced regional perspective on national policy making, there must be a significant shift in representation from both Ontario and Quebec to the eight smaller provinces. To complicate matters even more, there is every likelihood that the relative representation of two of the smaller provinces, New Brunswick and Nova Scotia, will also be diminished. Given these and other problems, it is questionable whether there would ever be a time when all eleven First Ministers would agree to a specific set of changes. To expect all eleven to rise simultaneously to the level of statesmanship required to ratify meaningful Senate reform as required under the Meech Lake Accord may be unrealistic, naive, or both.

It is instructive to recall that placing Senate reform on the national agenda required an implicit threat of blocking a constitutional change highly valued by both the federal and Quebec governments. If a simple acceptance of a commitment to Senate reform was obtained under extraordinary circumstances where the self interests of the federal and Quebec governments were key factors, what set of circumstances must pertain for meaningful reform? Proponents of Meech Lake have not addressed this matter. Opponents to Meech Lake have not only asked this question, but they have a disquieting answer, arguing that unless meaningful Senate reform takes place at the same time Quebec's demands are met, the only set of circumstances that would cause the central provinces and the federal government to agree to meaningful Senate reform is the existence of a viable and committed separatist threat from western Canada.[4]

Proponents of the Accord are equally adamant that the imposition of a unanimity requirement regarding Senate reform is not only reasonable but politically realistic for four reasons.[5] First, it is pointed out that the Meech Lake Accord itself attained unanimous agreement. Second, it is argued that the requirement gives Western and Atlantic provinces the ability to veto any attempts to reform the Senate in an unacceptable manner. Third, proponents point out that the probability of effecting fundamental change in Canada's national institutions without unanimous agreement is unrealistic. The problems created by the exclusion of Quebec from the 1982 constitutional changes is cited as a case in point. Finally, the interim appointment procedure is seen as a means by which Western and Atlantic provinces can ensure Senate reform will take place by recommending nominees who are themselves committed to seeing Senate reform take place and will therefore work within the Senate to this end.

Whether Meech Lake becomes a reality or not, the Accord has at least temporarily modified political practice in a way which, if used creatively by one or more provinces, could all but ensure that meaningful Senate reform will take place within the next decade or two. It is to this issue that we now turn.

Meech Lake and Senate Appointments

Undoubtedly, the most surprising and unexpected aspect of the Meech Lake Accord is the provision for an **immediate** change in the appointment procedure, a change which would become constitutionally binding if the Meech Lake Accord is implemented. The Accord provides that the selection of future appointees to the Senate be made by the Prime Minister from lists provided by the Premier of the province in which the vacancy occurs. Whether these lists are to contain one or more names is not stated. Nor is there any indication regarding the manner premiers might use to determine whose name(s) to submit.

Unlike the argument for entrenching a commitment to discuss Senate reform, and the delineation of what should be discussed, all of which had been discussed prior to the Meech Lake meeting,[6] the temporary change in the appointment procedure was an outgrowth of the First Ministers' discussions. Whether it grew out of a Machiavellian ploy by the Prime Minister and some premiers to reduce the chances of further Senate reform by sharing a highly valued patronage appointment, or was operationalized to provide evidence of a real commitment to reform is not clear. Yet regardless of the First Ministers' intent, it will be the actual practices which are followed by premiers and the Prime Minister in future appointments to the Senate which will determine whether this provision will enhance or hinder meaningful Senate reform. The decision to change Senate appointment procedures represents the first fundamental change in the makeup and, potentially, the powers of the Senate since Confederation. Ironically, at the same time that this provision could precipitate a significant breakup of the logjam facing Senate reform it could also create an Achilles' heel which will thwart further reform.

Models of Appointment

There are basically four models of appointment available to premiers in selecting nominees for the Senate, all of which have implications for further Senate reform. The first three models, which maintain previous Senate appointment practices, are discussed here while the fourth, which represents a fundamental change in Senate appointment procedures, is examined in the concluding section.

The first model available to premiers in making Senate nominees is the Triple P option: 'Premiers Perpetuating Patronage.' The patronage model has proven to be the most appealing to Prime Ministers over the past 120 years, and undoubtedly provides the greatest benefits to a premier. Unless a premier is ideologically committed to Senate reform, an unlikely possibility given that Alberta's Premier Don Getty is the only premier in the past two decades who has given evidence of such a commitment, the Triple P model offers a premier the best of both worlds. Premiers are now in a position to give evidence of the extent to which they value the services of several faithful party workers at once by submitting a list of two or more names. This would leave the premier with the benefits of having indicated his desire to reward several of the party faithful while at the same time saddling the Prime Minister with the unsavory task of choosing only one of the nominees.

If the 'Triple P' approach to Senate nominees is used by even one province it would effectively provide a near fatal blow to further reform. Not only would the individual premier using this approach be reticent to agree to meaningful reform in the future, but he or she would also have the absolute power to delay or stop Senate reform. In addition, the behavior of any individual premier would provide an appealing precedent for other premiers to follow. Because there is little or no precedent of political leaders foregoing patronage appointments, particularly of the magnitude of a Senate appointment, is it realistic to assume that ten premiers over an extended period of time will prove to be the exception to the rule in the name of meaningful Senate reform?

The second model of appointment is the 'qualified person' option. The rationale underlying this model is that the province and its citizens plus the Senate and the country would be well served by appointing a highly qualified individual to the Senate. This option has been used from time to time by Prime Ministers. For example, Prime Minister Trudeau appointed Ernest Manning, a former Social Credit Premier of Alberta, and Eugene Forsey, a constitutional law expert, neither of whom had Liberal party ties. If premiers adopt the 'qualified person' model in making Senate nominations it is conceivable that over time the prestige of the Senate would be enhanced marginally. There is little likelihood, however, that even with several dozen nominations and appointments of qualified and respected persons, the Senate would obtain adequate legitimacy to effectively represent regional aspirations within the national government. The problem with the Senate is not that there are too few well qualified senators. The problem is that any appointment, however made, simply reinforces the anachronistic nature of the Senate. Appointment to a legislative body is incongruent with modern democratic practices.

Over the past 120 years many appointments to the Senate have been made using a mixture of patronage and merit, a mixture which accomplishes two things at once. First, premiers obtain the prestige and power that goes with making appointments to individuals of their choice. Second, the public, the media, and even the opposition are satisfied the premier is working in the public interest. It is not surprising, therefore, that it is this mixed model of appointment that Newfoundland's Premier operationalized in making the first nomination under the provisions of the Meech Lake Accord in early 1988. The premier's behavior fits well within the best traditions of Senate appointments and gives good evidence of Premier Peckford's desire to maintain the status quo regarding the Senate.

The third model of Senate appointment available to premiers can be called either the 'do nothing' model or the 'no nominee' model. It requires only that a province refrain from making nominations to the Senate. The rationale behind this model is that over time the existence of vacancies in the Senate will increase demands for reform of the institution. The success of this approach is dependent primarily upon provincial premiers being able to withstand the pressures within their own party to provide 'jobs for the boys.'

While it is conceivable that a particular premier could on principle refuse to provide nominees over a period of several years, it is unlikely that such constraint could be maintained over a long enough period of time to exert adequate pressure for reform. Given the slow rate of turnover in the Senate, real pressure for reform would not be exerted until the number of senators dropped below 70, something that will not occur for well over a decade. For example, at one point in the 1970s there were 20 vacancies in the Senate and the only sustained demand to rectify the situation came from those seeking patronage appointments.[7] It would probably be well into the 21st century before this approach would exert adequate pressure to precipitate the necessary reforms. Further, for the 'no nominee' approach to take effect it would require that most if not all provinces take a similar approach, something which has not happened. While Ontario's Premier Peterson has already indicated that he is going to use this approach (Ontario presently has two vacancies in the Senate) there is no way for him to ensure that his own successor(s), much less any of the other premiers, will refrain from providing Senate nominees.

Alternate Approaches to Senate Reform

There are basically two alternate options open to proponents of Senate reform given the Meech Lake Accord: elect provincial nominees to the Senate, or place a political time bomb within the Accord. The first option requires that premiers use creatively the provinces' power to nominate senators, while the second option requires an amendment to the Accord.

Any one of Canada's ten premiers is presently in a position to provide for the election of a senatorial nominee. This option arises from the fact that the Meech Lake agreement is silent on the manner in which premiers obtain the names of their nominees. It is therefore open to any premier to pass provincial legislation providing for the election of senatorial nominees either at the time of a provincial election, or at some other convenient time. In addition, it is within the prerogative of a provincial government to informally limit the term of their nominees to whatever time they feel appropriate. This could be done by simply requiring a commitment from all candidates to resign after a specified period of time. In sum, no constitutional change of any kind is necessary to make the election of senators a reality.

There is no doubt but that the 'election of a nominee' option would in and of itself go a long ways towards creating a reformed Senate. The potential benefits of this option are considerable. Once one province elected a nominee there would be considerable pressure in other provinces to do likewise. In addition, the first two or three elected senators for a time would obtain a notoriety unparalleled by any other Canadian politician. This media exposure would dramatically increase awareness of the need for Senate reform and thus put pressure upon the First Ministers and their advisors to undertake the necessary constitutional changes to make meaningful Senate reform a reality. In addition, the election of a senatorial nominee would place within parliament a strong spokesman with a unique mandate for Senate reform.

While the Prime Minister retains the right to reject provincial nominees, for a Prime Minister to refuse to appoint an individual nominated by a majority of the electors of a province would have such serious political consequences that it reduces the likelihood of such an eventuality to nearly zero. In essence, the Prime Minister is placed in a Catch 22 situation. If he accepts the nominee the demand for Senate reform increases. If the Prime Minister chooses to reject an elected nominee his action would also dramatically increase the demand for Senate reform.

Although the election of nominees to the Senate holds out significant promise for creating an environment conducive to further Senate reform, there is also a potential dark side to this option. If all provinces were to adopt this approach over the next two decades, then it is possible to project the existence of a totally elected Senate which would further exacerbate the current maldistribution of seats in the Senate. The perpetuation of the existing distribution of seats would once again permit Ontario and Quebec to dominate national policy making and thwart the primary objective of enhancing regional input into the national policy making process. This possibility is highly unlikely, however, for it would be contrary to the self interests of all First Ministers to allow this state of affairs to pertain for any period of time. Such an elected Senate would also retain the existing senatorial powers and be able to challenge even the collective will of the First Ministers. Thus, given the First Ministers' power to reform the Senate without the Senate's concurrence, there is little doubt but that reform would take place well before the realization of an all elected Senate. A growing number of elected senators would provide an ever increasing incentive for First Ministers to undertake the necessary constitutional change.

The insertion of a legal timebomb with regards to Senate reform is a second approach. This could be done by simply constitutionalizing the 'no nominees' model discussed earlier. Rather than leaving it up to the discretion of premiers to refrain or indulge in Senate appointments, the Accord could be changed to require that no further appointments be made until Senate reform was realized. While this provision would have little effect over the next five years, thereafter the decreasing numbers in the Senate would increase the relative powers of the remaining Senators to the point where First Ministers would be obliged to act.

The key element in both alternatives is the creation of the necessary political incentive to induce First Ministers to reform the Senate. Experience indicates that the kind of constitutional changes necessary to realize Senate reform will only take place as a result of political necessity, not goodwill. Afterall, Senate reform was inserted into the Meech Lake Accord because it was the only way the federal and Quebec governments could obtain all province agreement to change the existing amending formula.

To expect that meaningful Senate reform will happen on the basis of goodwill among eleven heads of government all with differing constituencies and agendas is unrealistic in the extreme. Whereas the constitutional reforms of 1982 and the Meech Lake Accord dealt with more symbolic issues, Senate reform reaches to the very heart of the Canadian political system. It should therefore be expected that the practical political pressures upon First Ministers to undertake meaningful

Senate reform will have to be considerably more intense than the pressures which brought about either the 1982 constitutional changes or the Meech Lake Accord of 1987.

Notes

1 One of the foremost advocates of Senate reform is the newly created Reform Party of Canada. Their presentation to the Special Joint Committee of the Senate and the House of Commons on the 1987 Constitutional Accord, August, 1987, exemplifies the extent of dismay among Senate reform advocates regarding the Meech Lake Accord.

2 Premier Don Getty's defense of the Meech Lake Accord in the Alberta legislature provides an excellent example of the rationale underlying the defence of Meech Lake's Senate reform provisions. Alberta Hansard, June 17, 1987, pp. 1969-72.

3 This analysis was undertaken for a presentation to the Special Joint Committee of the Senate and House of Commons on the 1987 Constitutional Accord. See 'Western Perspective on the Meech Lake Accord,' Presentation of the Constitutional Reform Committee of the Canada West Foundation, August 11, 1987.

4 David Elton and Roger Gibbins, 'Western Alienation and Political Culture,' in R. Schultz et. al., editors, *Canadian Political Process*, 3rd ed. (Toronto: Holt, Reinhart and Winston 1979) 82-96.

5 James Horsman, 'Sorry, Ted, but you're wrong about the Meech Lake Accord,' *Alberta Report*, May 18, 1987, 15.

6 Peter McCormick and David Elton, 'The Western Economy and Canadian Unity,' *Western Perspectives* (Calgary: Canada West Foundation 1987) 18-19.

7 'Western Perspective on the Meech Lake Accord,' op. cit., 15.

Senate Reform:
Forward Step or Dead End?

Peter McCormick

The basic question of Senate reform in Canada is now, as it has always been, the matter of incentives: who wants what kind of Senate reform for what purposes and how much do they want it? Unless enough major political actors want similar or compatible reforms badly enough, nothing happens, and this is why Canadians today still enjoy the increasingly outmoded Senate that Sir John A. Macdonald designed for 1867. Meech Lake does not reform the Senate; it is not a decision, but only an agreement to talk about deciding. What is therefore critical is the way that Meech Lake alters the pattern of existing incentives to raise or lower the threshold of incentives necessary to move Senate reform forward.

There are three rather different aspects of the Accord that must be considered in these terms; Meech Lake addresses Senate reform three times from three different angles, and it is the combined impact of all three that must be assessed.

First, there is the constitutional guarantee of annual discussion of Senate Reform at a First Ministers' Constitutional Conference; the Triple E (Elected, Equal, Effective) Senate promoted by Premier Getty is not specifically mentioned in the Accord. Considering the resistance to including Senate reform on the agenda at Meech Lake, we should not lightly dismiss its constitutionally guaranteed inclusion in future gatherings, and unlike the obvious precedent of the native peoples, the Senate reform commitment is open-ended rather than being limited to two annual meetings. However, discussions are one thing and decisions are another, and the question of how likely the former are to yield the latter is a matter of incentives that is in no way altered simply by the decision to begin talking. Although this commitment represents a high water mark for Senate reform, as Premier Getty has claimed, it does not of itself put us any closer to substantive Senate reform, and the high water mark may still be so far down the beach that nothing will get moved except sand.

Second, there is the revision of the constitutional amending procedure to require unanimity among the eleven legislatures (Parliament plus all ten provinces) for amendments to 'national institutions' including (but not limited to) the Senate. Many have taken this to be the death knell of Senate reform, the hurdle of an absolute veto for each of eleven different participants being impossible to clear. Although the rigidity of unanimity is disturbing on principle, I personally doubt that the damage to Senate reform is particularly grievous. On the one hand, smaller provinces are unlikely to veto altering the Senate to give smaller provinces a more effective voice, so the spectre of a P.E.I. veto should not loom very large. On the other hand, the constitutional running sore of Quebec's solitary opposition in 1982 (which Meech Lake itself was intended to cure) makes it unlikely that a future national government would press substantive changes of any sort without at least grudging consent from the two major provinces. In practical terms, I think the central provinces probably already had a veto, and Meech Lake simply levels the playing field.

However, the unanimity requirement enables each of the actors to drive a harder bargain; enlarging the number of actors who have to be persuaded raises the ante of the incentives necessary for effective reform. It is no longer a question of putting together a package that will satisfy seven provinces and the federal government; after Meech Lake, there will have to be something for literally everyone, and the construction of the package becomes that much more challenging. Unanimity has made Senate reform a notch more difficult, although not necessarily prohibitively so.

In this context, settling for a pledge to keep meeting is a kind of defeat for Senate reform. For all the fine talk about principle and separating issues and all the rest of it, linkages are what constitutional reform in Canada is all about. With Quebec and the federal government firmly committed to the core of the Meech Lake package, an optimal solution would have been to force the inclusion of more specific and substantive Senate reform as the price of wider support; rather than starting half-way there, Senate reformers must now face much harder bargaining on a newly cleared table.

Third, there is the interim procedure whereby the Prime Minister is pledged to make Senatorial appointments only from lists of nominations submitted by the Premier of the relevant province. It is hard to see the need for this; it is like buying new seat covers for a car that you have decided to trade in as soon as possible. An appointed legislative chamber is so anachronistic that a simple sharing of the patronage hardly justifies its perpetuation, and it is disturbing to think that the push toward Senate reform could be deflected so easily. There is also something curious about a temporary interim procedure that must be constitutionally entrenched subject to a unanimity clause.

More to the point, this procedure is not just distracting but dangerous; its consequences will be far-reaching and ultimately harmful to the national government. To be sure, there will be little immediate impact, because the rate of turnover in Senate membership is low. But sometime early in the next century a majority of Senators will owe their position to the generosity of the provincial premiers who put their name in nomination, and coalitions of premiers will be able with impunity to defeat federal government policy. Even before that day arrives, there will be enough provincially nominated Senators to force delays of the type that has already infuriated the government with regard to borrowing powers, parole regulations, drug legislation, and the Meech Lake resolution itself. But the federal government will be on a slippery slope; it will be hard to refuse to make appointments without appearing to have negotiated in bad faith, and yet further reform to the Senate will be difficult because the status quo will then favour the provinces as much as it now favours Ottawa.

This is the point of looking at the situation in terms of incentives. Today, premiers will at least consider Senate reform precisely because the Senate means nothing to them: it is not 'their' patronage but Ottawa's, nor does it offer a useful access point to the federal policy process. They cannot lose from Senate reform because they have nothing to lose, but they might gain something. On the other hand, the federal government normally finds the Senate harmless or even useful; they can only lose from any reforms that would make the Senate stronger, because that strength must take the form of becoming a more effective check on the national government. Only public outcry against patronage has made the power to appoint Senators too hot to handle (at least temporarily) and the Prime Minister a luke-warm proponent of Senate reform.

But Meech Lake would dramatically transform the situation. Slowly but surely, it would substitute for the present deadlock and its ongoing price of regional disaffection a future deadlock whose price could be national governmental paralysis. Provincial premiers would then be reluctant to consider Senate reform because they would stand to lose the double plum: the power of patronage appointments that are not even paid from provincial coffers, and the power to obstruct undesirable federal legislation. The federal government could bring them to the table only by offering more concessions, and with the unanimity amendment rule the ante would be high. If Mulroney didn't give the store to the provinces at Meech Lake, a future Prime Minister might well have to do so to get out of the impasse it would create. People seldom drive hard bargains when they have a gun to their head.

The interim appointing procedure is the Achilles' heel of the Meech Lake Accord; it is (to switch metaphors) a ticking bomb in the heart of the national parliamentary system. By far the better arrangement is a simple constitutional prohibition on any further Senate appointments until substantive Senate reform is achieved; this would leave both federal and provincial governments with an incentive to negotiate, while the low turnover rate prevents it from being a formula for immediate chaos. The problem lies not with the commitment to Senate reform at Meech Lake, but with the fact that the bona fides the federal government has offered include a provincial share in the appointment process, something which once attained cannot be changed without unanimous consent. Temporary arrangements always tend to become permanent, but this 'temporary' measure is virtually guaranteed permanence by being entrenched in the constitution without any sunset clause.

The real problem of Meech Lake is not that it subjects Senate reform to a unanimity requirement, although this is on principle objectionable. Nor is it that Senate reform is scheduled for future discussion rather than accomplished immediately, although this too is clearly second best for those who want to replace an increasingly outmoded Senate. Instead, the real problem is that it would replace the present archaic direct appointment with an ill-considered provincial nomination process, and thereby paralyze future impetus for Senate reform. The big gainers are the premiers and the loser is the national government; it is not clear why Ottawa made the offer, but it is transparently obvious why the provinces accepted. If Meech Lake was the best that Getty could do for the Senate reformers by speaking up at the conference, then they would have been better off if he had kept quiet.

The Flaws of the Meech Lake Accord: An Alberta Perspective

Howard Palmer

While there are many troubling aspects of the Meech Lake Accord, I would like to discuss four problems: its impact on Senate reform; its wider potential for creating constitutional stalemate because of the unanimity rule; its potentially negative impact on immigration policy; and the undemocratic process of its ratification as revealed in the debate in Alberta leading up to the legislature's unanimous ratification of the Accord in December of 1987.

Senate Reform

Many westerners have come in the past few years to see the need for a reformed and elected Senate in order to enable smaller provinces and regions to have a stronger voice at the center of national government. When so many decisions vital to the interests of westerners such as those related to transportation, grain and energy policy, and international trade and banking will inevitably be made in Ottawa because of the nature both of the Canadian constitution, and of the realities of the economic world, westerners need more input there. While it is possible that the vital interests of Quebec may be guarded by building up isolationist walls and gaining more power for its provincial government, it is doubtful that greater power for the provincial government is going to safeguard the vital economic interests of Alberta. What westerners need is more control over what goes on in Ottawa, and an equal, effective and an elected Senate is likely the best way of achieving that end.

Just at a point when there was growing enthusiasm for Senate reform not only in Alberta, but elsewhere in the country, Premier Getty agreed to a constitutional arrangement that will make creating an elected Senate even more difficult. Bringing about effective Senate reform was certainly going to be an uphill battle before the Accord. But with the need for unanimity of all the provinces for Senate reform, implementing a Triple E Senate has become extremely unlikely, no matter how many meetings Prime Minister Mulroney promises for the discussion of Senate reform.

Getty supposedly went to Meech Lake with Senate reform as his priority. He emerged with a promise for talks on Senate reform, which was an important step. But that was coupled with a constitutional amending formula requiring unanimity, thereby totally undermining the achievement. Even more troubling, he agreed to a supposedly interim measure, which gives provinces the right to appoint senators. It seems very unlikely that all premiers are going to be willing to give up this right in order to make way for an elected Senate.

Despite the position of the federal and Alberta governments to the contrary, there is no reason that the appointment of senators by the provinces is inextricably linked with the other compromises that make up the supposedly 'seamless web' of Meech Lake. If changes to the Senate were removed from the unanimity requirement, and if all appointments to the Senate were simply suspended until talks on Senate reform achieved something, then Alberta's chances of achieving Senate reform would dramatically improve.

Alberta's Minister of Intergovernmental Affairs, Jim Horsman, is undoubtedly right in his repeated contention that under the Meech Lake Accord, other provinces won't be able to 'impose' on Alberta a Senate Albertans don't like. This argument is based however on a totally negative view of how to achieve the changes that Alberta wants. What Horsman forgets to mention is that under Meech Lake, Alberta probably won't get a EEE Senate either. Given that many of the same constitutional experts who advised Lougheed are still advising the Getty government, and that the Lougheed government consistently opposed the idea of an elected Senate, one is left wondering if these advisors are simply paying lip service to Senate reform, but don't really believe in it.

With the passage of the Meech Lake Accord, Alberta will lose almost all its bargaining power for Senate reform. Until the point that Quebec was brought into the 1982 Constitution Act, Alberta still had a great deal of leverage in constitutional talks to further the cause of Senate reform. But with the current Accord, which removes the incentive for other provinces to agree to an elected Senate, Alberta's lever has disappeared.

The Getty government has agreed to an Accord which will likely entrench western alienation because it further hinders the one clear possibility for changing the structural weaknesses in the Canadian political system that have consistently accentuated regional grievances. Under the guise of achieving something for Alberta, Getty has condemned Albertans to ongoing political frustration at the national level.

Getty placed the Alberta-based Triple E Senate committee in a difficult position because Getty was the only premier championing their cause, even though he did so in a way that made Senate reform even more difficult. The Triple E Committee, which is made up predominantly of Conservatives, went along with Getty's strained logic about Meech Lake helping, or at least not hindering Senate reform. In the rather limited public debate in Alberta over the Meech Lake Accord, it was left to politically weak forces – the provincial Liberal party, the Canada West Foundation, and Preston Manning's new Reform Party of Canada – to point out the weaknesses of the provincial government's position on Senate reform.

The Unanimity Requirement

The added difficulty of creating an elected Senate under the Meech Lake agreement is symptomatic of a larger problem with the Accord. The formula requiring unanimity of all provinces is, on the surface, an appealing one since it recognizes the equality of all provinces. However, when one examines it more closely, it becomes apparent that it will, in all likelihood, freeze Canada's constitution and prevent its further evolution. Canada already has a good deal of historical experience with unanimity in the long and tortuous negotiations over the patriation of the constitution. Constitutional talks on patriation failed in 1927, 1931, 1935-36, 1950, 1961, 1964, 1971, 1975-76, 1978-79, because of the informal agreement requiring the unanimity of all provinces. The only way out of this impasse was for the federal government to forge ahead on its own as it did in 1980-81. Had it not done so, and broken with the unanimity requirement, we still wouldn't have our own constitution today, because Quebec would have vetoed the agreement in 1981.

Giving all provinces a veto over changes in national institutions hinders the development of a flexible constitution, capable of responding to the changing needs of an evolving nation. Canada's history since confederation has been marked by a shifting of power back and forth between Ottawa and the provinces in response to changing economic and social conditions, the circumstances of war, and changing political alliances and judicial interpretations. The Meech Lake Accord will likely hamstring future constitutional change. What if future economic, social or international circumstances such as economic depression or war show a clear need for greater power at the federal level? Canada's experience during the depression of the 1930s and during the Second World War shows the need for constitutional flexibility to allow the federal government to act in time of national need.

Under the guise of coming together as a family, the Accord, by giving all provinces a veto, puts in place a system based on the 'everyone is out to get us' school of Canadian history. It could be argued that giving everyone a veto is not based on mutual trust and equality, but on mutual distrust. The Alberta-inspired amending formula in the 1982 Constitution Act introduced a flexible plan that provided for opting out of constitutional amendments. The Alberta government's current position that everyone now needs a veto in some areas is an implicit statement that something was wrong with the amending formula they pushed so hard for in 1980-81.

Impact on Immigration and Multiculturalism

That the Accord may undermine federal strength in areas where it is necessary is clear when one examines its potential impact on immigration policy and multiculturalism. Under the Meech Lake Accord, Quebec will be guaranteed a certain number of immigrants in relationship to its population and will play a role in selecting immigrants. In addition, the Canadian government will withdraw services for the reception and integration of 'all foreign nationals wishing to settle in Quebec...with such withdrawal to be accompanied by reasonable compensation'[section 2(c)]. While a case can be made for Quebec having more control over immigration policy, there are some troubling implications to the possibility of more provincial governments wanting to play an aggressive role in immigration policy: Canada could end up with several different immigration policies.

Even if this scenario does not develop, it is possible that the federal multicultural policy could be gutted by the Accord. If the federal government is to turn over the money that it has been spending for the integration of immigrants to the Quebec government, why wouldn't other provincial governments press for the same thing? As the Accord itself states 'Nothing in this Accord should be construed as preventing the negotiation of similar agreements with other provinces...' If provincial governments can take credit for programs paid for by the federal government, why not do so? But then we must ask: will the programs established by the provincial governments promote identification with Canada as a whole? While provincial and national identity can be complementary, it undoubtedly remains true that provincial governments are limited in what they can do to promote a national identity.

These concerns about immigration and multiculturalism however, played little role in the Meech Lake debate in Alberta. The provincial Conservatives have developed strong support among almost all ethnic groups, and new ethnic groups, like most Albertans, are willing to put their faith in the provincial government. While some ethnic groups in Alberta expressed concern over the implications of Meech Lake for the multiculturalism policy, their concerns were largely allayed through Conservative party reassurances. The introduction by the federal Tories of a Multiculturalism Act in December, 1987 reaffirmed the federal government's commitment to multiculturalism and assuaged the fears of some ethnic leaders that multiculturalism was being forgotten. Such promises may however ultimately be rendered meaningless by the impact on political structures of an Accord that creates a profoundly centripetal framework for Canada.

The Process

The process of negotiation and ratification of the Meech Lake Accord has been as flawed as the agreement itself. The 'behind closed doors' approach to the Meech Lake agreement has left many groups out of the process of shaping the future framework of Canada. Women, northerners, natives, French-Canadians outside Quebec, and other ethnic groups all have legitimate concerns about the way in which their interests were not taken into account by the eleven men who sat down to decide Canada's future.

The refusal of the Alberta Conservatives to hold public hearings on the Meech Lake Accord is symptomatic of the undemocratic way in which the whole process has evolved. Their refusal aroused suspicions in some circles that they were afraid of providing a platform for Albertans' views on the subject. Perhaps they were afraid that public hearings, in which the Accord's distinct society clause would undoubtedly be scrutinized, might provide a focus for strong anti-French Canadian feelings that surface periodically in the province.

The provisions in the Accord that gave a veto to all provinces and not just Quebec removed one element that might have aroused anti-French feelings in the province. In addition, it may be that the intense opposition of many Albertans in 1987 and 1988 to Bill C-72, the amendments to the Official Languages Act, channelled anti-French feelings that might otherwise have been mobilized against the Meech Lake Accord.[1] In its reaction to the Piquette affair in the Alberta legislature, the Getty government also demonstrated clearly that the Accord did not provide any additional guarantees for French language rights in Alberta.[2] These factors hindered an anti-French backlash to the Accord.

Prior to introducing the Accord for debate in the legislature, the provincial Conservatives held a few 'public' meetings on the agreement in September, 1987. It seemed clear at these meetings that the Tory MLA's who massed to praise the Accord hoped these gatherings would be a substitute for real public hearings. People in the audience were told that if they didn't like the Meech Lake Accord, or even if they simply wanted public hearings, that they were either centralists, or worse, Liberals. The genuine concerns that many people at these meetings expressed that the whole Meech Lake process had been fundamentally undemocratic, and that the Meech Lake Accord would make a 'Triple E' Senate virtually impossible, were summarily dismissed.

Jim Horsman, the Minister of Intergovernmental Affairs stated that all-party public hearings weren't necessary since they would simply allow constitutional experts a place to have their say. Perhaps this position reveals something about the provincial government's attitude toward experts on Canadian history, politics, and law at Alberta's universities. Was the government simply afraid of having to face some hard questions?

Women's and native groups in Alberta mounted some opposition to the Accord, but neither group had much impact. Their natural political ally, the New Democrats, held public hearings in September which provided a platform for the concerns of women, natives, academics and other concerned individuals. All but one of the over 130 briefs presented to the hearings criticized the Accord on various grounds, repeating concerns elsewhere in the country with regard to the process, the inflexibility of the amending formula, its impact on Senate reform, and its neglect of women, natives and northerners. These concerns received very little public attention since the Alberta media largely ignored the NDP hearings.

Opposition to the Accord within the Alberta NDP was hindered by the national party's decision to support it. While the Alberta New Democrats proposed amendments (virtually identical to the amendments introduced by the NDP in the House of Commons) to take into account some of the concerns raised at the hearings, they nonetheless unanimously voted for the Accord when their amendments lost.

The provincial Liberals, with four MLA's in the legislature, broke with their national party to oppose the Meech Lake Accord. They felt it would kill Senate reform, that it slighted aboriginal rights, eroded federal power, undermined the charter of rights and would make the establishment of new provinces extremely difficult. But their anti-Meech Lake petition campaign in the summer of 1987 calling for public hearings on the Meech Lake Accord didn't get far. The Liberals were organizationally weak, they were still tainted by the memory of the widely hated Trudeau and the National Energy Policy, and they were hindered by the disinterest of the Alberta media in the Meech Lake debate at the provincial level. They were also caught flat-footed when the time came to vote on the resolution in the legislature and they managed to miss the vote.

Consequently, with the support of the NDP, the Meech Lake resolution passed unanimously in the Alberta legislature. Individual NDP and Conservative MLAs who had doubts about the Accord simply stayed away from the vote since they didn't want to break with national party solidarity; just over half of the MLAs were in fact present for the vote on the Accord.

Conclusion

The reaction in Alberta to the Meech Lake Accord demonstrates some of its flaws and those of the Alberta government's constitutional strategy. At one level, the Accord was greeted positively as a statement of national unity that was consistent with the constitutional views of many Albertans. The Accord embodied many of the longstanding views expressed by Alberta Conservatives, at both the provincial and federal levels, about the need to turn more power over to the provinces, and have fewer decisions made in Ottawa. The Accord also seemed, at least on the surface, to embody the principle of the equality of all provinces which has been a position strongly held by both the Lougheed and Getty governments.

But the Alberta government's position has been contradictory and self-defeating. Demanding vetoes for all provinces, and at the same time a Triple E Senate, has set up a process that will lead almost inevitably to frustration and disappointment. Despite the widespread appeal of an elected Senate to individual Canadians, and the nearly universal agreement among Albertans about the need for a EEE Senate, the Meech Lake Accord is much more likely to result in a Senate which is a provincially appointed patronage body, which most Albertans don't want.

With regard to the process of ratification, Albertans who wanted to participate in the public discussion of the Meech Lake Accord had very few avenues for doing so. National party loyalties stifled dissent within the party systems. The provincial government's decision not to hold public hearings choked off debate. The failure of the media in Alberta to understand and explain to the public either the content, or the importance of the Meech Lake debate also contributed to public apathy.

The Meech Lake Accord was put together by people who thought they were building a better Canada. On closer examination, it seems more likely that, if ratified, it will turn out to be a disastrous formula for deadlock, regional fragmentation and continuing western alienation.

Notes

1 For examples of the intense opposition to Bill C-72, see *Alberta Report*, May 16, 1988 p.12-14.

2 For a discussion of the Piquette affair, see the introduction to section V of this book, and the article by Karen Taylor-Brown.

The Courts: Toward a Provincial Role in Judicial Appointments

Peter McCormick

The Meech Lake Accord is a surprisingly comprehensive document, and contains a number of provocative suggestions that deserve careful scrutiny rather than blanket condemnation as 'giving away the shop' to the provinces. One of those suggestions deals with the Supreme Court of Canada, and with a provincial role (although not a unilateral one) in appointments to that court.

In principle, I fully support giving provincial premiers such a role. It has always been a constitutional anomaly that our Supreme Court frequently acts as a final arbiter in federal-provincial jurisdictional conflicts despite the fact that it was unilaterally created by the federal Parliament, has its size and jurisdiction set by federal legislation, and is staffed by unilateral federal appointment. When federal-provincial disputes loom large on the Court's dockets, the situation is not unlike a hockey game where one team brings its own referees. Peter Hogg has carefully examined the record to see if the Supreme Court has in fact been biased in such cases, and he concluded that it has not[1]; however, he undertook the analysis only because such Supreme Court decisions as CIGOL[2] and Potash[3] put the question on the political and academic agenda in an immediate and forceful way. In the 1982 constitutional amendments, the controversy issued in a splendid compromise: section 41 of the Constitution Act includes 'the composition of the Supreme Court' as one of the matters requiring unanimous agreement from all eleven governments for amendment, but no one knows for sure what the phrase means or what is included in or excluded from this rigorous and difficult amending procedure.[4]

The idea of a provincial role in Supreme Court appointments has been discussed ever since the constitutional debate began heating up in the 1970s. However, many of the proposals for bringing the provinces into the process have been so cumbersome (such as the Victoria Charter formula), or so public and so overtly political (such as a straight copy of the American procedure of public Senate ratification), that they would create more problems than they would solve. The procedure contemplated in the Meech Lake Accord has the distinct advantage of being both plausible and workable, a minimal adjustment of present procedures that carries a qualified potential for maximal benefits.

The Meech Lake Accord contemplates a process whereby a vacancy on the Supreme Court of Canada would trigger nominations from the provincial premiers, and the Prime Minister would make the appointment from the list of nominees. As I read it, a premier is not necessarily limited to only one nomination, although it might well turn out this way, nor does it seem that the nomination must necessarily come from the same province as the premier, although it is hard to envision a situation in which this would not be the case. The dynamics and implications of such a process cut in two significantly different directions, one for Quebec and another for the rest of the country.

The process suggested for filling non-Quebec vacancies on the Court is promising. Because the Prime Minister could choose only from the pool of provincial nominees, the Supreme Court could not be blatantly stacked by the appointing government — not that the Court ever has been routinely stacked in such a way, but it could be, and Supreme Court decisions unfavourable to the provinces can create a politically exploitable appearance that it has been. At the same time, because nine different premiers could be suggesting candidates, each would have an incentive to propose strong and credible judicial candidates. To do otherwise, to waste the nomination on a personal crony or provincial party hack or a flaming provincialist who will be rejected out of hand, would be to throw away an opportunity to influence the composition, and derivatively the direction, of the highest court in the land.

The dynamics of the process are promising, with premiers having an incentive to nominate on merit, and a Prime Minister cut off from direct patronage with no incentive not to appoint on merit. The balance between the two levels of government is potentially a constructive one, although this would be the case only if the current conventional practices of the regional allocation of Supreme Court judges (three to Ontario, one to the Atlantic provinces, one to the Prairies, and one to British Columbia) do not become too rigid to permit temporary departures from the preferred pattern. Were it to be too clearly the case that a Supreme Court seat 'belongs' to a particular province, then the boundary line between nomination and appointment would become blurred, and the pressures of patronage could overwhelm the dynamics of merit.

Presumably, a provincial premier need not treat the nomination as a personal prerogative, but could both broaden the field of choice and enhance the nominee's credibility for the final selection by adopting a more formal and explicitly non-partisan mechanism. The Quebec provincial nominating committees, or the provincial judicial councils that are involved in the appointment process in many of the provinces[5], might well provide a model attractive for both political and practical reasons. A judicial nominating committee could be devised for choosing provincial Supreme Court nominees, preferably with a fairly stable and largely ex officio membership (to ensure maximal impartiality and minimal possibility of stacking a committee) meeting to consider nominees for a specific vacancy on the Court.

But Supreme Court vacancies occur rather infrequently, and a judicial nominating committee could perform other functions as well. One in particular that recommends itself is making nominations for section 96 courts (that is, provincial superior courts) as well. Unlike provincial courts, which in six provinces use an impartial screening body of judges, lawyers and laypeople to approve candidates for judicial appointment, and unlike the post-Meech Lake Supreme Court, which would require cooperation between two governments for appointment, section 96 courts are still staffed unilaterally by the federal government. The legally arbitrary appointment power is buttressed by recruitment, consultation and screening procedures that are highly effective but purely customary in nature. An objective and non-partisan judicial nominations committee could deal with Section 96 appointments without compromising the selection process or unduly overloading the committee.

For the nine provinces other than Quebec, the procedure suggested in the Meech Lake Accord for appointing judges to the Supreme Court of Canada is both positive in itself and a possible bridge to other desirable developments. However, the proposals have quite a different dynamic and quite a different set of implications as they would apply to Quebec. The Supreme Court Act requires that three of the judges on the Supreme Court must be appointed from the bar of the province of Quebec, not to represent Quebec as a province or as a distinct language community, but to acknowledge the difference between Quebec's civil code and the common law of the other nine provinces. No corresponding provision exists for other parts of the country. This means that a 'Quebec vacancy' is clearly designated as such, that there can be no departure, temporary or otherwise, from the quota, and that the nominee or nominees for the Quebec vacancy can come from only a single provincial government.

The dynamic of a provincial role for other provinces is potentially positive, if the nine premiers compete to put forth the strongest candidate. The dynamic for Quebec is quite different, and one can easily imagine scenarios including political confrontation, deadlock, 'leaks' to the media from both governments, and the total politicization of the selection process. A provincial premier of no matter what political party or policies would find the pull of a nomination tantamount to appointment a powerful allure, whether for party patronage or for political advantage. The potential for damage in the hands of a separatist premier is even more obvious, although one should be careful not to overstate the power that resides in the power of judicial appointment; it was after all President Eisenhower who appointed much of the Warren Court, including the Chief Justice, and he was as surprised as anyone by that Court's judicial activism. It is also worth pointing out that one would have to remain premier of Quebec for quite a long time to have a reasonable prospect of being able to nominate all three of the Quebec Supreme Court judges, and the electorate of Quebec defeats provincial governments more often and more regularly than that of any other province.

There may be a 'contagion effect' as well; if the premier of Quebec is to enjoy an unimpeachable claim to virtual appointment to a bloc of Supreme Court seats, then the premiers of Ontario and British Columbia might well demand a similar lock on 'their' seats, and for them as well the competition of merit could be supplanted by the manipulative logic of straightforward appointment. The constructive and positive dynamic of merit implied by several premiers trying to present the most credible nominee would then apply only to the Atlantic and Prairie 'representatives' on the Supreme Court, and even there the pull might be toward a formal rotation that would allow each premier in turn a share in the power enjoyed by the 'big three.' The 'worst case' scenario of provincial premiers actually appointing Supreme Court judges according to their own priorities and purposes, with the Prime Minister of Canada having little more than a nominal ratifying power, is unfortunately a possible outcome, although in my opinion it is not an inevitable one.

The Meech Lake proposals for Supreme Court appointments are therefore splendidly flawed. They are splendid because they are easily implemented, practical to carry through, and built upon a realistic dynamic of merit that involves both levels of government; as a further bonus, they have some potential for improving the appointment process for other federally-appointed judges as well. They are flawed because the firm assignment of a fixed quota of seats to a single province, subject to the 'nominations' of a single premier, is tantamount to having a provincial premier appoint one-third of the court on his/her own criteria to serve his/her own plans and priorities, and will create either a dangerous 'special status' for Quebec of the sort that has long been resisted, or a contagion effect as other provinces scramble for a comparable status.

A splendidly flawed idea is at best a gamble; the tragedy is that the Supreme Court of Canada has never had a stronger claim to being thought so important that we cannot afford to gamble with it. The Canadian Charter of Rights and Freedoms has given the Court a larger and more pervasive role than it has ever enjoyed before, and the measured daring of its early Charter decisions show that it is not taking lightly the revolutionary potential of its new responsibilities. We are living in the narrow transition zone when the old appointment procedures are still being accepted for the newly powerful court because neither the implications of the power nor the flaws in the procedures have come fully to public attention. When they do, the demand for a revised method for appointing Supreme Court judges is liable to be irresistible, and the three-ring circus of the Bork nomination shows some of the dangerous possibilities that loom in the future; Meech Lake ideas might well forestall such developments.

If the Meech Lake package were to be opened up for amendment, an option that the federal government is firmly resisting, a few modest revisions would allow us to hedge our bets by minimizing the risks and maximizing the gains. The premiers could accept the narrowing of their options by building provincial nominating commissions into the constitution, and the federal government could in return 'sweeten the pot' by adding the section 96 provincial superior courts (or at least the provincial Court of Appeal) to the appointments that would be made by this procedure. Failing such amendment, we can evaluate the judicial appointment procedures only by falling back on the famous test for distinguishing an optimist from a pessimist: should we think of the glass as half full, or as half empty?

Notes

1 Peter Hogg, 'Is the Supreme Court of Canada Biased in Constitutional Cases?' in *Canadian Bar Review* 52 (1979) 721-739.

2 Canadian Industrial Gas and Oil v. Saskatchewan (1978) 2 S.C.R. 545.

3 Central Canadian Potash Co. v. Saskatchewan (1979) 1 S.C.R. 42.

4 c.f. Peter Hogg, Constitutional Law of Canada (2nd ed.) 63; Cheffins, 'The Constitution Act 1982 and the Amending Formula' in *Supreme Court Law Review* 4 (1982);

Lederman, 'Comment Concerning Reform of the Supreme Court of Canada,' in Cahiers de Droit (1984).

5 c.f. Peter McCormick, 'Judicial Councils for Provincial Judges in Canada' in *Windsor Yearbook of Access to Justice* 7 (1987) passim.

Manitoba and
the Meech Lake Accord

Gerald Friesen

Manitoba has been a forum for several debates of national importance. Premier John Norquay opposed Sir John A. Macdonald in the struggle over the federal power to disallow provincial legislation and fell from power as a result. The Manitoba school law of 1890 provoked a national crisis, the implications of which are still being worked out. The federal amendments to the Criminal Code definition of seditious intent (Section 98), a response intended to suppress the revolutionary socialism of the 1919 Winnipeg General Strike, was repealed only in 1936 after repeated criticism by civil rights and labour representatives. The 1983-84 debate over French-language services in Manitoba received national attention because the participants were addressing the changed circumstances of bilingualism in modern Canada. And, in 1987-88, the commencement of a Manitoba debate over the Meech Lake Accord received national attention. Once again, the province seemed to be in a position to clarify a national issue and even, perhaps, to determine its outcome.

The apparent importance of Manitoba's role in the Meech Lake debate has prompted this volume's editors to commission a progress report. Several qualifications must accompany my paper. The debate itself is not over. Indeed, it has yet to have a proper beginning. Moreover, because this is written in May of 1988, as a new provincial government assumes power and public hearings are delayed, uncertainty will prevail for many more months. Finally, having participated as a critic of the Meech Lake Accord in the events that are described in these pages, I should acknowledge that this is not an objective account. The paper offers one perspective on a provincial discussion that may eventually have national significance.

Why should the Meech Lake Accord have run into resistance in Manitoba? One obvious answer is the composition of the provincial population. The prominence of natives and ethnic groups and French-speaking citizens in Manitoba's public affairs is reason enough to believe that some of the Accord's clauses would receive careful scrutiny. Another plausible explanation is the relative ease of debate in a small, centralized province. Manitoba has just over one million citizens, 70 percent of whom live in Winnipeg or in its shadow; its public discussions are dominated by a small number of media outlets and by well-organized party networks that can generate interest remarkably quickly. A third explanation is the intense partisanship of recent politics. The competitiveness of the Conservative and New Democratic parties after twenty years of increasingly heated debate, and the complications introduced by a revitalized Liberal party ensure that most issues receive attention as the parties jockey for position. None of these answers is sufficient. The crucial factor in the emergence of a Manitoba debate lies in the nature of the constitutional amendment process itself and the response to that process by former Manitoba premier Howard Pawley. Pawley's insistence that Manitobans have an opportunity to consider the amendments at public hearings provided the occasion for the debate. And the apparent haste with which other parties to the agreement, including both the federal Conservative government and such provincial allies as Alberta and Saskatchewan attempted to entrench the changes (neither held hearings), provoked the suspicion of Manitobans.

Howard Pawley's role in the Meech Lake process reflected his position as Canada's only New Democratic Party premier. Pawley attended the first bargaining session at Meech Lake expecting that the talks would end in failure. He had no idea that the federal government preparations included considerable discussion of Quebec's aspirations with other western premiers. Closeted in an upstairs room in the conference cottage and without the benefit of advice from his three Manitoba colleagues who were in another part of the building, Pawley felt isolated, not for the first time at such federal-provincial meetings. Though interpretations of the Meech Lake agreement differ, Pawley left the meeting with the assumption that the constitutional proposals were flexible and would almost certainly be revised at the next conference. Other leaders did not share this impression. As the odd man out in party terms, Pawley had no one to defend his perspective.

Pawley's commitments as a social democrat underlie his role in the Langevin Block amendments to the Accord. He had returned to Winnipeg after the Meech Lake meetings to a mixed but generally favourable reaction. However, a few critical comments had reached his office, particularly as a result of disquiet among aboriginal leaders, and he had immediately prepared a list of specific amendments to be presented at the next round. This list included a clearer clause on the federal spending power, defenses of northern Canadian participation in national institutions, a clause on aboriginal government, a clause on multicultural rights, and a firm commitment to public hearings before the constitutional revisions came into effect. Once again, when the nation's leaders convened at the Langevin Block to consider the Meech Lake document, Pawley apparently found himself in a minority of one. He won sufficient support on some parts of his list to make several changes but on a matter dear to his heart, aboriginal rights, he was flatly rejected. In the wee hours of the morning, he sat on the back stairs with Premier David Peterson of Ontario debating whether to jettison the entire Accord. The two men returned to the conference room, Peterson endorsed the Accord, and Pawley, too, gave his assent. He then returned to the unstable political situation in Manitoba knowing that he was committed to holding provincial hearings before a final decision was made on the entire Meech Lake package.

The New Democratic government was situated precariously. In the 1986 provincial election it had won 30 seats to the 26 held by Gary Filmon's Conservatives and the one seat occupied by the Liberal leader, Sharon Carstairs. Then, in the autumn of 1987, a veteran NDP minister whose health was uncertain decided to leave the government, his resignation to take effect on the opening of the 1988 session. A second crucial NDP vote was also in question. James Walding, NDP backbencher and former Speaker of the Assembly, was no longer attending caucus meetings and was rumoured to be hostile to the government. If one vote was lost and the other switched sides, the Pawley administration would collapse.

The Meech Lake Accord was not one of the pressing issues on the NDP government's agenda during its final six months. Plans for the legislative hearings into the Accord were slowly taking shape and a paragraph on the hearings was drafted for the Throne Speech. Premier Pawley had not wavered in his support. Then, between October, 1987, and January, 1988, members of his party, including, it was said, a sizeable proportion of his caucus, began to question the so-called 'seamless' web woven by Canada's other First Ministers. This dissenting movement was drawn from almost every region and interest group in the party. Moreover, despite the conventional wisdom that constitutions are not the stuff of popular debate, the Accord's Manitoba opponents discovered a remarkable degree of interest in and concern about the proposed changes. In January, 1988, at least fifteen constituencies passed resolutions critical of the Meech Lake Accord which were forwarded in turn to the provincial executive for consideration at the annual party convention in early March. At this point, Pawley recognized that he could no longer assume endorsement of the Meech Lake principles in the Manitoba legislature.

Pawley had commenced discussions with representatives of the party dissenters in December but, at that early stage, his main concern was to ensure that they were not motivated by anti-French sentiments and that they appreciated the difficult situation of the national party leader, Ed Broadbent, who had to acknowledge Quebec views. As the convention approached, however, Pawley acted to avert a contest over the Accord. This was a wise move because, whether he knew it or not, the dissenters believed that a motion rejecting the Accord would easily win party approval. A resolution was drafted and re-drafted to meet the views of the various groups and resulted in a composite statement presented to delegates at the provincial convention. It called on the government to hold hearings before it decided whether to support the Accord in the Legislature. Pawley was able to speak in favour of the resolution, Broadbent avoided an embarrassment, and the opponents of the Accord were encouraged to launch a campaign at the public hearings in the expectation that the party was on their side and that the party caucus could be persuaded to reject the constitutional resolution.

Three days later, Walding deserted his party on the budget vote and the government fell. Pawley resigned, the New Democratic Party commenced a leadership campaign and the province entered a general election. Given the disastrous state of the New Democrats — February was the month of large increases in government-controlled automobile insurance rates, April the month to calculate increased tax payments — all signs pointed to the demise of the NDP government. The sudden turn of events implied rapid passage of the Accord under a new Conservative government.

The people of Winnipeg chose to confound the electoral experts. A cautious and uninspired Conservative campaign actually lost votes for the party's candidates in Manitoba's capital city. The New Democrats, clearly out of favour with the people despite a new leader, Gary Doer, lost even more votes. These losses and an unusually large turnout favoured the Liberals. Final standings in the election were 25 Conservatives (a minority government), 20 Liberals (all but one from Winnipeg), and 12 New Democrats. Suddenly the fate of the Meech Lake Accord was in doubt.

The Liberal leader, Sharon Carstairs, was an emphatic opponent of the Accord. Now that she held the balance of power, she could happily declare to the media that Meech Lake was 'dead.' It was hyperbole but, in the first flush of success, it was an understandable exaggeration. And, because the sudden rise in her party's fortunes could be attributed to her forceful leadership, presumably no one in her caucus of neophytes would want to challenge her conclusion. Certainly, Premier Filmon was not about to test her resolve. He assured questioners that the Accord was not a legislative priority of his new government. He would take no action to precipitate an unnecessary crisis – even the hearings seemed to be in doubt – and would await the unfolding of national political events. The leader of the New Democrats, Gary Doer, continued to advocate that hearings take place and, like his predecessor, seemed determined to introduce amendments on such matters as aboriginal, northern and women's rights.

Why was the Accord stalled in Manitoba? On the surface, the Pawley government's sudden fall and the unexpected rise of a third party seemed to account for the pause. But this was not the full story. In addition to Pawley's determination to proceed slowly and with due attention to public consultation, one must emphasize that many Manitobans were now suspicious of the proposal. The very absence of public debate in English-speaking Canada and the failure of national political representatives to articulate the strengths and weaknesses of the measure roused doubts. The concerns of Manitobans probably reflected those of many other western and English-speaking Canadians. These concerns may be placed in five categories: the social democrats, the Charter of Rights coalition, native and northern citizens, constitutional critics and the anti-French.

Members of unions, mostly affiliated with the Canadian Labour Congress, may be taken as representative of the social democratic strain. These union members concluded that the Accord, by decentralizing Confederation, was part of a neo-conservative agenda that included the proposed Canadian-American trade deal, the deregulation of some industries and the privatization of certain government-controlled companies and services. In this view, the Accord was striking at the nation's social democratic foundation, a community consensus that offered a strong defense of unions, in favour of a market-based, American-style social system. Those in service sector occupations, including members of civil service unions and of day-care teachers' and nurses' associations, were particularly interested in these discussions. The fact that the Canadian workforce was much more unionized than the American (about 37% of non-agricultural workers compared to about 18%) lent strength to the arguments as well as to the numbers of those sympathetic to the cause.

Affiliated with the unions in these social democratic concerns were members of the left-wing farm movement, the National Farmers' Union, and numerous members of the New Democratic Party. The farmers believed that several crucial principles for which they had fought throughout the twentieth century, including supply managementment and freight rate controls, were challenged by the Conservative agenda. Though the Meech Lake Accord was less pressing than several other federal initiatives such as the free trade deal and the dismantling of the Crow's Nest Pass freight rate agreement, it seemed to these farm families, as it did to the union members, part of a larger perspective with which they disagreed. The New Democrats added to this list their concern that the federal spending power, which had created and maintained national standards for the medical care system, could not in a post-Meech Lake era play the same role in the establishment of, for example, a national non-profit day-care system of the type that Manitoba's NDP government had been pioneering. Such concerns motivated social democrats to question the Meech Lake Accord rather than to reject it outright. However, given the absence of a public forum for this debate, questions often became criticism and then hardened into opposition.

The 'Charter' concerns with the Accord crossed all party lines but the term is appropriate because it reflects the concentration on particular rights that are enshrined in Canada's Charter of Rights. These concerns included women's rights and the place of multiculturalism in the national fabric. Representatives of the women's movement and of ethnic groups were divided in their analysis of the Accord; in each case, some regarded it as benign and others believed that it contained potential problems that should be addressed before it became law. When the Accord's supporters rejected amendments, however, increasing numbers in these groups moved into the opponents' camp.

The single clearest flaw in the Accord was its failure to acknowledge the rights and aspirations of northern Canadians. Tony Penikett, New Democratic Party leader of the Yukon territorial government, won sympathy across the country when he challenged the proposed rules for the nomination of Senators and Supreme Court judges and for the creation of new provinces. His case was made stronger by another crucial omission from this round of constitutional talks, aboriginal rights. Having failed to win agreement on aboriginal self-government in the preceding five years, the Premiers and Prime Minister had simply left the issue out of their discussions in this so-called 'Quebec round' or 'provinces' round.' Native leaders resented this silence on a pressing issue but, more important, they regarded the rule for the creation of new provinces as a serious setback to the aboriginal cause. If ever a native-controlled territory was to have a test, it would probably be in some portion of the North and under some version of provincial status. The new Meech Lake rules would ensure that southern provinces, some of which would inevitably be closely aligned with international resource corporations, could forever block the establishment of a predominantly native province in northern Canada. Once again, aboriginal leaders felt betrayed.

The concerns of constitutional analysts would never generate a campaign in the streets or even stir up a flurry of calls to a radio open-line show (the modern Canadian equivalent), but these legal specialists also played a role in the Meech Lake debate. Conducted in newspaper columns and public speeches as well as private correspondence, the Manitoba discussions reflected national concerns. Bryan Schwartz, a law professor, lamented the rigidity of the Accord in a book, *Fathoming Meech Lake* (1987). Israel Asper, former Liberal leader, and Jack London, law professor, debated Senator Nathan Nurgitz and Member of Parliament Leo Duguay, both Conservatives, in a televised battle of celebrities that offered more misinformation than one might have expected but also a good deal of popular entertainment. Behind the public talks, which were at best sporadic and inconclusive, an informal private circulation of briefs, drafts of scholarly articles (including some written for this book), and copies of letters kept the issue to the fore. This was not a clandestine activity, by any means, but the academic network did add fuel to the debate. Thus, a speech to the Alberta NDP task force on Meech Lake by retired Senator Eugene Forsey, to take one example, was distributed privately in Manitoba because it was a forceful criticism of the Accord and because there was insufficient room or interest in the popular media for such extended discussions of these matters. Thus, the academic analysis of the Accord was conducted in parallel with the public political campaign. Inevitably, criticisms spilled over into the partisan arena and fuelled further controversy.

The debate provoked in the New Democratic Party was the largest popular movement against the Accord in 1987 but another important expression of public opposition came from the Union of Manitoba Municipalities. Based in the local governments of small-town and rural Manitoba, the UMM had fought the extension of French-language services in the province in 1983-84 and perceived the Meech Lake proposals as another concession to French-language interests. The distinct society clause, in particular, was anathema to citizens who insisted on a one-nation rather than two-nation definition of Canadianism. These rural political leaders also believed the Accord would undercut their campaign for a new Senate based on equal regional or provincial representation, an issue that had preoccupied some western Canadians in recent decades. Though the UMM was close to the Conservative party on many issues, the Meech Lake Accord threatened to divide the rural electorate and to fuel a renewed round of western separatist activity. The founding of a new western Canadian party under the leadership of Alberta's Preston Manning in the autumn of 1987 even gave brief public prominence to this sentiment but rural Manitobans did not rally to the Reform Party of Canada in succeeding months.

Disquietude and uncertainty remained in rural Manitoba but it had not found political expression.

It might be argued that the Liberals and New Democrats mobilized opinion against the Meech Lake Accord in the 1988 provincial election campaign. It is true that both parties and particularly the Liberal leader, Mrs. Carstairs, criticized its flaws and emphasized the importance of public hearings. Nonetheless, the Accord was never a significant issue in the campaign, except, perhaps, in northern Manitoba where unionized workers and aboriginal voters re-elected five New Democrats. The real story of the Manitoba response to the Accord lay in the problems associated with establishing an informed public debate. Nowhere were the failures of the Meech Lake process more evident. The refusal of the federal Opposition parties to oppose, an obligation of Her Majesty's Loyal Opposition, placed significant constraints on provincial wings of the national Liberal and New Democratic parties. The federal government's insistence that the Accord was a seamless web, not open to amendment or to complementary clauses, frustrated provincial Conservatives. Movements of dissent arose in all three parties, however, and in extra-political circles. Ironically, an agreement reached in private by eleven individuals was pronounced dead by a twelfth individual, the leader of the Manitoba Liberal party.

As this article is written, Manitobans have not yet conducted a truly province-wide discussion of the merits and shortcomings of a crucial constitutional revision. However, it is likely that the commitment of their former premier, Howard Pawley, will eventually be honoured by his successors and a genuine exchange of views will occur. Until then, however, it cannot be said that Manitobans, any more than their counterparts in the other western provinces, have come to terms with the Meech Lake Accord.

Meech Lake and Quebec

'Quebec has won one of the greatest political victories of its history, a victory recognized beyond doubt by most objective observers as one of its greatest in two centuries.' Robert Bourassa.[1]

'I do not feel pleased, as a French Canadian, that the rest of Canada says, Well, you poor guy, you are not as good as the rest of us so we will give you a few more powers to run your province. That is what special status is.' Rt. Hon. Pierre Trudeau.[2]

'I have no problems with the notion of Quebec as a distinct society. It has always seemed to me that this was a sociological reality of the Canadian system of government. Good constitutional law like any good law reflects society.' Edward McWhinney.[3]

'When you combine the distinct society provisions with the present proportion of population guarantee, plus Supreme Court entitlements, plus Senate appointment powers, [and] the constitutional amendment veto for Quebec, I suggest that it gives a chuckling René Levesque almost everything he ever wanted without any of the trauma.' Israel Asper.[4]

INTRODUCTION: MEECH LAKE AND QUEBEC

In important ways the Constitution Act of 1982 was a paradox for Quebec. On the one hand it was initiated by Pierre Trudeau, and strongly supported by the 74 Liberal MPs from Quebec (the province has 75 seats in the House of Commons). The Act constitutionalized the key components of the Official Languages Act of 1969, legislation which had been designed to protect linguistic minorities across the country, to create a functionally bilingual public service, and to ensure that the symbols, signage and communications of the federal government were bilingual. For many Canadians, and particularly for those in the West, the Constitution Act seemed to fulfill the longstanding constitutional aspirations of Quebec, or at the very least those aspirations as they had been articulated by Pierre Trudeau.

On the other hand, the Quebec government of the day, led by René Levesque, refused to sign the Constitution Act, arguing that it failed to meet the federal government's promise during the 1980 referendum campaign to 'renew' Canadian federalism. While it might be argued that Levesque's leadership of a party and government committed to Quebec's independence may well have precluded agreement to any constitutional arrangements short of separation, it is nevertheless clear that opposition to the Constitution Act was more broadly based in Quebec. Although the Act provided constitutional protection for francophone minorities across Canada and for the anglophone minority in Quebec, it did not address the linguistic concerns of the francophone majority in Quebec, and indeed challenged some of the popular features of Quebec's language policy as embodied in Bill 101. Nor did the Act address, except by silence, the constitutional status of the Quebec government and National Assembly within the Canadian federal state. Quebec's ability to protect and nurture a distinctive francophone community in North America was not enhanced. For Quebecers, however, the most disturbing aspect of the Constitution Act was that it had been enacted despite the opposition of the Quebec government. Even though the Act stemmed directly from Ottawa's 1980 pledge to Quebecers to renew Canadian federalism, Canadians had been willing and able to rewrite the basic constitution of the land without Quebec.

It is against this backdrop of the Constitution Act, and the constitutional principles of Pierre Trudeau, that Guy Laforest and Dale Thomson place the Meech Lake Accord. Thomson traces out the history of constitutional negotiations in Quebec, and the changed political circumstances after 1984 which allowed the new Liberal government in Quebec to succeed where the Parti Québécois government had failed. Both Thomson and Laforest maintain that the constitutional demands of Quebec reflected in the Accord are relatively modest when compared to the historical stance taken by Quebec nationalists, that they do little more than constitutionalize the political status quo while recognizing the sociological reality of Quebec's distinct society. As Laforest argues, however, the modest character of the Accord should not conceal the great symbolic value that has been attached to the Accord in Quebec, and which would be attached to the Accord's rejection outside Quebec. Thus the specific conditions of the Accord must be seen in light of the role they play in expressing a new constitutional vision of Quebec, and of Quebec's position within the Canadian federal state. For Quebecers, the Meech Lake Accord addresses symbolic and constitutional concerns which go to the very heart of Quebec's relationship with the broader Canadian community.

Those symbolic and constitutional concerns are also addressed by Pierre Trudeau's contribution to this section. However, Trudeau's analysis of the Accord comes to a very different conclusion than that advanced by Laforest and Thompson. Canada's chief architect of the 1982 Constitution Act is in no sense apologetic for what others see as shortcomings in the Act, nor does he see the Accord as a positive step for Quebec or Canada. For Trudeau, the Accord bids adieu to the national vision around which the Constitution Act, and Canada, was constructed.

Notes

1 Premier of Quebec. Minutes of Proceedings and Evidence of the Special Joint Committee on the 1987 Constitutional Accord, September 1, 1987, 16:27.

2 Minutes of Proceedings and Evidence of the Special Joint Committee on the 1987 Constitutional Accord, August 27, 1987, 14:131.

3 Q.C. Minutes of Proceedings and Evidence of the Special Joint Committee on the 1987 Constitutional Accord, August 31, 1987, 15:60 – 15:61.

4 Q.C. Minutes of Proceedings and Evidence of the Special Joint Committee on the 1987 Constitutional Accord, August 18, 1987, 8:8.

Say Goodbye to the Dream of One Canada[1]

Pierre Elliott Trudeau

> We have in our country the patriotism of Ontarians, the patriotism of Quebecers and the patriotism of westerners, but there is no Canadian patriotism, and there will not be a Canadian nation as long as we do not have a Canadian patriotism.
>
> The late Henri Bourassa, journalist and politician.

The real question to be asked is whether the French Canadians living in Quebec need a provincial government with more powers than the other provinces.

I believe it is insulting to us to claim that we do. The new generation of business executives, scientists, writers, film-makers and artists of every description has no use for the siege mentality in which the cities of bygone days used to cower. The members of this new generation know that the true opportunities of the future extend beyond the boundaries of Quebec, indeed beyond the boundaries of Canada itself. They don't suffer from any inferiority complex, and they say good riddance to the times when we didn't dare to measure ourselves against 'others' without fear and trembling. In short, they need no crutches.

Quite the contrary, they know that Quebecers are capable of playing a leading role within Canada and that — if we wish it — the entire country can provide us with a powerful springboard. In this, today's leaders have finally caught up to the rest of the population, which never paid much heed to inward-looking nationalism — that escape from reality in which only the privileged could afford to indulge.

Unfortunately, the politicians are the exception to the rule. And yet one would have thought that those who want to engage in politics in our province would have learned at least one lesson from the history of the last 100 years: Quebecers like strong governments, in Quebec and in Ottawa. And our most recent history seems to establish beyond question that if Quebecers feel well represented in Ottawa, they have only mistrust for special status, sovereignty-association and other forms of separatism. They know instinctively that they cannot hope to wield more power within their province without agreeing to wield less in our nation as a whole.

How, then, could 10 provincial premiers and a federal prime minister agree to designate Quebec as a 'distinct society.' It's because they all, each in his own way, saw in it some political advantage to themselves.

1   Those who have never wanted a bilingual Canada — Quebec separatists and western separatists — get their wish right in the first paragraph of the Accord, with recognition of 'the existence of French-speaking Canada...and English-speaking Canada.'

Those Canadians who fought for a single Canada, bilingual and multicultural, can say goodbye to their dream. We are henceforth to have two Canadas, each defined in terms of its language. And because the Meech Lake Accord states in the same breath that 'Quebec constitutes, within Canada, a distinct society' and that 'the role of the legislature and government to preserve and promote (this) distinct identity...is affirmed,' it is easy to predict what future awaits anglophones living in Quebec and what treatment will continue to be accorded to francophones living in provinces where they are fewer in number than Canadians of Ukrainian or German origin.

Indeed, the text of the Accord spells it out. In the other provinces, where bilingualism still has an enormously long way to go, the only requirement is to 'protect' the status quo, while Quebec is to 'promote' the distinct character of Quebec society.

In other words, the government of Quebec must take measures and the legislature must pass laws aimed at promoting the uniqueness of Quebec. And the text of the Accord specifies at least one aspect of this uniqueness: 'French-speaking Canada' is 'centred' in that province. Thus Quebec acquires a new constitutional jurisdiction that the rest of Canada does not have: promoting the concentration of French in Quebec. It is easy to see the consequences for French and English minorities in the country, as well as for foreign policy, for education, for the economy, for social legislation, and so on.

2   Those who never wanted a Charter of Rights entrenched in the Constitution can also claim victory. Because 'the Constitution of Canada shall be interpreted in a manner consistent with...(Quebec's) role to preserve and promote the distinct identity' of Quebec society, it follows that the courts will have to interpret the Charter in a way that does not interfere with Quebec's 'distinct society' as defined by Quebec laws.

For those Canadians who dreamed of the Charter as a new beginning for Canada, where everyone would be on an equal footing and
where citizenship would finally be founded on a set of commonly
shared values, there is to be nothing left but tears.

3   Those who want to prevent the Canadian nation from being
founded on such a community of values are not content merely to
weaken the Charter. They are getting a constitutionalized — that is
irreversible — agreement 'which will commit Canada to withdrawing
from all services...regarding the reception and the integration (including linguistic and cultural integration)' of immigrants. We can guess
what ideas of Canada will be conveyed to immigrants in the various
provinces, with Canada undertaking to foot the bill for its own balkanization, 'such withdrawal to be accompanied by fair compensation.'

What's more, this principle of withdrawal accompanied by 'fair compensation' is to be applied to all 'new shared-cost programs.' That will
enable the provinces to finish off the balkanization of languages and
cultures with the balkanization of social services. After all, what provincial politician will not insist on distributing in his own way (what remains, really, of 'national objectives?') and to the advantage of his
constituents, the money he'll be getting painlessly from the federal
treasury?

4   For those who — despite all the Canadian government's largesse with power and with funds — might still have been hesitant to
sign the Meech Lake Accord, the Prime Minister had two more sur-
prises up his sleeve. From now on, the Canadian government won't
be able to appoint anyone to the Supreme Court and the Senate except people designated by the provinces! And from now on, any province that doesn't like an important constitutional amendment will have
the power to either block the passage of that amendment or to opt out
of it, with 'reasonable compensation' as a reward!

This second surprise gives each of the provinces a constitutional veto.
And the first surprise gives them an absolute right of veto over Parliament, since the Senate will eventually be composed entirely of persons who owe their appointments to the provinces.

It also transfers supreme judicial power to the provinces, since Canada's highest court will eventually be composed entirely of persons put
forward by the provinces.

What a magician this Mr. (Brian) Mulroney is, and what a sly fox!
Having forced Mr. Bourassa (Quebec Premier Robert Bourassa) to take
up his responsibilities on the world stage, having obliged him to sit
alongside the Prime Minister of Canada at summit conferences where
francophone heads of state and heads of government discuss international economics and politics, he also succeeds in obliging him to pass
laws promoting the 'distinct character' of Quebec.

Likewise having enjoined Mr. Peckford (Newfoundland Premier Brian Peckford) to preside over the management of Canadian seabeds, having compelled Mr. Getty (Alberta Premier Don Getty) to accept the dismantling of Canadian energy policy, having convinced Mr. Peterson (Ontario Premier David Peterson) to take up his responsibilities in the negotiation of an international free trade treaty, having promised jurisdiction over fisheries to the East and reform of the Senate to the West, Mr. Mulroney also succeeds in imposing on all these fine folks the heavy burden of choosing senators and Supreme Court justices! And all this without even having to take on the slightest extra task for the Canadian government, be it national regulation of securities markets, be it the power to strengthen the Canadian common market, be it even the repeal of the overriding ('notwithstanding') clause of the Charter.

In a single master stroke, this clever negotiator has thus managed to approve the call for Special Status (Jean Lesage and Claude Ryan), the call for Two Nations (Robert Stanfield), the call for a Canadian Board of Directors made up of 11 first ministers (Allan Blakeney and Marcel Faribeault), and the call for a Community of Communities (Joe Clark).

He has not quite succeeded in achieving sovereignty-association, but he has put Canada on the fast track for getting there. It doesn't take a great thinker to predict that the political dynamic will draw the best people to the provincial capitals, where the real power will reside, while the federal capital will become a backwater for political and bureaucratic rejects.

What a dark day for Canada was this April 30, 1987! In addition to surrendering to the provinces important parts of its jurisdiction (the spending power, immigration), in addition to weakening the Charter of Rights, the Canadian state made subordinate to the provinces its legislative power (Senate) and its judicial power (Supreme Court) and it did this without hope of ever getting any of it back (a constitutional veto granted to each province). It even committed itself to a constitutional 'second round' at which the demands of the provinces will dominate the agenda.

All this was done under the pretext of 'permitting Quebec to fully participate in Canada's constitutional evolution.' As if Quebec had not, right from the beginning, fully participated in Canada's constitutional evolution!

More than a half-dozen times since 1927, Quebec and the other provinces tried together with the Canadian government to 'repatriate' our Constitution and to agree on an amending formula.

'Constitutional evolution' presupposed precisely that Canada would have its Constitution and would be able to amend it. Almost invariably, it was the Quebec provincial government that blocked the process. Thus, in 1965, Mr. Lesage and his minister at the time, Mr. René Levesque, withdrew their support from the Fulton-Favreau formula (a plan to amend the British North America Act) after they had accepted and defended it. And Mr. Bourassa, who in Victoria in 1971 had proposed a formula which gave Quebec a right of absolute veto over all constitutional amendments, withdrew his own endorsement 10 days after the conference. In both cases, the reason for backing off was the same. Quebec would 'permit' Canada to Canadianize the colonial document we had instead of a Constitution, only if the rest of Canada granted Quebec a certain 'special status.'

The result was that 10 years later, when the Canadian government tried once again to restart the process of constitutional evolution, it faced the roadblock of 10 provinces which all wanted their own 'special status'; inevitably, they had enrolled in the school of blackmail of which Quebec was the founder and top-ranking graduate.

The rest of the story is well known. The Canadian government declared that it would bypass the provinces and present its constitutional resolution in London. The Supreme Court acknowledged that this would be legal but that it wouldn't be nice. The Canadian government made an effort at niceness that won the support of nine provinces out of 10. Mr. Levesque, knowing that a constitutional deal would interfere with the progress of separatism, played for broke, refused to negotiate and turned again to the Supreme Court to block 'the process of constitutional evolution.' He lost his gamble: the court declared not only that Quebec had no right of veto (Mr. Bourassa had in any event rejected it in Victoria, and Mr. Levesque had lost it somewhere in the west of the country), but also that Quebec was fully a party to 'Canada's constitutional evolution.'

A gamble lost, a gamble won — big deal! Quebec public opinion, with its usual maturity, applauded the players and then, yawning, turned to other matters.

But not the nationalists! Imagine: They had tried blackmail once again, but Canada had refused to pay. It was more than a lost gamble, it was 'an attack in force' (law professor Léon Dion and many others) it was 'an affront to Quebec' (Paul-André Comeau, assistant editor of Le Devoir). Because in addition to being perpetual losers, the nationalists are sore losers. For example, they didn't lose the 1980 referendum: the people made a mistake, or were fooled by the federal government. Likewise, after Robert Bourassa and René Levesque had foolishly passed up a right of veto for Quebec, it was necessary to somehow blame it on the federal government; attack in force, affront!

The provincialist politicians, whether they sit in Ottawa or in Quebec, are also perpetual losers; they don't have the stature or the vision to dominate the Canadian stage, so they need a Quebec ghetto as their lair. If they didn't have the sacred rights of French Canadians to defend against the rest of the world, if we could count on the Charter and the courts for that, they would lose their reason for being. That is why they are once again making common cause with the nationalists to demand special status for Quebec.

That bunch of snivellers should simply have been sent packing and been told to stop having tantrums like spoiled adolescents. But our current political leaders lack courage. By rushing to the rescue of the unhappy losers, they hope to gain votes in Quebec; in reality, they are only flaunting their political stupidity and their ignorance of the demographic data regarding nationalism.

It would be difficult to imagine a more total bungle. Mr. Bourassa, who had been elected to improve the economic and political climate in the province, chose to flail around on the one battlefield where the Péquistes have the advantage: that of the nationalist bidding war. Instead of turning the page on Mr. Levesque's misadventures, he wanted to make them his own. Instead of explaining to people that, thanks to the ineptitude of the Péquistes we were fully bound by the Constitution of 1982, Mr. Bourassa preferred to espouse the cause of the 'moderate' nationalists.

A lot of good it does him now! The Péquistes will never stop demonstrating that the Meech Lake Accord enshrines the betrayal of Quebec's interests. And a person as well-informed as (newspaper columnist) Lysianne Gagnon was able to twit Mr. Bourassa thus: 'Quebec didn't achieve even a shadow of special status...the other provinces fought tooth and nail for the sacrosanct principle of equality. And they too will have everything Quebec asked for' (La Presse, May 2, 1987). Does not the very nature of immaturity require that 'the others' not get the same 'trinkets' as we?

The possibility exists, moreover, that in the end Mr. Bourassa, true to form, will wind up repudiating the Meech Lake Accord, because Quebec will still not have gotten enough. And that would inevitably clear the way for the real saviors: the separatists.

As for Mr. Mulroney, he had inherited a winning hand.

During the earlier attempts to Canadianize the Constitution, prime ministers MacKenzie King, Saint-Laurent, Diefenbaker, Pearson and Trudeau had acted as if it couldn't be done without the unanimous consent of the provinces. That gave the provinces a considerable advantage in the negotiations and accounted for the concessions that the Canadian prime ministers had to contemplate in each round of negotiations. It is likely, for instance, that if King had been prepared to accept unanimity (Mulroney-style) as the amending formula, the Constitution could have been repatriated as early as 1927.

But since 1982, Canada had its Constitution, including a Charter which was binding on the provinces as well as the federal government. From then on, the advantage was on the Canadian government's side; it no longer had anything very urgent to seek from the provinces; it was they who had become the supplicants. From then on, 'Canada's constitutional evolution' could have taken place without preconditions and without blackmail, on the basis of give and take among equals. Even a united front of the 10 provinces could not have forced the federal government to give ground: with the assurance of a creative equilibrium between the provinces and the central government, the federation was set to last a thousand years!

Alas, only one eventuality hadn't been foreseen: that one day the government of Canada might fall into the hands of a weakling. It has now happened. And the Right Honorable Brian Mulroney, PC, MP, with the complicity of 10 provincial premiers, has already entered into history as the author of a constitutional document which — if it is accepted by the people and their legislators — will render the Canadian state totally impotent. That would destine it, given the dynamics of power, to eventually be governed by eunuchs.

Notes

1 This article first appeared in the *Toronto Star*, May 27, 1987, pp. A1, A12.

The Meaning and Centrality of Recognition

Guy Laforest

As a Québécois intellectual living and working in Alberta, I find myself in a peculiar, rather uncomfortable position with regards to public discussions of the Meech Lake Accord. Sharing the company of historians who believe Meech Lake to be a full-blown disaster, of political scientists who perceive in it seeds of instability, of Western spokespersons who compare it to the Aids virus, and finally of Trudeau nostalgics who keep on wondering who spoke for Canada and lamenting the transformation of Ottawa into a city of political eunuchs, I am more or less compelled to mute my own misgivings concerning the Accord. I have to set aside the considerable amount of public discussion which took place in Québec during the past few months, with people like former P.Q. leader, Pierre-Marc Johnson, denouncing the monster of Meech Lake, and numerous observers deploring either the emptiness of the distinct society clause, or the insufficient limitations of the spending powers of the federal government.[1]

However, while the Meech Lake Accord represents an imperfect agreement, I believe that it offers Canada an extraordinary opportunity, unforeseen by almost all commentators, to fill the gaping hole in legitimacy persisting in the political system since that fateful November night, in 1981, when a province at the heart of the Canadian duality, representing more than a quarter of the population of the country, was isolated and excluded from the process of constitutional reform.[2] René Lévesque, who was buried exactly six years after the patriation deal, and the members and sympathizers of his government-party, were not the only ones to have felt betrayed at that time. Speaking for the federalists and moderate nationalists who had voted 'No' in the 1980 sovereignty-association referendum, Solange Chaput-Rolland argues that the Accord had provided her and like-minded persons with their first adequate justification for their momentous decision at the beginning of the decade.[3] They had been promised reforms during the referendum, and these had meant much more than the Trudeau scheme of patriation coupled with a Charter of Rights and Freedoms.[4] Critics of the Accord argue that the agreement was reached in an undemocratic way, is bad for the West, could jeopardize human rights in Québec, endangers mobility rights through its provisions on immigration, creates an imbalance in the Supreme Court by entrenching the presence of three Québec judges, threatens the equality rights of women, ignores multicultural groups, aboriginal peoples, the demands of the Territories and those of francophones outside Québec. I must say that I remain unperturbed by these arguments. They ask of Meech Lake a level of perfection that has never been reached in the history of Canadian constitutionalism. They also mistakenly see this agreement as an immutable end-point. Meech Lake could more appropriately be called the Québec round in our process of reform. This is certainly how it was seen by the Premiers meeting in Edmonton in August, 1986, when they first responded to advances made by the Bourassa government, notably by Gil Rémillard's Mont-Gabriel declaration.[5]

Because Meech Lake is the Québec round, I would like to center my reflections on the aspect of the Accord which has been most vehemently attacked by former Prime Minister Pierre Trudeau, by his former ministers and intellectual acolytes Donald Johnston, Jean Chrétien, George Radwanski and others. Meech Lake adds an additional device to the interpretive basket of the constitution by formally and explicitly recognizing Québec as a distinct society. Moreover, it imposes on the government of Québec and the National Assembly the obligation to defend and promote such a distinctiveness. Symbolically, this is quite important. But it means much more than a token recognition, a generous but empty gesture offered to 'our friends in Québec.'

Etymological Aspects of Recognition

Meech Lake recognizes Québec, within Canada, as a distinct society. But what does this mean? What does an individual, or a group, really do in granting recognition to another partner in a relationship? In the world of political science in Canada, few people have insisted on the importance of etymology with the persistence of Gérard Bergeron.[6] With him, I deem it fundamental that Canadians should know what they are about to do at this crucial juncture in our history. Recognition can mean a plurality of things. Jacques Cartier was involved in recognition when he explored an unknown land for Europeans. So were the settlers of the West when they proceeded with detailed examinations of the new territories.[7] But in the case of the recognition of Québec as a distinct society, a different layer of meaning is implied. The action involved here covers the admission that something is real, legal, true, authentic, certain.

It is often said that everybody in Canada knows that Québec is distinct, that it is not a province like the others. Historians have said so, private citizens concur in their conversations. It is an accepted convention in our country that Québec is different. But contemporary Québécois are not satisfied by conventions. They were taught by the Supreme Court earlier in this decade, in the patriation affair, that conventions are a tricky business; they are hard to invoke, at the mercy of political circumstances, and not enforceable by the judicial system.[8] Meech Lake, however, has the enviable quality of formality and clarity: it **recognizes**, at the heart of the fundamental law of the country, for our own consumption and for the world, the specificity of Québec.

Aside from the formal recognition of the authenticity of Québec's distinctiveness, I hope there is another relevant layer of meaning in such an action. I am thinking of recognition as an expression of gratitude. At the present conjuncture in the history of the country, dominated by the free trade debate, partisans and opponents of a comprehensive deal with the Americans swear their allegiance to the Canadian brand of distinctiveness. Now one central element of that phenomenon is the French fact. Roger Gibbins expresses the situation in these terms:

> On the more positive side, French Canada makes a valuable contribution to English Canadian nationalism as it is Canada's bilingual and bicultural character that more than anything else sets it apart from the United States. The question that arises is what English Canada has to offer French Canada in return.[9]

One element of the answer resides in the recognition of linguistic duality. However, the at times artificial nourishment of French minorities outside Québec is an insufficient rampart for the integrity of a thriving French Canada. This needs a strong territorial base where the dynamism furnished by the concentration of a French population, joined with the tools of government, can be used to countervail the conditions of an English-speaking North America. The recognition of Québec is thus a second element in the answer. It gives Québec the ability to defend and promote not only what constitutes a significant part in the identity of Québécois, but also the identity of all Canadians. If this recognition cannot be granted in a spirit of what I have called gratitude, or generosity, then indeed this country is in great danger.

This question has a particular relevance in the West. The recent founding of the Reform Party indicates that the West continues to feel considerable alienation, stemming from the belief that the region as a whole is not adequately represented in federal institutions, that it does not receive its fair share in the federal politics of economic redistribution. Admittedly, Meech Lake has nothing to do with the first element of this alienation, although it does place senate reform on the constitutional agenda, and it fails to rectify the second one. But if Westerners refuse Meech Lake mostly because it fails to satisfy their own grievances, then in my opinion they miss the point about the agreement. By patriating Québec, Meech Lake reduces the rigidity of the constitutional reform process itself, and it strengthens the specificity of both Québec and Canada. It seems to me that this is beneficial to Westerners **qua** Canadians.

Cultural Nationalism, Recognition, Language

Some years ago, Donald Smiley was lamenting 'the non-philosophic nature of Canadian political discourse.'[10] He thought our tradition was conservative and legitimist, more turned towards historical reflections than philosophical considerations. However, he did concede an exception in Charles Taylor, who in the spring of 1979 delivered the keynote address at a conference of philosophers debating Confederation in Montréal. Taylor had been extremely active for ten years in the N.D.P., trying to build bridges for the party in Québec, working towards inter-cultural dialogue.[11] Known for his studies in German philosophy, Taylor chose on that day to focus his presentation on the philosophical roots of linguistic and cultural nationalism. He did so by drawing on a group of concepts borrowed from Herder and his followers in German post-Romantic thought: expression, realization or achievement, and **recognition**.

Taylor thinks language and culture can blend to form a significant pole of identity for individuals in the modern world. In his address to philosophers in Montréal, he thus evaluated positively the phenomenon of Québec nationalism.[12] For individuals who consider their linguistic and cultural affiliation an important pole of their identity, it will become crucial that the language in question receives adequate room for expression.[13] They will be highly concerned with the vitality of their language, knowing that a crippled idiom would undermine their own personal identity. Such a language is much more than a mere instrument for communication. It possesses a constitutive dimension.

On such a requirement for linguistic expression, as Taylor well realized, French Québécois have based their demands for collective language rights.[14] What they ask for here is certainly not expression for expression's sake. Such space for expression, in cultural nationalism, is desired in order to make a number of contributions in fields that are highly valued by moderns: arts, science, technology, along with economic and political achivements.[15] Twenty-five years ago, Québec held an election over the nationalization of private hydro-electrical companies, in order to demonstrate, symbolically and practically, that it wished to embark upon a fully modern life in French in North America, making the kind of realizations Taylor had in mind. The intense debate in Québec in the late seventies involved intellectuals and politicians who agreed on the need for expression and modern achievements in French (Trudeau and Lalonde included), but who disagreed on the means, on the political infrastructures more likely to facilitate the actualization of these objectives.

Taylor is particularly eloquent when discussing recognition, which goes to the heart of post-1960 Québec nationalism:

> This is especially evident when we appreciate how important is the self-respect of a culture. This self-respect is gained through realization; but the value of realization depends also to a great degree on the recognition of others, on how a people is seen internationally, by the world at large....There is therefore among a small people, whose self-confidence has been shaken by living in the shadow of the contemporary world's most powerful language/culture/technology, a tremendous hunger for international recognition.[16]

On the eve of the 1980 referendum on sovereignty-association, Taylor felt caught between extreme positions. He could not accept the arguments of the anti-nationalists, who rejected the notion of group identification, denied that Québec was a nation, and conceived Canada mostly as a country of individuals whose rights should be protected by the federal state. Nor did Taylor feel more sympathy for the ultra-nationalists, who conceived of language and culture as the fundamental, most important pole of identification, and who starting from that premise justified the status of nation-state for Québec, seen as the only way to obtain appropriate levels of realization and recognition. Taylor took the intermediate position according to which language and culture did constitute an important pole of identification, even more so in the light of Québec's situation in North America. Allying himself with the members of the Task Force on Canadian Unity, or the Pépin-Robarts Commission, he argued for a revision of Canadian federalism which would respect the spirit of duality, making room for Québec's specific need for recognition, outside as well as inside Canada.[17] As Québécois, according to Taylor, 'We have a right to demand that others respect the conditions of our language/community being a viable pole of identification.'[18]

In the spring of 1980, a majority of Québécois decided they could settle for less than the zenith, that is political independence, in terms of international recognition. This did not mean the eradication of Québec nationalism. Moreover, it did not signify the end of the thirst towards recognition. The external aspect of that thirst has manifested itself in the past few years in visits made in Québec by the pope, the American and French presidents, by the secretary-general of the United Nations. More tangibly, it was expressed by the participation of Québec in the 'Sommets de la francophonie,' in Paris in 1986 and in Québec in early September 1987. The Québec government, under the Liberals of Robert Bourassa, has continued to assert its presence in international relations.

External recognition, however, is only one dimension of the whole affair; the internal aspect is equally important. In Québec, the basic perception concerning the nature of this country is dualistic,[19] and as long as such a perception endures, it will contribute to the extreme dissatisfaction of many Québécois with the constitutional settlement achieved under the stewardship of Pierre Trudeau in 1981-1982. The Constitution Act, 1982, recognized the fundamental rights of individuals and the democratic rights of citizens. It protected the multicultural heritage of the country, contained a number of dispositions on the rights of aboriginal peoples and stated some obligations of the political system towards them. It gave strong guarantees to provincial governments, for instance with the notwithstanding clause and the amending formula, came to the rescue of the educational rights of linguistic minorities, and made the provisions for equality in the direction sought by various organizations representing women. The only basic reality which was blatantly neglected was the collective identity of Québécois. With Meech Lake, these Québécois will see a reflection of this part of their identity enshrined in the Constitution. They have been finally recognized by the Other, or Others, with whom they share the country.

Meech Lake thus works towards the satisfaction of something very profound in the soul of most Québécois. We should not let merely utilitarian concerns cause us to forget this. We should not let ourselves be seduced either by the strong rhetoric of former Prime Minister Trudeau.

Meech Lake and Pierre Trudeau

One month after the Meech Lake agreement had been tentatively reached, Pierre Elliott Trudeau put an end to the religious silence he had held for three years on Canadian public affairs. The Accord obviously contradicted major elements of his vision of the country. Trudeau was under intense pressure from his friends and political supporters. On this issue, he had to speak out. He did so with his sharpest polemical pen, using extreme language laced with sexual connotations. Prime Minister Mulroney was a weakling who had yielded to the blackmail of Québec nationalists.[20] The balancing act of 1982 had been lost. Henceforth, the country would be governed by eunuchs and would suffer from impotence. Provincializing politicians were bad losers needing the Québec ghetto in lieu of a den.[21] Here, however, I shall concentrate my efforts on the criticisms Mr. Trudeau addressed to the recognition of Québec as a distinct society and the additional powers implied by this acknowledgment.

It is not insignificant to note this was the very first point discussed in Trudeau's letter to Montréal's *La Presse* and *The Toronto Star*. The real question, as he rhetorically put it, is whether or not French Canadians living in Québec need a provincial government with more powers than the others. In his answer, Trudeau was faithful to his reputation as a champion of individualism.[22] Québécois, argued Trudeau, should feel insulted by a constitutional scheme that would grant more powers to their province. They have acquired a new self-confidence and feel enough security to compete on an equal footing with the rest of the country. The new class of businessmen storming the province, the likes of Pierre Lortie, Bertin Nadeau, Michel Gaucher and the Lemaire brothers, have abandoned the state of siege mentality which burdened the thought of nationalist elites prior to and after the Quiet Revolution. They do not need crutches provided by the Québec state to go out and face the world. Following the leadership of people like them, Québécois can play a key role in Canadian affairs. This is Trudeau's individualistic politics of the will, which has accompanied him since his Brébeuf days, at his very best.[23] It is a grand ideal, noble and valiant. But it is equally misguided and, I believe, wrong.

Trudeau's vision possesses plausibility on the blackboard of a university classroom. However, it illegitimately abstracts from the context of North American life. An individualistic scheme like his, insisting on the rights and mobility of Canadian citizens, would be more relevant if Canada and Québec were located right in the middle of the European continent, surrounded by numerous countries and as many different languages. But this is not the case. Québec belongs to North America. It tries to maintain its identity, to live modernity in a comprehensive way, surrounded by rather perilous circumstances. Its only neighbour in its linguistic environment is an idiom dominating French by a ratio of fifty to one, and that happens to be at the same time the *lingua franca* of the modern world. This language trumps French by a ratio of three to one in Canada, and it is also the idiom of the United

States, the greatest power in the history of mankind in the strategic, technological and economic spheres. Québec does not find itself in the controlled conditions of experimentation typical of a university laboratory. It lives in the real world of North America, its truth is that of French as it stands on the linguistic battlefield of our continent. I think Trudeau often forgets the *hic et nunc*, the here and now, of the whole problem.

It takes more than goodwill, and a few tens of millions of dollars, to maintain the integrity of modern French societies in North America. Surveying the situation in our country, informed Québécois can realize soon enough that protections granted to French Canadians, as individuals, cannot reverse the trends revealed by statistics.[24] In the West, for example, assimilation rates of French minorities oscillate between 60% and 70%. In such circumstances the gamut of services in French, along with the actions of the Secretariat of State, are comparable to those costly treatments administered to agonizing patients facing a terminal disease. While the lives of French communities outside Québec — in St. Boniface, Windsor, Sudbury, Acadia or the Eastern townships of Ontario — may be prolonged by the infusion of federal funds, they will not be saved.

But meanwhile Québec is compelled to live with the facts and the forces at work since the late nineteenth century.[25] Things cannot be changed by a simple operation of the will. The ideals, the ambitions of Pierre Trudeau have not been transformed into realities. At the present time, then, the government of Québec must assume its responsibilities towards its French majority, the only population in North America capable of living all the facets of modernity in a language other than English. It is quite justified therefore, for this government to have the additional, supplementary powers that Trudeau rejects, powers for the protection of the language and culture of a distinct society.

Those politicians who refused to sign the Canadian Constitution, 1982, do not seek the 'guettoization' of Québec. They do not manifest a preference for walking with crutches. They are simply realists who confront lucidly, in an enlightened way, the peculiarities of Québec's situation. In the terms of Aristotelian philosophy, they display prudence, or practical wisdom. In the best of all worlds, Québec would not need a security net like the one provided by Bill 101. In ideal circumstances, it could let a hundred flowers bloom with regards to the language of public signs. But because we live in America, it would be excessively dangerous for Québec to succumb to Trudeau's universalizing and abstract liberalism.[26] Trudeau forgets the teachings of Aristotle when he fails to confront his own thought with the practical parameters of a situation. In the field of morals and politics, Aristotle rejected the Platonist doctrine of the fixity of truth.[27] He underlined the importance of application, inviting us to deliberate within the confines of our rootedness.

It is possible to understand why Trudeau can brush off so rapidly the greater dependence of the individual upon the community that characterizes Québec, why he can absolutize the capacities of any French Canadian or Québécois to act and to compete successfully without additional state protection.[28] To become what he now is, in the words of Christina McCall-Newman, 'a kind of racial hermaphrodite, the unmatchable bicultural man,' Trudeau, beyond his undeniably strong will and vigorous moral character, benefited from exceptional familial and educational circumstances.[29] He came from a rich bilingual family in the most bilingual and bicultural of Canadian cities. His college and university years in Québec and abroad, which would still be considered exceptional in our own times, took place while the rest of the country, and certainly Western Canada, was humbled by the abyss of the Depression. In such fortunate circumstances, it is easy to forget what one owes to one's inheritance. In his remarkable political career and in his recent text on Meech lake, Trudeau extrapolated the potentialities associated with his own personal story to all French Canadians and Québécois individuals. Projecting, universalizing his own case, he postulated that these people only need courage and will.

The problem of course is that Trudeau, even with the best of intentions, cannot transfer to all of them the incredible advantages that were his from the start. His uncommon means explain his ability to outdistance the community without losing his identity. This is obviously very praiseworthy. But it is not correct to ask, to demand the same thing of the average citizen of Québec. State protections for language and culture are not aimed towards persons like Pierre Trudeau. They have to take into account the conditions of most Québécois.

It is not the virtue of courage which is being asked of each and every Québécois by Pierre Trudeau when he suggests they should disregard Meech Lake's distinct society clause and its concomitant additional powers. Courage and other moral virtues are not immutable essences that one could possess once and for all. These virtues are realized through practice. They imply the creation of good habits through repetitive actions. Aristotle defines them as dispositions to choose the mean between extremes, between deficiency and excess.[30] Moreover, the mean in question is always with regards to the particular situation in which we are involved. What can be defined as courage for Pierre Trudeau, the mean between fear and confidence for him in the Canadian context, would become for a considerable number of Québécois something contrary to the virtue in question, namely rashness (témérité, for us...).[31] Rashness is vicious behaviour marked by an excess of confidence. It would lead these Québécois to undertake actions without proper deliberation. It is impossible to deliberate about things which are impervious to change. There are no such things, repeats Aristotle, as abstract and eternal deliberative conditions. Québécois should therefore choose the mean according to their own situation.

Deliberating about the best means for achieving both individual success and the maintenance of their identity, they would do well in my judgment to ignore the arguments of Pierre Trudeau. Huge differences in life conditions should warn them about the necessity of circumspection. As a virtue, courage is something that one shows paradigmatically in front of death.[32] As members of a linguistic and cultural community, French Québécois transmit to each other from generation to generation the awareness that their condition corresponds to a constant battle between life and death.[33] In Hegelian terms, it is part of the *Bildung*, of the formation of our collective consciousness to have experienced fear of death, the absolute master.[34] Acting courageously in front of this is drawing a line between fear and confidence. Cowardice, here, is not absence of fear; it is excessive fear.

Québécois will not suddenly become cowards, nor will they have any reason to feel ashamed, in the eventuality of a strengthening of the Québec state through Meech Lake's distinct society clause. Realistically, there can be no such thing as a battle on an equal footing for Québécois in the linguistic landscape of North America. We understand that. However, many of us feel the recognition of Québec as a distinct society would create room for greater provincial legislative autonomy, thus making things somewhat less unequal.

This view has been championed by Claude Ryan, who actualizes the rich tradition of pan-Canadian, federalist Québec nationalism. In his lengthy reply to Trudeau's Meech Lake statement, Ryan pointed out that Trudeau's position has extremely shallow roots in French Québec.[35] When they are federalists, French Québécois do not believe the relationship between their provincial government and its federal counterpart should be one of subordination. As Ryan explained it, they would prefer to describe the relationship in terms of 'collaboration,' 'concertation,' and 'coordination.'[36] In this context, the recognition of Québec as a distinct society would not only have formidable symbolical consequences. It would have important juridical effects as well. Their spirit, I surmise, will be one of intergovernmental collaboration rather than subordination.

Special Status and Asymmetrical Federalism

It would be futile to try to summarize in the present context the history of the special status option in our constitutional evolution, particularly since the Quiet Revolution in Québec. This option was certainly embraced by the second Lesage government, by the 'Etats-Généraux du Canada francais' in 1967, by an intellectual like Claude Ryan when he was editor of *Le Devoir*. It has been criticized not only by centralists like former Prime Minister Trudeau and his supporters, but also by decentralists, and by intellectuals and politicians in the West who favor strict equality for all the provinces.[37]

Legally however, the Constitution Act, 1867, did grant a special status to the province of Québec.[38] It was the only original province touched by institutional bilingualism, in its legislature and judicial system (art. 133). It was the only province excluded from the provision allowing the federal government to standardize civil law in the country (art. 94). It was also the only province where a minority was protected with regards to the delimitation and the allocation of seats in the provincial legislature and in the Senate (articles 80, 21 and 23). For these reasons alone, and the list is far from exhaustive, it would be legally correct to say that Québec has always had a special status in the Canadian federation.

Meech Lake will not alter this basic fact, but will build upon it. The distinct society clause will increase the asymmetry of Canadian federalism in that Québec will be the only province to be constitutionally distinct. The government of Québec and the National Assembly will have the power to promote this distinctiveness. No other province will have anything resembling this. This certainly means the Charter of Rights and Freedoms should be interpreted differently in the case of Québec. The distinct society clause therefore adds an additional element to the basket of interpretive devices at the disposal of Supreme Court judges, who will not be able to ignore the entrenchment of Québec's specificity in the fundamental law of the land. Those who fear for the very survival of human rights in Québec should note that the clause in question will not systematically override the Charter and other interpretive principles. But it undeniably means there will be occasions, particular circumstances, where such an override will be justified. The first article of the Constitution Act, 1982, allows room for the common good to prevail at certain occasions over individual rights. There are reasonable limits to the exercise of rights, even in a free and democratic society. The distinct society clause acknowledges that there is no perfect identity in Canada between the common good for most of the country and the common good for Québec.

The Supreme Court will have to use its own brand of practical wisdom, of prudence, in this dimension of its activity. A relevant example is the Brown, McKenna, et al. affair regarding bilingual signs, currently in front of the Supreme Court. I suggest that the distinct society clause would help the tribunal decide in favor of the Québec government. The dispositions of Bill 101 pertaining to the language of public and commercial signs had one principal target: the area of greater Montréal. It is imperative that Montréal should continue to present a French visage to the thousands of immigrants who settle in the city every year. Greater Montréal holds almost half of the population of Québec. For us, it is the place where the linguistic battle will be either won or lost. I believe the Supreme Court should in this instance respect the decision which comes from the electoral, democratic process in Québec.[39]

Is this a form of the tyranny of the majority over the minority? I doubt it. The linguistic group in question has access to the best minority system of education in North America, to a remarkable array of social, cultural and economic services. Many French minorities outside Québec would like to be tyrannized in this way.

The distinct society clause will foster asymmetrical federalism in other ways, as it is the pillar which grants further legitimacy to other important dimensions of the Meech Lake Accord. It is because it is distinct that Québec will fully exercise its powers following the provisions of the agreement concerning immigration, along with its prerogative on the percentage of immigrants. The same basic reality justifies the position of Québec vis-a-vis the entrenchment of the composition of the Supreme Court. Finally, Meech Lake will enable Québec to be better equipped as a distinct society to resist the encroachments of the federal government upon its jurisdictions, with the limitations of the federal spending powers in conjunction with larger opting out provisions.

I refered earlier to the existence of discrepancies between the common good for most of the country and the common good for Québec. One of the greatest factors of resistance to the recognition of Québec as a distinct society is a tendency to deny these divergences. This tendency manifests itself in post-referendum aspects of Canadian nationalism.

Nation and Identity

There are perceptions which are wrong in Canadian history and politics, and French Canada is responsible for a number of them. For instance, it has certainly been wrong to assume that what it called English Canada shared its homogeneity. Our historians have tended to minimize the regional, ethnic and religious diversity of English-speaking Canadians. There were also problems with a thesis that had great currency in French Canada, the compact theory of Confederation. It is hard to identify the contracting parties; the Québec Resolutions were in addition modified in London; and the law which was the ultimate result of this process was after all enacted by the British

Parliament.[40] More recently, the two-nation thesis came under stringent attack by Canadians of neither British nor French origin, and by aboriginal peoples as well. French Canadians and Québécois have thus been forced by political events to recognize the weakness of some of their visions of the country, to rethink their perceptual allegiance to Canadian federalism.

The recognition of Québec as a distinct society is rendered difficult by an equally erroneous perception which was fostered in the aftermath of the referendum by the Trudeau government, and which has now acquired great credibility among English-speaking Canadians. This perception suggests there is indeed such a thing as a single pan-Canadian national identity at this time in our history. In the latter part of his career, Pierre Trudeau evolved towards a strong advocacy of a political Canadian nationalism based on the individual rights of citizens.[41] The 1982 Charter of Rights and Freedoms was an adventure in nation-building, and it will have strong effects in this direction despite the concessions the federal government was forced to make. The Charter, according to Knopff and Morton, stresses popular sovereignty rather than relationships between governments; it will foster judicial policymaking promoting national unity, and it puts forward 'a public discourse based on the language of rights' which will have 'nationalizing and centralizing implications.'[42] English-speaking media in Canada give their audiences the impression this nation-building process has already achieved its goals. *The Globe and Mail* presents itself as 'the national newspaper.' The C.B.C. invites the public to listen to *The National*; one hour later, its competition airs *The C.T.V. National News*.

Intellectuals and academics seem to have followed in the same direction. Ottawa for them represents the 'national government.'[43] It is interesting to remark that in Québec political science, Ottawa is systematically associated with the federal or central government, but almost never with the national one.[44] The same thing applies to political parties. For Québécois, John Turner heads the federal wing of the Liberal Party, not the national one. The boisterous nationalism of English-speaking Canadians goes hand in hand with an interpretation of the reverse fortunes of Québec nationalism. The latter phenomenon is seen to be declining in the atmosphere of moroseness overtaking Québec since the referendum, in the anti-state and individualistic context of neo-conservatism.[45] Some observers have proclaimed the end of the Quiet Revolution, others have underlined the collapse of a separatism which has proven to be nothing more than a paper tiger.[46] In this context, it has become possible to write an introductory textbook in Canadian Studies optimistically stressing the roots of unity, frankly situated around the historical, political and cultural dimensions of the Canadian nation, and its corresponding expressions in the regions; Québec, in this interpretation, becomes a region like the others.[47] Some political scientists go even further. In a renowned text-book on Canadian politics, the absence of Québec from the 1982 constitution is nothing more than a marginal issue, mentioned only obliquely in a section on federalism.[48]

The belief that Canada before Meech Lake had achieved a comprehensive national identity is a serious mistake.[49] It creates unfounded illusions about the solidity of the country, for Québécois in the eighties continue to see themselves as members of a nation. *Stricto sensu*, the 1980 referendum meant this nation had decided, in exercising its right to self-determination, to maintain its allegiance to Canada as a country. Nationalists were not to be found only on the Yes side. The slogan of the No side, 'Mon non est québécois,' and the leaders of its campaign in Québec, were firmly rooted in the tradition of Québec nationalism. No Québec government sitting in the National Assembly, Péquiste, Liberal, or even N.D.P., would accept to be a full partner in a country in which the basic infrastructure remains the unmodified Constitution Act, 1982. In the field of culture, the Québec of the eighties has reached the threshold, the critical mass allowing analysts to talk about its national music, theatre, cinema and literature. In this general context, it is presumptuous to talk about a pan-Canadian national identity involving Québec.

Something like Meech Lake, with the recognition of Québec as a distinct society, is a fundamental precondition for the eventual emergence of a common Canadian identity. I must repeat this would be a rather unique or original form of 'nationhood.' It would not mean the eradication of the primary allegiance of French Québécois to their homeland. In the conditions of North America, these Québécois would be extremely foolhardy ever to surrender this. The understanding of such a reality would considerably increase the chances for a successful dialogue in contemporary Canadian politics.

The recognition of Québec as a distinct society is not a matter that should be taken lightly. Other provinces should not do it simply as a way to advance their own personal objectives and priorities. They should embrace it only if they authentically believe a more securely distinct Québec can enrich Canada, in the knowledge this recognition would establish a special status for Québec and move the federation in an asymmetrical direction, in the belief a strong Québec nationalism could be reconciled with a Canadian identity which would be unique, unparalleled in the concert of peoples and states. This is the real challenge posed by Meech Lake.

Notes

1 Le Devoir (dossier), *Le Québec et le Lac Meech*, Montéal: Guérin Littérature, 1987. See in particular the reservations of Léon Dion on the distinct society clause, 89 and those of Jacques Parizeau on the spending powers clause, 179.

2 Gérard Bergeron, 'Québec in Isolation,' in Keith Banting and Richard Simeon, *And No One Cheered: Federalism, Democracy and the Constitution Act* (Toronto: Methuen 1983) 64-67. See also Daniel Latouche, 'The Constitutional Misfire of 1982,' in Banting and Simeon, 96.

3 The Report of the Special Joint Committee of the Senate and the House of Commons, *The 1987 Constitutional Accord* (Ottawa: Queen's Printer for Canada) 139-140.

4 Gérard Bergeron, *A nous autres: Aide-mémoire politique par le temps qui court* (Montréal: Québec/Amérique 1986) 26-27.

5 Le Devoir (dossier), *Le Québec et le Lac Meech*, 56-57.

6 Bergeron gives us an example of his etymological passion in his detailed analysis of the notion of 'governance,' in Gérard Bergeron, *La gouverne politique* (Québec-Paris-La Haye: Les Presses de l'université Laval-Mouton 1977) 19.

7 'Reconnaissance,' in *Grand dictionnaire universel Larousse du XIX-siècle* (Genève-Paris: Slatkine 1982) 791.

8 Edward McWhinney, *Canada and the Constitution, 1979-1982* (Toronto: University of Toronto Press 1982) 85-86.

9 Roger Gibbins, *Conflict and Unity: An Introduction to Canadian Political Life* (Toronto: Methuen 1985) 219.

10 Donald Smiley, *Canada in Question: Federalism in the Eighties* (Toronto: McGraw-Hill 1980) 284.

11 See for instance Charles Taylor, *The Pattern of Politics* (Toronto: McClelland and Stewart 1971) 126.

12 Charles Taylor, 'Why Do Nations Have to Become States?' in Stanley G. French ed. *Philosophers look at Canadian Confederation* (Montréal: The Canadian Philosophical Association 1979) 19-35.

13 Ibid., 26. For a revealing formulation of linguistic identity, see the novelist Jacques Godbout, 'En français d'Amérique, *Possibles* XI(3) (1987) 185:

> La langue, n'est-ce pas, c'est ce que d'autres appellent l'âme, je crois. C'est le seul héritage indiscutable, démocratique et commun que se transmettent les générations. Parfois, (c'est extraordinaire!) quand j'écoute bavarder comme une pie trotteuse la fille de mon fils, j'entends le discours de mon père. Parfois, c'est moi que j'entends. Notre voix. J'écris pour ne pas mourir, sachant que la langue me survivra.

14 Taylor, 'Why Do Nations Have to Become States?' 26.

15 Ibid., 26-27.

16 Ibid., 29.

17 Report of the Task Force on Canadian Unity, *A Future Together* (Hull: Supply and Services Canada 1979) 124-125.

18 Taylor, 'Why Do Nations Have to Become States?' 33.

19 There is a historical sketch of the duality thesis in Edwin Black, *Divided Loyalties: Canadian Concepts of Federalism* (Montréal and London: McGill-Queen's University Press 1975) 173ff.

20 Pierre Trudeau, in Le Devoir (dossier), *Le Québec et le Lac Meech*, 341.

21 For a devastating criticism of Trudeau's ghetto image when he refers to the Québec of nationalists, see Lise Bissonnette, 'Le Ghetto vous salue bien,' in *L'Actualité* XIII(8) (1987) 57.

22 George Radwanski, *Trudeau* (Toronto: Macmillan of Canada 1978) 121.

23 Ibid., 35-36.

24 Réjean Lachapelle and Jacques Henripin, *The Demolinguistic Situation in Canada* (Montréal: Institute for Research on Public Policy 1982) 310.

25 For an understanding of the perceptions of those who pushed towards linguistic homogenization in Western Canada, see David Hall, *Clifford Sifton (vol. I): The Young Napoleon* (Vancouver: University of British Columbia Press 1981) 95-96.

26 For a detailed analysis of Trudeau's political philosophy, see Reginald Whitaker, 'Reason, Passion and Interest: Trudeau's Eternal Liberal Triangle,' *Canadian Journal of Political and Social Theory* IV(1) (1980) 5-31.

27 Aristotle, *The Nicomachean Ethics* (Oxford: Oxford University Press 1980) Book I, Chapters 2-4.

28 On a philosophical level, Trudeau has internalized what Charles Taylor has named the modern disengaged identity. See Charles Taylor, *Human Agency and Language, Philosophical Papers (vol. I)* (Cambridge: Cambridge University Press 1985) 8.

29 Christina McCall-Newman, *Grits: An Intimate Portrait of the Liberal Party* (Toronto: Macmillan 1982) 62.

30 Aristotle, Book II, Chapter 6.

31 Ibid., Book III, Chapter 6.

32 Ibid., Book III, Chapter 6.

33 Gérard Bergeron, *Pratique de l'Etat au Québec* (Montréal: Québec/Amérique 1984) 18. See also Louis Balthazar, *Bilan du nationalisme au Québec* (Montréal: L'Hexagone 1986) 205.

34 Hegel, 164. This is at the beginning of the famous passage on fear, in the section on independence and dependence of self-consciousness: domination and bondage.

35 Claude Ryan, in Le Devoir (dossier), *Le Québec et le Lac Meech*, 349.

36 Ibid., 350.

37 Roger Gibbins, 'Constitutional Politics and the West,' in Banting and Simeon, 127-128.

38 Smiley, 218-2

39 This issue illustrates the role to be played by the courts in fleshing out the distinct society provision of the Meech Lake Accord.

40 Black, 151ff.

41 Alan Cairns and Cynthia Williams, 'Constitutionalism, Citizenship and Society in Canada: An Overview' in Alan Cairns and Cynthia Williams, *Constitutionalism, Citizenship and Society in Canada* (Toronto: University of Toronto Press 1985) 40.

42 Rainer Knopff and F.L. Morton, 'Nation-Building and the Canadian Charter of Rights and Freedoms' in Cairns and Williams, 146.

43 See for instance Gibbins, *Conflict and Unity: An Introduction to Canadian Political Life*, 69, 71, 77, 107, 128.

44 Bergeron, *Pratique de l'Etat au Québec*, 173ff.

45 Dominique Clift, *Quebec Nationalism in Crisis* (Montréal-Kingston: McGill-Queen's University Press 1982).

46 Donald Smiley, *The Federal Condition in Canada* (Toronto: McGraw-Hill Ryerson Limited 1987) XI. See also Ramsay Cook, 'Has the Quiet Revolution Finally Ended?' in Eli Mandel and David Taras, *A Passion for Identity: An Introduction to Canadian Studies* (Toronto: Methuenn 1987) 298.

47 Eli Mandel and David Taras, 'Preface' in Mandel and Taras, 7.

48 Richard Simeon, 'Federalism in the Eighties' in Paul Fox and Graham White, *Politics: Canada* (Toronto: McGraw-Hill 1987) Sixth Edition, 267ff.

49 Charles Taylor, 'Alternative Futures: Legitimacy, Identity and Alienation in Late Twentieth Century Canada,' in Cairns and Williams, 216-217.

Quebec and Meech Lake

Dale C. Thomson

The principal purpose of the Meech Lake Accord is, in Prime Minister Mulroney's words, to bring Quebec back into the Canadian family. More precisely, it is to obtain the adhesion of Quebec to the Canadian Constitution as up-dated in 1982.

Other matters, including some important ones crying out for attention, were injected into the negotiations leading up to the Accord. However, as the ten provincial premiers concluded at their annual conference in Edmonton in 1986, the Quebec situation had to be resolved first. Other concerns were not to be allowed to place in jeopardy the paramount objective of correcting the potentially dangerous situation resulting from Quebec's self-exclusion from the constitution-making process.

To understand this position, it is useful to review the previous attempts to up-date and repatriate the Canadian constitution. Since 1950, four attempts had been made to find a consensus of the federal and provincial governments. In 1950, Quebec Premier Duplessis turned down a federal proposal without even giving it serious consideration. In 1965, Premier Jean Lesage initially agreed to the Fulton-Favreau amending formula. However, he back-tracked in the face of Quebec nationalist opposition and did not present this tentative constitutional agreement to the Quebec National Assembly. In 1971, Premier Bourassa did precisely the same thing with regard to the Victoria Charter.

Finally, in 1982, Prime Minister Pierre Trudeau, in the last phase of his political career and still dreaming of achieving his greatest ambition, decided to ride rough-shod over Quebec's objections. With the approval of nine provinces but not Quebec, the British North America

Act was patriated and the Charter of Rights was integrated into the constitutional structure of the Canadian federal state. While the manoeuvre was perfectly legal, it was hardly designed to make Quebecers, always uneasy about their relationship with the rest of the country, feel secure about their future. Had the sovereignty association referendum not already been held, had not Premier Rene Levesque accepted the verdict of that referendum, had the Prime Minister of Canada not been a French-speaking Quebecer, and had Canadians generally not been sick and tired of the constitutional wrangling, the constitutional decision in 1982 might have been deadly serious for Canada. As it was, the 'coup de force,' as it was widely described in Quebec, became a festering sore in the Canadian political system. It also provided precious ammunition for the nationalist supporters of independence.

The wheel of Canadian political fortune, however, continued to turn. In 1984, Brian Mulroney became Prime Minister. Half French-Canadian, not identified with the 'coup de force,' and more flexible, less confrontational in dealing with Quebec, he was well suited to lead another attempt to win that province's approval for constitutional change. He was aided by the fact that he had welcomed a number of Quebec nationalists, and even former separatists, into his caucus. In 1985, furthermore, Robert Bourassa again became Premier of Quebec, this time on an unequivocally federalist programme and with a strong enough majority in the legislature not to have to worry very much about the separatists. The scene was set for a reconciliation.

Understandably, the other Premiers were skeptical when they learned that Bourassa was ready to start constitutional negotiations again, and had to be convinced that he would go the course. However, Bourassa had matured a lot in what he called his 'years of purgatory.' Shortly after his election, he drew up a list of five conditions that needed to be met if Quebec was to be brought into the constitutional fold:

- recognition of Quebec as a distinct society.
- guarantees for Quebec's cultural security, particularly with regard to immigration.
- limitations on the federal spending power.
- a Quebec veto on constitutional amendments deemed contrary to its interests.
- the right to participate in the selection of Supreme Court judges from Quebec.

The last three of those conditions, he pointed out to the other premiers, could apply to all provinces, and the first two would have no direct effect on the other provinces. In short, Bourassa argued, the other premiers had quite a lot to gain, and nothing to lose.

In return for the support of the other premiers, Bourassa made a firm commitment to have the Accord approved by the Quebec legislature even before it was ratified by Parliament or the other provincial legislatures. That task was made easier for him by the fact that he and Mulroney collaborated closely in the Meech Lake and Langevin negotiations, devising wording to balance concerns for national and provincial interests. In the end, Quebec received more than its bottom line, and more in fact than it expected. Bourassa made good on his commitment, and Quebec's legislature was the first to approve the Meech Lake Accord, approval that was also facilitated by the disorganized state of the opposition Parti Québécois.

At this point, it appears that the other provinces will all follow suit, although the new Premier of New Brunswick, Frank McKenna, remains a wild card in the deck. Elected after the eleven first ministers had initially endorsed the Accord, McKenna is not personally committed to the agreement. In fact, during his victorious election campaign in the fall of 1987, he promised to seek some revisions to the Accord. Here it is worth noting that the Confederation agreement of 1864 almost went awry when power changed hands in New Brunswick; the new government's defeat had to be manipulated by the pro-Confederationists, including the British authorities, to get the agreement back on track. That seems unnecessary this time. In his campaign against Premier Richard Hatfield, who had signed the Accord, McKenna used all of the ammunition in his arsenal, including an assault on the Accord. As it turned out, however, he need not have mentioned the subject at all, winning as he did every seat in the legislature. McKenna, I would argue, has proven too loyal a Canadian, and too conscientious an administrator, to break the consensus unless other provinces also decide to do so.

It should be stressed that opposition to the Accord will be watched closely within Quebec. In 1988, the relatively moderate leader of the Parti Québécois, Pierre-Marc Johnson, was replaced by separatist hardliner Jacques Parizeau. The new PQ leader would be pleased indeed if the Meech Lake agreement were blocked, or if it was opened up for re-negotiation. The possibility of a PQ comeback in that event is reason enough, in the eyes of many federalists, to ratify the Accord post-haste.

The Terms of the Accord

The clause that has stirred most debate is the one recognizing Quebec as 'a distinct society,' and thus recognizing the dual character of Canada. Many people have seen in the recognition of Quebec's 'distinctiveness' a step towards separatism. That has always been former

Prime Minister Trudeau's position, that any constitutional differentiation of Quebec would be an invitation for Quebec to go all the way to independence. By taking advantage of such a provision, it is argued, the Quebec authorities could move step by step to make the province so different from the others that de facto separation would occur, followed eventually by de jure independence. That was, in fact, the strategy of certain 'gradualist' separatists such as Claude Morin and Jacques Parizeau long before the Parti Québécois was formed. Parizeau has recounted that, while he was economic adviser to Premier Jean Lesage, he and his colleagues sought incrementally to strip the federal government of its financial and other powers. He has compared the process to tearing a sheet: when the rip gets deep enough, it is no longer worth repairing and has to be thrown away.

For many Quebecers, however, the distinctive society clause has important symbolic value. Quebecers have long had a visceral reaction against Quebec being treated as 'a province like the others.' For them, the survival of the French way of life depends not only on being different from other North Americans, but being recognized as different by those who feel that the assimilation of francophones is in the logic of history.

At a Montreal conference of the Canadian Bar Association, held in November 1987, there was a vigorous debate over the distinct society clause. Does the latter provide largely psychological satisfaction or, as Trudeau has argued, is it a step towards independence? At the conference, opinions were sharply divided. Pro-federalist supporters of the Accord noted that the distinctive society clause is merely 'interpretative' in nature, that it cannot over-ride other clauses while at the same time other clauses must not contradict it. They felt that its principal effect would be to enable the Quebec authorities to take special measures to protect the French language. Pro-separatists, including Parti Québécois tenors Claude and Jacques-Yvan Morin, denounced the clause as a meaningless sham designed to conceal another constitutional straightjacket.

Much of the discussion revolved around the scope of the word 'distinctive.' Does it refer to the predominantly French character of Quebec society, or does it encompass English-speaking and other Quebecers as well? (After all, the same paragraph in the Accord refers specifically to the English-Canadians 'present in Quebec.') How does the distinct society clause square with the undeniable fact that Quebec society is pluralistic, not homogeneous?

The scope of the word is a matter of considerable importance at a moment when the Supreme Court of Canada seems likely to decide, on the basis of the Constitution as it presently exists, that English-speaking Quebecers have the right to signs in their language. Will the

Meech Lake Accord, as presently worded, remove that right in the name of the province's 'distinctiveness?' With the Accord in place, how far would the Supreme Court go in letting a Quebec government reduce non-francophones' rights in order to protect the French character of the society? Such questions in turn underscore the importance Quebec has attached to attaining provincial input into Supreme Court appointments.

Concern has been expressed that the distinctive society clause could be invoked to limit the rights of groups other than linguistic minorities in Quebec. For instance, one of the most serious threats to the survival of a distinctive Francophone culture comes from the low birth rate in Quebec, which has gone from being the highest to the lowest in the country. Indeed, the birth rate has dropped to the point where the Francophone proportion of the Canadian population is expected to drop to twenty percent early in the twentieth century. To counter this trend, a number of possible measures have been discussed, including outlawing abortions and pressuring Francophone women to resume the role of homemakers and child-bearers. Women outside Quebec, however, seem more upset by this discussion than do those inside; Francophone Quebecers have made such great progress in so many respects since the 1950s that they are hardly likely to submit to authoritative measures for the alleged requirements of the 'race.'

A companion piece to the distinctive society clause, and one which has also caused concern, is the 'opting out' clause. Section 7 would enable a province to withdraw from a federal-provincial programme, establish its own, and still receive the amount of money the federal government would have spent. This possibility has existed since the early 1960s when the government of Lester Pearson allowed Quebec to not participate in a number of federal-provincial programmes and to receive the equivalent to the federal expenditure in tax points. When Trudeau assumed office he put an end to this trend which he considered, quite rightly, as a dangerous erosion of federal authority. The difference in the Meech Lake Accord, however, is that the opting-out province has to provide a programme 'compatible with the national objectives.' As with so many other parts of the Accord, it is not clear who will decide the matter of compatibility.

For those who fear that this provision will encourage the gradualist separatism pursued by Parizeau and Claude Morin in the 1960s, it is worth nothing that at the Bar Association meeting, Morin denounced the provision as too circumscribed to be used effectively for that purpose. Furthermore, he pointed out that the Accord does not limit in any way the federal spending power. In sum, then, the potential impact of the Meech Lake Accord remains unclear.

The Accord also modifies the procedures for selecting Supreme Court judges. Prior to the Accord, selection had been a federal responsibility, although the provinces have been consulted on occasion. Quebec's objections to that arrangement have been three-fold. First, while traditionally three of the nine Supreme Court justices came from Quebec, that number was not constitutionally guaranteed. Second, judges could be chosen to represent a federal or centralist viewpoint, a matter of some consequence given that the Supreme Court is the final arbiter of federal-provincial conflicts. Third, Quebec has been concerned that at least three judges are competent to hear cases based on Quebec's distinctive civil code. The changes proposed in the Accord meet these objections; the provinces will submit names for the federal government's approval, thus creating a double veto. Although this could lead to some difficult negotiations and even delay appointments, it is not likely to change the federal system per se.

Quebec was also able to get agreement to strengthen its control over immigration to that province, both in the matter of selection abroad and in the integration of new arrivals. There already exists an arrangement between Ottawa and Quebec City called the Cullen-Couture Agreement that provides for joint selection of immigrants. Through its officials abroad, Quebec makes the first selection, taking into account the applicant's likelihood of integrating into the francophone community; federal officials give final approval. The Accord arrangements call for Quebec to receive a number of immigrants each year proportionate to its percentage of the Canadian population. It can also have a monopoly over integration programmes in order to ensure that the new arrivals do indeed join the francophone community, and thus offset the low birth-rate among resident Quebecers.

Whether or not this increased control over immigration will be effective is an open question, since a landed immigrant can still decide to move into the anglophone community in order to broaden his or her career opportunities. Nor does the proposal close the Quebec border to people from other parts of Canada. All in all, one can understand and sympathize with Premier Bourassa and his colleagues in their attempt to bolster the francophone community in this way, but the experience even among French-speaking Quebecers has shown that there are limits to the ability of governments to determine the language of individuals. Notwithstanding Bill 101, which made French the sole official language of the province, more Quebecers are speaking English today than ever before. For many people the attraction of English-speaking North America is greater than political decrees.

The final measure in the Meech Lake Accord designed to meet Quebec's demands is the veto, accorded to all provinces, on an extended number of constitutional changes. Historically, Canadian law-makers have avoided the need for unanimous consent, fearing excessive rigidity in the face of changing conditions. Certainly Canada's first Prime Minister, Sir John A. Macdonald, would not have approved. Once again, however, the objective of the extended veto is to give Quebec a feeling of security within Canada, and to avoid a situation in which matters vital to Quebec are decided outside its borders.

Conclusion

In sum, Premier Bourassa, closely allied with Prime Minister Mulroney, got a deal that he could sell without serious difficulty to Quebec's National Assembly. The other Premiers went along for a variety of reasons. Certainly they were willing to do their part to bring Quebec back 'into the Canadian family,' providing they were convinced that Bourassa would not back out again. Second, the gains for Quebec did not adversely affect the interests of other provinces. Indeed, some provisions strengthened provincial governments generally. That, it seems to me, was the *quid pro quo*.

But over and above the Premiers' self-interests, the questions remains whether the Accord was a good deal for Canada. On balance, I believe it is acceptable. Granted, it might be better if it also dealt with some of the pressing issues of native rights, women's rights, Senate reform and multiculturalism. But, as I suggested earlier, the primary objective was to obtain Quebec's approval of the updated constitution. To do otherwise was to allow feelings of frustration and insecurity to grow and to feed the forces of separatism. In dealing with an insecure group of fellow-citizens, there is only one realistic policy in a democracy, and that is to err, if at all, on the side of generosity. French-speaking Quebecers have an on-going problem of living and working in their own language and environment; it is up to the majority group to demonstrate their understanding and their support. Canadian support for the equality of rights and opportunities requires such an attitude; political realism does too.

As an Anglo-Quebecer, I realize that my particular group may pay the heaviest price for the Meech Lake Accord since our language rights may be further restricted. Perhaps, though, that is the price that we may have to pay to make this country work. At any rate, we survived the PQ government, adapted by becoming bilingual, and are living as good lives as anywhere in Canada. We can adapt again.

In short, although the Meech Lake Accord is an imperfect thing, conceived and brought forth in an atmosphere of haste and political opportunism, it does meet a fundamental objective for Canada. We can live with it, even continue to grow under it, because no political deal can outweigh the basic strength of this country. And — a final word — the price of failure at this stage would be unacceptably high.

The
Political
Process

> *[T]he proposed changes strike at what is, in a way, the very essence of the Canadian federation. They undermine the three fundamental components of any modern democratic state: executive power, legislative power and the judiciary.* Pierre Elliot Trudeau.[1]

> *Eleven men sat around a table trading legislative, judicial, and executive power as if engaged in a gentlemanly game of poker, with little regard for the concerns of individual Canadians.* Deborah Coyne.[2]

> *There will be those who will describe the Meech Lake Accord as another example of the great Canadian art of compromise. I have no quarrel with those words. Rather, I view them as a compliment that should be directed to the Prime Minister and all of the other participants.* Bill Vander Zalm. [3]

> *Free societies are not those which seek unanimity. It is quite the contrary. Free societies are those which institutionalize conflicting opinion, reason and desire.* Ed Broadbent.[4]

INTRODUCTION:
THE POLITICAL PROCESS

Much of the debate over the Meech Lake Accord has arisen from the impact that specific provisions might have on the interests of particular groups, such as women, linguistic minorities and Northerners, or on the attainment of broader goals such as Senate reform or Quebec's integration into the Canadian federal state. There is, however, a second dimension to the debate which centres upon the political process which produced the Meech Lake Accord, and the potential impact of the Accord on the Canadian political process in the years ahead. It is this second dimension which is addressed by the authors in the following section.

Claude Rocan argues that the Accord does little more than reflect the political reality of a country in which the provinces have assumed a progressively larger role in the governance of the country, in which the federal and provincial governments are increasingly entangled across a broad policy domain. Thus Rocan concludes that the Accord should have a positive impact on intergovernmental relations without having any adverse effective on the federal government's ability to pursue national programs and objectives. This conclusion, however, is challenged by Malcolm Brown whose economic assessment paints a much bleaker picture of the Accord's impact on the federal government.

The chapters by Alan Cairns and Roger Gibbins explore the impact of the Accord on Canadian executive federalism. While agreeing with Rocan that the Accord reflects important **governmental** realities within the Canadian federal state, they argue that the Accord does not reflect the social underpinnings of the Canadian federal state, that it distorts rather than reflects the realities of Canada as the country moves towards the twenty-first century. This conclusion is shared by William Gold and Doreen Barrie who argue that while the voices of the provincial premiers echo throughout the Accord, the voice of Canada has been distorted if not lost altogether.

In total, the chapters in this section emphasize the importance of the political process through which the Accord was produced, and through which ratification is proceeding. Regardless of the Accord's fate, that process warrants close examination for it casts into bold relief the principal features, and principal flaws, of executive federalism as it has come to be practiced in the Canadian federal state.

Notes

1 Minutes of Proceedings and Evidence of the Special Joint Committee on the 1987 Constitutional Accord, August 27, 1987, 14:117.

2 Faculty of Law, University of Toronto. Minutes of Proceedings and Evidence of the Special Joint Committee on the 1987 Constitutional Accord, August 27, 1987, 14:8.

3 Premier of British Columbia. B.C. Debates of the Legislative Assembly, May 1, 1987, p. 915.

4 Leader of the Federal NDP Party. Commons Debates, May 11, 1987, p. 5938.

Ottawa, The Provinces, and Meech Lake

Alan C. Cairns

The Many Difficulties of Criticizing Meech Lake

> when you have matters as significant as defining the nature and character of Canada being set behind closed doors and then simply run past the people after the fact, then I have some difficulty with that. (A. Wayne MacKay)[1]

Two statements from Lord Acton's Inaugural Lecture on 'The Study of History' have not lost their cogency in the more than ninety years since they were delivered to a distinguished Cambridge audience in 1895: 'The living do not give up their secrets with the candour of the dead,'[2] and:

> There is a popular saying of Madame De Stael, that we forgive whatever we really understand. The paradox has been judiciously pruned by her descendant, the Duke de Broglie, in the words : 'Beware of too much explaining, lest we end by too much excusing.'[3]

The first statement reminds us that the student of unfolding events is not aided by being a contemporary of the politicians whose work he evaluates. The reverse is true, for the living continue to seek glory, ever striving to protect and enhance their reputation, and if politically active still struggling to change the goals of the state. They often prefer, accordingly, serviceable fictions to a potentially damaging candour. Hence their disclosures of motive and purpose are typically coloured by their ongoing pursuits.

In democracies, as elsewhere, politicians give themselves the benefit of the doubt when their policies appear questionable or even sullied to outside observers. The criticisms of the latter are, indeed, often discounted on the ground that those who make them are naively unaware of the pressures which buffet men of action. The world of decision-making, it is implied or asserted, is another country, an alleged fact which disqualifies those who have never travelled in it from judging the behaviour of its inhabitants.

A stratagem highly appropriate to this defence is to make policy in secret, deprive the public of information on what went into its making, and then rebuff critics for not understanding the necessities that attend statecraft. Of course, the practice of confidentiality and of cabinet solidarity are conventional attributes of responsible government. However, the dangers of elite conspiracy, to which that system if unchecked might lead, are normally countered by the system of adversarial politics which accords high status to the official opposition. The parliamentary battle challenges the seductions of power with the searchlight of criticism. The public is thus provided with flows of information and many-sided commentary which are essential tools of a thinking citizenry. For the Meech Lake Accord, the atypical fact that both the Liberals and the NDP officially supported the agreement in the House of Commons has greatly restricted the information and alternative analyses available to the public.

The situation was succinctly summarized by Pat Nowlan, a Conservative dissenter on Meech Lake:

> there really has not been a debate in the House of Commons. When all three Leaders and Parties are together on principle and have a hearing during the summer there is not time for it to percolate out from coast to coast. It is very politically astute to get the measure through, but that is not the way to have a meaningful debate and a better Constitution.[4]

The compliance of the opposition parties mutes their normal inquisitive aggressiveness, to the disadvantage of public knowledge. Further, the agreement of all three national parties to the Accord adds to the psychological sense of isolation and impotence which often accompanies the role of critic.

When policies emerge from the intergovernmental arena, as in Meech Lake, a supplementary checking arrangement often, but not always, operates. The different vantage points and hence interests of the eleven major governments of the federal system, allied with the recurring temptation for particular leaders to 'go public' to enhance their bargaining power, or to reassure their constituents, often increase public awareness of the nature of controversies among elites. Such elite division also stimulates public involvement as well as public understanding. That was emphatically the case for the major intergovernmental constitutional discussions from the late 60s to the 1982 Constitution Act. In the words of one participant in those earlier struggles, the 1982 Constitution Act amendments

> ...were the product of years of public debate, countless federal-provincial conferences, hundreds of hours of debate in Parliament and legislatures, thousands of newspaper articles, many election campaigns and the Quebec referendum. The debates centered on fundamental concepts, and equally important, on wording of proposed texts.[5]

This has not been the case with Meech Lake, for the politics of reaching agreement were held to require lengthy backroom negotiations and soundings prior to the 'official' negotiating sessions in order to minimize the possibility of failure. Further, the actual Meech Lake/Langevin discussions took place in the absence of advisors in the bargaining room, with only two note-takers present from the federal and provincial sides.

The secrecy and deliberately low profile of a process which was carefully designed to ward off unwelcome probes or queries from non-participants were graphically underlined by the statements of both Lowell Murray and Prime Minister Mulroney two weeks before the Meech Lake meetings: that the purpose of the pending session was simply to see if a basis existed for serious discussion. Mulroney stated in the House of Commons that the meeting would not be 'a constitutional conference, it will be a normal meeting.' Lowell Murray, Minister of State for Federal-Provincial Relations, 'stressed,' according to a *Globe and Mail* report, 'that the gathering will not be a formal negotiating meeting.'[6] The day after what had been publicly defined as an exploratory meeting Canadians were informed that an agreement in principle had been reached which was to be quickly transformed 'into a constitutional text' to be transmitted to a constitutional conference 'within weeks to approve a formal text.'[7] A few weeks later at Langevin House the Accord was given legal clothing and the eleven first ministers 'committ[ed] themselves and the governments they represent' to seek approval of their separate legislatures for a resolution to amend the constitution accordingly.[8] Thus five weeks after a declared exploratory conference Canadians were confronted with a definitive constitutional text, described as inviolable, and to be opened up only if egregious errors, as defined and agreed to by eleven first ministers, were discovered. Thus the intergovernmental process, moving from secrecy to unanimity, and protected by confidentiality did little to enlighten the public beyond making available the actual words of successive intergovernmental agreements struck and refined in slightly over a month. Within another three weeks the Quebec National Assembly approved the Accord and Premier Bourassa asserted that Quebec would not consider proposals for change arising from hearings in other provinces.[9] The process was beginning to look more like a military manoeuvre by governments to keep the citizens at bay than an acceptable process of constitution-making in one of the world's oldest liberal democracies.

The remarkable mustering of elite support for the second most comprehensive package of constitutional change since 1867 by all three parties in the House of Commons and by the first ministers of eleven governments has drastically reduced the base of information and competing analyses available to the non-participants. The threatened breach of intergovernmental solidarity by the new Liberal government of Frank McKenna, which replaced the Hatfield Conservatives in New Brunswick, and the wavering of Premier Pawley of Manitoba have not yet effectively broken down the united front of governing elites and the undersupply of information to which it leads.

In spite of these constraints, the politics of a free society has partially lifted the veil. The servants of this task essential to our democratic health include a handful of politicians who have broken party ranks, and paid a price, a former Prime Minister who has defended the constitutional vision which informed much of the 1982 Constitution Act, various members of the Liberal dominated Senate who have balked at being rubber stamps, a few academics who have performed their duty of disrobing emperors, various citizen activists who dislike the provincialist vision of Canada embodied in Meech Lake, and a number of interest groups whose shotgun criticisms reflect their fear that their ox has been gored. Nevertheless, a contemporary Lord Acton could only agree that those who wield power over us have not been forthcoming in explaining exactly what they have done to the constitution. The overwhelming justification offered for the Accord has been political, the necessity of getting the willing agreement of the government of Quebec to the constitution.

The consequences **for** the constitution of accommodating Quebec and placating the other nine provinces in the process have been treated as secondary phenomena. The phrase 'equality of the provinces' has done yeoman service in justifying why Newfoundland, Manitoba, British Columbia and the other provinces should have received so much constitutional largesse from what the federal government misleadingly called the Quebec round.

The 'Quebec round' label underscores the tendency for the defenders of Meech Lake to dwell on its overriding political purpose, healing the wounds left by the 1982 Constitution Act which the Quebec government opposed. Since the Meech Lake critics frequently focus on the negative consequences of particular clauses, rather than on the noble objectives they are alleged to support, the resultant debate has been unproductive. In general, critics resent being labelled anti-Quebec when they question the ambiguities, vagueness and other weaknesses which they feel mar the Accord.[10] On the other hand, the federal government resists defending and explaining the Accord on its merits, preferring the high ground and unassailable criterion of reuniting the Canadian family.

A related aspect of the process gravely hampers the successful performance of the honourable role of constitutional commentator. With the exception of the known position of the Liberal Government of Quebec there is an absence of position papers explaining the rationale for particular changes as appropriate means for explicit constitutional ends. From the federal government, which must assume the primary responsibility for the overall health of the constitutional order, there has been a virtual total silence on the implications of particular changes involving, for example, the Senate, the Supreme Court, the spending power, and immigration. We have only a handful of descriptive documents, public relations releases, and reassuring speeches which put down the critics as anti-Quebec or as negativist nay-sayers. The Meech Lake Accord process represents an oracular, ex cathedra style of governing more appropriate to theocratic rulers dictating to the faithful than to elected political leaders explaining themselves to the citizens to whom they are accountable.[11]

For students of Meech Lake, Lord Acton's approving citation of the admonition of the Duke de Broglie, 'Beware of too much explaining, lest we end by too much excusing,' is also highly apposite. The defenders of Meech Lake, by defying its critics to come up with a 'better' package which could obtain the requisite agreement of the other provinces and bring Quebec back into the constitutional family on honourable terms, suggest not only that this was a minimum package of concessions, but that it was an inevitable package, the best that could be achieved in the circumstances. The argument that the agreement is a seamless web, so interdependent and so fragile that an amendment will shatter it, also suggests that Meech Lake is what it is because it could be no other.

The fact that our leaders provide negligible information on what went on at Meech Lake and Langevin House means that their claim can only be accepted on faith. We simply do not know what alternative package, reflecting different leadership and a different group chemistry, might have gained the requisite agreement. We know that the federal government bargaining strategy was to keep adding concessions until agreement was reached. Whether there was a stopping point beyond which Ottawa would not go is unknown. According to one journalist, the Prime Minister gave Lowell Murray 'carte blanche to negotiate away whatever federal powers were necessary to get Quebec into the constitution.'[12] If this assessment, which differs little from that of Jeffrey Simpson,[13] is even approximately true it is unreasonable to imply that if critics cannot come up with modifications that will get unanimous agreement that Meech Lake is better than any alternative. Any agreement that occupies the field and has the backing of eleven governments has a practical advantage over a contender lacking any official support. However, such a statement implies neither the superiority nor the inevitability of the Meech Lake Accord, only that it has all the advantages that go with incumbency. Had the federal government conceded twice as much to the provinces the resultant agreement would have been even more difficult to dislodge, although even less attractive to many of its critics. Accordingly, the outside analyst is wise not to accept the self-interested explanations of political leaders at face value.

The barriers suggested by the preceding paragraphs, which stand in the way of seeing clearly what happened and why, are supplemented by an additional impediment, the politicization of the academic community of commentators, many of whom have worked for governments, and most of whom have taken sides in the constitutional battles of recent decades. I exempt myself from neither of these categories. So the reader is to be warned that clinical detachment may be engaged in a losing struggle with partisan commitment and official connexions in the minds of those who, in person or on paper, address audiences while wearing the protective garb of scholarship.Lord Acton's ideal, detached historian, whose 'most sacred and disinterested convictions ought to take shape in the tranquil regions of the air, above the tumult and the tempest of active life'[14], does not find a congenial environment at conferences which discuss divisive contemporary issues.

What Really Happened, or How the Quebec Round Became the Provincial Round

The first half-truth to be held up to the light is the reiterated assertion that this was the Quebec round, intended in the words of the Meech Lake communique 'to allow Quebec to resume its place as a full participant in Canada's constitutional development.'

The fact that the government of Quebec did not give its approval to the 1982 Constitution Act, and denied its legitimacy, raised political rather than legal problems for the constitution clearly applied to Quebec. Nevertheless, it was obviously eminently desirable to have the Quebec government signal its formal allegiance to the Canadian constitutional order. After all, the catalyst for nearly two decades of constitutional introspection culminating in the 1982 Constitution Act had been the nationalist demands of the government and people of Quebec. While the willing allegiance of the citizens and Quebec government might have incrementally developed with the passage of time, and the grievances of 1980-82 might have become faded memories as new political generations emerged, it was probably a safer course of action for the other governments of Canadian federalism to work towards a constitutional rapprochement with the government of Quebec. To achieve such a reconciliation would presumably strengthen Canada by eliminating a grievance which would otherwise remain available for exploitation in the next wave of Quebecois nationalist fervour.

In the great political compromise which produced the 1982 Constitution Act both the federal government and the governments of the other nine provinces had achieved some of their objectives. The Charter and other provisions of the 1982 Constitution Act also responded to women, aboriginals, visible minorities, and multicultural Canadians. The major actor whose claims were still unaddressed was the government of Quebec. Thus both concern for the health of the Canadian constitutional order and an elementary sense of justice suggested that, when circumstances allowed, a judicious statesmanship should seek the reconciliation of the Quebec government. Hence, that there should be a Quebec round of constitutional discussions when the time was ripe seemed to be no more than common sense.

Quebec's ambivalent status was not a trivial matter for the other governments of Canadian federalism. The Parti Québécois government had signalled its constitutional alienation and defiance by systematically employing the notwithstanding clause (s.33) of the Charter wherever possible, and by limiting its participation in the intergovernmental arena, including constitutional conferences. The other provincial governments knew that without Quebec's participation in the constitutional process their own demands for constitutional change could only be met with difficulty. Immediately prior to the federal announcement of the Meech Lake meetings Premier Bourassa had announced that Quebec was boycotting the pending first ministers' conference on aboriginal rights as a sign of its dissatisfaction with the slow response to its own constitutional proposals. In effect the government of Quebec employed its disagreement with the 1982 Constitution Act as a resource to embarrass its government partners in the federal system, and to hamper the system's effective functioning. It was evident that the national unity/integration purposes of the 1982 Constitution Act, especially of the Charter, would be ill-served by the continuing official estrangement of the Quebec government.[15]

The other nine provincial governments, however, were not passive spectators as the federal government orchestrated a response to the Quebec's government's constitutional demands. The threat of their power to block gave them significant constitutional leverage, which they employed for their own interests.

In the Meech Lake Accord, the governments of the other nine provinces gained new powers and responsibilities for the nomination of Supreme Court judges and Senators, a potentially enhanced role in immigration, an increased blocking power with respect to constitutional amendments, protection against the 'abuse' of the federal spending power – including guaranteed compensation for non-participation in certain circumstances – and an enlarged role in the federal-provincial partnership through the constitutional requirements for two annual federal-provincial conferences, one on the constitution and one on the economy. Alberta was given the side payoff of having 'Senate reform' identified as a mandatory agenda item for future annual constitutional conferences. Newfoundland received the supplementary constitutional gift of having 'roles and responsibilities in relation to fisheries' placed on the agenda of the annual constitutional conferences in perpetuity, or until resolved.

Along with this overflowing cornucopia of constitutional blessings the premiers of the provinces outside Quebec have been lauded by the Prime Minister for their self-restraint, altruism and discipline in suspending their own constitutional demands while those of Quebec received prior attention. This is a somewhat restrictive definition of self-restraint. Much of the Accord is a response to the ambitions of provincial elites outside of Quebec who enhanced the status of their governments on the coattails of Quebec. By inference, they were prepared to leave Quebec out of the Canadian constitutional family until they received significant payoffs. Their self-restraint was relative.

The Quebec government received essentially the same constitutional treatment as the governments of the other nine provinces, with the significant exception of a new interpretation clause tailored to its requirements which stated, *inter alia*, that the Constitution of Canada was to be interpreted in a manner consistent with 'the recognition that Quebec constitutes within Canada a distinct society,' (s.2(b)), and 'The role of the legislature and Government of Quebec to preserve and promote the distinct identity of Quebec...is affirmed.'(s.3)

Further, Quebec was to be the first province to have increased powers in immigration given constitutional protection. The negotiation of similar agreements was held out to the other provinces. With respect to the provincial government's nominating role for Supreme Court judges, the Quebec government received the right to nominate three

Supreme Court judges, while the rights to nominate the remaining six were not allocated to specific governments in the other nine provinces. The right of appointment, of course, remains with the federal government.

Overall the Meech Lake constitutional outcome is best characterized as a provincializing round. The role of the Quebec government was to set the terms for the enhancement of the powers of all the provinces. This outcome was rationalized in terms of the principle of the equality of the provinces. This principle, however, was elaborated and strengthened in the very process of bargaining which produced Meech Lake.

The requirements of the 1982 amending formula, as modified by the policy of the Mulroney government to treat the whole package of constitutional change as requiring unanimous provincial government agreement, gave an equality of veto power to each provincial government. Constitutional bargaining translated this into equal treatment of the other nine provinces as beneficiaries of whatever the federal government was willing to concede to Quebec. Thus the means employed to respond to Quebec transformed the Quebec round into a provincial round. The provincial governments of English Canada which had profited from the 1982 Constitution Act compromise which left the government of Quebec on the sidelines, profited again from the reconciliation of Quebec.

The staggered two-stage process of constitutional change in 1980-82 and 1987, in conjunction with the amending formulas applicable to the separate stages, strengthened the provincializing tendencies in the composite package of 1982 and 1987. The 1981 Supreme Court decision, which allowed Quebec to be left out of the patriation package while requiring, by convention, a substantial measure of provincial consent, led to a 1982 Constitution Act which was a true compromise. Both the dissenting provinces and the federal government gained some of their objectives, but had to concede in other areas. The Meech Lake response to the flaw of 1982, given a new amending formula which required unanimity to satisfy some of Quebec's demands, imparted an overall provincializing thrust to this second round which was not initially anticipated.

This provincializing outcome was facilitated by the Mulroney bargaining style, which appears to put a higher premium on getting agreement than on the substance of the agreement reached. Certainly in this constitutional round the federal government promoted no national vision, nor sought to strengthen a pan-Canadianism derived from the Charter. This absence may be partly attributed to a bargaining process which suggested that a federal government assertiveness requiring provincial government concessions would simply have made agreement impossible. Given the very strong desire of the federal government for an agreement, the provincial governments held most of the bargaining chips. On the other hand, there is little evidence of the existence of a Mulroney vision of a national community that was suppressed as a statesmanlike gesture in support of the higher objective of bringing Quebec into the constitutional family.

In sum, the general tenor of the Meech Lake Accord is unquestionably provincializing, although not always decentralizing. A number of commentators, seeking to find some confirmation that the flow of power was not entirely from Ottawa to the provinces, cite the recognition of the spending power in areas of 'exclusive provincial jurisdiction' as a net gain for the federal government. This interpretation, however, rests on the premise either that there was a serious risk that the constitutionality of the federal spending power in provincial areas of jurisdiction might be successfully challenged in court, or that a more restrictive amendment than the Meech Lake proposal would otherwise emerge in the future. While neither of these can be discounted it is relevant that both Lowell Murray and Prime Minister Mulroney repeatedly described their objective and achievement as the civilizing of the federal spending power.[16] Whether or not this is desirable it clearly suggests constraining and limiting its future use.

The provision for annual conferences on the constitution and on the economy enhances the provincial government role in executive federalism. The provincial government roles in the nomination of Senators and Supreme Court judges are examples of intrastate reforms designed, in the language of the 70s, to federalize the centre.[17]

The extension of the unanimity principle for amendments to new areas, beyond those covered by the amendment provisions of the 1982 Constitution Act, reflects similar constitutional tendencies – provincial government input receives greater recognition and federal government discretion is correspondingly reduced from what it was prior to the Accord. With respect to the creation of new provinces the federal government has experienced successive encroachments on the discretionary power it formerly enjoyed. Prior to 1982 the creation of new provinces was a matter for the federal government alone. The 1982 Constitution Act subjected the creation of new provinces to the 7/50 amending formula, the agreement of at least two thirds (out of 10) provinces with 50 percent of the population, and that of the federal government. Meech Lake requires the unanimous consent of all eleven governments, and thus gives the smallest province a constitutional weight equivalent to that of Ottawa. It is symptomatic of the Meech Lake process that it has been left to the governments and citizens of Yukon and the Northwest Territories to resist this encroachment on federal government constitutional powers. The federal government itself has been mute; unwilling to direct attention to its own losses it prefers to speak of gains for the federal system.

Other defenders of the Accord also resist the language of winners and losers and prefer to describe the Accord in terms of a more effective intergovernmental partnership. Interdependence, so the argument goes, requires a higher degree of intergovernmental cooperation and coordination if the single citizenry served by both governments is not to be damaged by counterproductive clashes between competing governments. While there is some validity to this perspective, it should be noted that the new stress on interdependence is purchased almost entirely at the cost of reducing the autonomy and the discretion of the federal government, and strengthening the role of provincial governments in virtually every area touched by the Accord.

The Meech Lake vision is one of intensified executive federalism and intergovernmental contact within which the relative power of provincial governments is enhanced. This is true of the new procedures for Senate and Supreme Court appointments, for immigration, and for the annual conferences on the economy and the constitution. In sum, the Meech Lake vision of federalism postulates more provincialized central government institutions, an enhanced provincial government role in an enlarged intergovernmental arena, and a federal government which has voluntarily fettered much of the discretion it formerly enjoyed and wielded. This enhanced provincial role is not the product of a triumphant political theory which irresistibly champions this direction of change, nor of a sensitive judgement of the most appropriate structure of federalism to respond to the policy demands of the future. These possible rationales are conspicuously absent from the Meech Lake discussions. Meech Lake is a product of the internal dynamics of the intergovernmental arena responding to a problem within the constitutional system itself.

The Emerging Constitutional Culture and the Challenge to Government Domination of the Amending Process

The Meech Lake/Langevin Accord was an affair of governments. In Quebec the well-publicized constitutional policy of the Quebec Liberal party became government policy after the provincial Liberals replaced the Parti Québécois as the government of Quebec. The proposals were subsequently refined at a carefully staged and well-reported conference in Mont Gabriel, Quebec. Elsewhere there was negligible public involvement leading up to Meech Lake. A brief flurry of lobbying between the Meech Lake and Langevin meetings resulted in some limited changes from the initial version to protect the interests of aboriginal

Canadians and supporters of multiculturalism. The post-Meech Lake role of the public in Joint Committee hearings was defined by the federal government as 'explor[ing] the implications of the Constitution Amendment, 1987 so it is well understood by everyone' and thus helping to set the agenda for future constitutional conferences.[18]

Government domination of the Meech Lake process meant that the outcome would reflect the interests of governments. This domination, perhaps natural in earlier periods of Canadian history, turned out to be much less so in the Canada of the Charter. At this Calgary conference, as in some of the journalistic commentary that attended the interventions of former Prime Minister Trudeau, there has been a tendency to define Trudeau as a figure from yesterday, and his views and concerns as almost medieval so drastically has the *Zeitgeist* allegedly been transformed. These assessments, however, rest on a profound misunderstanding of the significance and consequences of the 1982 Constitution Act, and particularly of the Charter, which is Trudeau's major legacy. The process leading up to the 1982 Constitution Act and much of its content – the symbolism as well as the substance of s. 28 dealing with gender equality, s. 27 with its provision that the 'preservation and enhancement of the multicultural heritage of Canadians' is a criterion for Charter interpretation, s. 25 recognizing the rights of aboriginals, along with other clauses dealing with aboriginals, and s. 15 (1) and s. 15 (2) with their identification of particular groups in the equality and affirmative action provisions – have transformed the Canadian constitutional culture in a manner that explains much of the hostility that Meech Lake has aroused.

These groups identify with particular clauses of the 1982 Constitution Act, primarily those found in the Charter. They no longer therefore see the constitution and its amendment as an affair of governments. Typically, although aboriginals resist easy categorization, these groups are sympathetic to the federal government; they, or at least their elites, think of themselves as Charter Canadians. They have acquired a constitutional recognition which gives them status and supports aspirations for an improvement in their socio-economic condition. Accordingly, they are disturbed when they see or fear that the recognitions they have so recently won are threatened by constitutional changes worked out in secret and reflecting government concerns.

In brief, they view government domination of the constitutional amending process as illegitimate. Their anger confirms that the Trudeau government's nation-building purposes for the Charter are already being realized, at least at the level of non-governmental elites. In that sense Trudeau is not a museum piece for he speaks through the numerous groups which have attached themselves to the Charter, which he was so influential in fashioning.

Thus although Meech Lake may be seen correctly as a Quebec round which became a provincial round, it should also be seen as highlighting a constitutional incoherence which will have to be worked out in coming decades. The Charter and the groups it has brought into the constitution have weakened the status of federalism as a constitutional organizing principle. This has reduced the legitimacy of government domination of the amendment process, especially when it is employed by governments to serve their own interests as governments.

In this constitutional culture which is beginning to take shape as a result of the 1982 Constitution Act, especially of the Charter, government control of the amending process, once considered natural, now appears as an arrogant elitism. The rights and recognitions entrenched in the Charter have generated beliefs that their possessors are entitled to participate in constitutional change. The Charter fosters a participatory ethic, the frustration of which, as in Meech Lake, reveals a basic contradiction in the Canadian constitutional culture. At the present time the historic government domination of the formal procedures of constitutional change confronts a new set of actors who have acquired a presence in the constitution – women, aboriginals, linguistic minorities, multicultural groups, the disabled, and a more diffuse category of rights bearers who support the Charter as a progressive advance.

The reforms of 1982 have changed the relation of the Canadian constitution to Canadian society. The post-1982 written Constitution is a much more comprehensive instrument than was the BNA Act. It incorporates and responds to various cleavages to which the BNA Act was indifferent. This enhanced constitutional sensitivity to Canadian social diversity diminishes the pride of place that governments based on territorial diversity formerly enjoyed in the constitutional order. The written constitution is now a major instrument for the regulation of the relative social status of different categories of Canadians. Failure to recognize that fact is the fundamental shortcoming of Meech Lake. That is why Meech Lake, both in its process and in its vision, is an anachronism, out of touch with what Canada has become.

Notes

1 Minutes of Proceedings and Evidence of the Special Joint Committee of the Senate and of the House of Commons on the 1987 Constitutional Accord, August 5, 1987, 3:64.

2 'The Study of History,' 505, in *Selected Writings of Lord Acton, Vol. II, Essays in the Study and Writing of History* by John Emerich Edward Dalberg-Acton, First Baron Acton, edited by J. Rufus Fears (Indianapolis 1985).

3 Acton, 'Study of History,' 550.

4 House of Commons Debates, October 5, 1987, 9684.

5 Edward S. Goldenberg, 'Debate needed to make sure accord is right,' *Globe and Mail*, July 14, 1987.

6 'PM invites 10 premiers to discuss Quebec constitutional proposals,' *Globe and Mail*, March 18, 1987.

7 Meech Lake Communique, April 30, 1987, in Bryan Schwartz, *Fathoming Meech Lake* (Winnipeg 1987), 232.

8 Schwartz, *Fathoming Meech Lake*, 238.

9 'Vote to ratify accord hailed as great victory for Quebec,' *Globe and Mail*, June 24, 1987.

10 See 'PM's comment on motive angers women's groups,' *Globe and Mail*, August 20, 1987 and Sergio Marchi, House of Commons Debates, October 6, 1987, 9742.

11 The comments of Sergio Marchi in the House of Commons, although lengthy, merit extensive citation. House of Commons Debates, October 6, 1987, 9742:

> The absence of any true public input in the development of this resolution is a national tragedy. The package was not only assembled and hastily ratified in secret by the First Ministers, it was accomplished by marathon talks which continued into the early hours of the morning-two characteristics which are certainly not conducive to drafting the most essential piece of legislation governing Canada which is expected to meet the aspirations of all Canadians and the tests of time and circumstance.
>
> To further aggravate the situation, the public hearings before the joint parliamentary committee were held during the summer months, the worst possible time of the year for any Government to encourage the participation, involvement and attention of Canadians. In addition, before the first witness had a chance to appear before the committee, government spokespersons made it painfully clear that the government-dominated committee would not be in any mood to accept any changes or consider any amendments. For once, unfortunately, the Government kept its word.
>
> We saw the spectacle of individual Canadians and an impressive spectrum of organizations representing various constituencies travelling to the nation's capital to provide Members of Parliament and Senators with very moving and passionate presentations of their vision of Canada and of their dreams. All of these counted for absolutely nothing.
>
> Canadians did not have a meaningful opportunity to share their dreams and their wishes for their country. This is a staggering and remarkable shortcoming because this stage in our constitutional evolution as a nation excluded the very people whom our Constitution is to serve and protect. There was no partnership. There was no give and take. The process was secret and dictatorial. It was a take-it-or-leave-it proposition from start to finish.
>
> This approach, unfortunately, also gripped the elected Chamber. It was regrettable that many Members of Parliament of all stripes responded to those seeking changes and improvements by alleging that they were anti-Quebec or by promoting the concept that the inclusion of a new clause or the amendment of a current clause would scuttle the entire deal. The language and strategy used assumed that if the Accord could not convince Members on its own

merit there was a need to intimidate individuals into accepting the Accord's version of Canada. This tack was not only unfortunate and misleading, it also depicted an air of desperation and insecurity as well as an attitude which was prepared to tolerate glaring and recognizable shortcomings in the Accord.

12 Charlotte Gray, 'Clever Lowell Murray,' *Saturday Night*, November 1987, 14.

13 Jeffrey Simpson, 'Anatomy of a Deal,' *Globe and Mail*, June 2, 1987.

14 Acton, 'Study of History,' 550.

15 Much of this paragraph is taken from another paper: Alan Cairns, 'Meech Lake, Federalism and the Provinces,' mimeo, 9-10, prepared for a conference on 'Meech Lake: From Centre to Periphery: The Impact of the 1987 Constitutional Accord on Canadian Settlements,' January 7-8, 1988, organized by the Centre for Human Settlements, University of British Columbia.

16 See, for example, 'Notes for an Address by Prime Minister Brian Mulroney on the Meech Lake Agreement,' House of Commons, Ottawa, May 11, 1987, mimeo, 7; and Lowell Murray, in Proceedings...on the 1987 Constitutional Accord, No. 2, August 4, 1987, 23.

17 For a discussion of intrastate federalism see Donald V. Smiley and Ronald L. Watts, *Intrastate Federalism in Canada*, Vol. 39 of the research studies of the Royal Commission on the Economic Union and Development Prospects for Canada (Toronto, 1985).

18 Government of Canada, *Strengthening the Canadian Federation*, 9 (no place, no date).

A Sense of Unease:
The Meech Lake Accord and
Constitution-Making in Canada

Roger Gibbins

The intent of this paper is to explore a disquietening sense of unease I have about the Meech Lake Accord. Admittedly, 'unease' is a relatively mild term, one that stops well short of 'outrage' or 'alarm,' and indeed there are many aspects of the Accord with which I have difficulty finding fault. But the term 'unease' also stops well short of 'satisfaction,' for I am unable to convince myself that the Accord provides a satisfactory point of departure for the future shaping of Canadian constitutional and political life.

Many criticisms of the Accord focus on its failure to offer adequate protection for women, for Aboriginal peoples, for multicultural communities, for francophone minorities outside Quebec, and for the provincial ambitions of the Northern Territories. These are criticisms that I do **not** embrace, and only in part perhaps because I am not a woman, I am not of Aboriginal descent, I am an anglophone of British stock, and I am fortunate enough to live well south of the sixtieth parallel. I see these defects as at worst minor ones that can be addressed through the ongoing constitutional process. They may be seen, admittedly, as warts or blemishes on the Accord, but they stop well short of being fundamental weaknesses of principle or design. In any event, they do not explain the sense of unease that lingers in my own mind as I try to come to grips with the Meech Lake Accord.

Nor, I should stress, does that sense of unease spring from the Accord's recognition of Quebec as a distinct society. I am quite prepared to recognize Quebec's distinctiveness as an historical, sociological and linguistic fact, although it is ironic that its distinctiveness gains constitutional recognition at a time when Quebecers, in their enthusiasm for free trade, are embracing more than ever before the cultural and commercial values of the broader North American society, when the Québécois are less distinct than they have ever been. Here I should also note in passing that Quebec's exclusion from the 1981 Accord and the subsequent Constitution Act of 1982 has been exaggerated by defenders of the Meech Lake Accord. Quebec per se was **not** left out; what happened was the Parti Québécois **government**, a government committed to the independence of Quebec, did not sign the 1981 Accord or the 1982 Constitution Act as it would not have signed any agreement endorsing Quebec's continued participation in the Canadian federal state. That decision by René Levesque and the Parti Québécois cannot and must not be confused with the exclusion of Quebec in any broader political or cultural sense.

Yet, be that as it may, the fact that the Quebec government did not endorse the 1981-82 constitutional agreement meant that our Constitution was unfinished, and in this sense Quebec's exclusion can be seen as an important loose end. Thus when Robert Bourassa's Liberals replaced the Parti Québécois government in Quebec and Brian Mulroney's Progressive Conservatives captured the federal government in Ottawa, when Quebec's signatory to the Constitution became a possibility, Canada's First Ministers are to be praised for pursuing the possibility. Undoubtedly Mr. Mulroney deserves particular praise. If constitutional recognition of Quebec as a distinct society was the price to be paid for Quebec's inclusion, I do not feel that the price was too high.

Where the price may have been too high, however, is in the Accord's implicit recognition of the remaining nine provinces as distinct societies in their own right. The Meech Lake Accord went well beyond the inclusion of Quebec to expand significantly the powers of all provincial governments. Thus the Accord recognizes the constitutional equality of all provinces, provides for an expanded provincial role with respect to immigration, gives provincial governments the dominant role in appointments to the Senate and Supreme Court, makes it easier for provinces to opt out of future national programs, and provides for an expanded provincial veto on future constitutional change. While it is one thing to recognize Quebec as a distinct society, it is something else entirely to entrench constitutionally a provincialist view of the country for which there is much less sociological, cultural or political support. In short, my quarrel is not with what the Accord says about Quebec, but rather with what it says about Canada.

The Meech Lake Process

In assessing the political process which produced the Meech Lake Accord, it is useful to compare that process to the one which produced the Constitution Act of 1982. In both cases the First Ministers were the prime movers and principal players. In both cases the decisive First Ministers' Conferences were conducted in secret, and in both cases the final accords were the product of nearly exhausted men wrestling early into the morning with some of the most intractable problems in Canadian political life. Not surprisingly, in neither case was the Accord perfect and in neither case was the process in any sense an open process; the accords were hammered out by a handful of men working in a private, intensely personal political arena. As Alan Cairns has pointed out with respect to the 1981 Accord:

> there are no constitutional utopias. We have to be satisfied with the stumbling efforts of imperfect men to keep our problems at bay.[1]

The First Ministers' process had, admittedly, a secretive, masculine air, but perhaps this is as accurate a reflection of the realities of Canadian political life as is the recognition of Quebec as a distinct society.

There is, however, an important distinction to be made between the process leading up to the 1981 Accord and that leading up to the Meech Lake Accord. Prior to the 1981 Accord, the Canadian public had been involved, and often intensely involved, in the constitutional process. Canadians had gone through at least five years of protracted constitutional debate that reached well beyond the First Ministers to embrace seemingly endless task forces, televised confrontations, townhall meetings, editorial commentary, articles in *Saturday Night*, and the groves of Academe. There had been a genuine, prolonged and often intense public debate in which the sovereignty association referendum in Quebec was but one milestone. It was also a debate in which competing visions of the Canadian political community were vigorously promoted by the likes of Pierre Trudeau, René Levesque, Brian Peckford and Peter Lougheed. While this debate **culminated** in the more secretive deliberations of the First Ministers, it set the context for and unquestionably shaped the outcome of those deliberations.

No such public debate preceded the Meech Lake Accord, although undoubtedly this statement is more correct for Canada-outside-Quebec than it may be for Quebec itself. Constitutional concerns had slipped from the Canadian political agenda to be replaced with a new set of largely economic concerns, led by the growing national soul-searching on free trade. Thus in a sense Meech Lake was sprung on Canadians; they were not, in any emotional sense, part of the process leading up to the Meech Lake Accord. As a consequence, Canadians are more uneasy with the executive federalism process in 1987 than they had been with essentially the same process in 1981. It is one thing for the First Ministers to come together in private to tie together a constitutional package whose components have been subjected to intensive and even exhaustive public debate. It is something else for the First Ministers to come together in private to create a new constitutional accord in the absence of any such debate.

To stretch the point, the 1981 Accord bordered on constitutional **ratification** while the Meech Lake Accord was closer to constitution **making**. Admittedly, the First Ministers played a central and creative role in both instances. At the same time, however, the constitutional product was more uniquely theirs in 1987 than it was in 1982.

If this difference in process accounts for some of the unease with which many Canadians have greeted the Meech Lake Accord, so too does the content of the Accord when compared to the Constitution Act of 1982. The Constitution Act was sold to Canadians, and sold legitimately, as a **people package**. The essence of the Act is not to be found in its restructuring of intergovernmental relations or in its tinkering with the constitutional division of powers in the Canadian federal state, both of which were almost completely ignored. Rather its essence is to be found in the act of patriation, which was a highly emotive issue, and in the Charter of Rights and Freedoms which set forth the rights of individual Canadians vis-à-vis governments, federal or provincial. Elements of the Charter were designed to appeal and did appeal to both large and symbolically important blocs of the Canadian electorate – to women, Aboriginal peoples, multicultural communities, linguistic minorities, civil libertarians, and the beneficiaries of equalization payments. The Charter was pitched to individual Canadians and not to governments, and particularly not to provincial governments. Thus no matter that the details of the Constitution Act may have been hammered out in private by the First Ministers; the final product could be presented to Canadians as their constitution, as one that enshrined their individual rights and freedoms.

The Meech Lake Accord, however, has no such intrinsic public appeal, or at least it has not been promoted outside Quebec as a 'people package.' The Accord addresses a number of issues of considerable importance to the governments of Canada, but issues of less direct relevance to average Canadians. Thus because Canadians have not been sold on the product they have become uneasy about the process, even though that process has changed little if at all since 1981-82. To put the matter more bluntly if somewhat unfairly, at least some Canadians see the First Ministers meeting in private to reshape the constitution to their advantage and not to the advantage of Canadians at large.

It is the Accord's character as an intergovernmental **document** that generates unease about the intergovernmental **process** through which the Accord was produced.

Some note should also be made of the political process which followed the signing of the 1981 and 1987 Accords. After the Accord had been signed in 1981, a number of groups were successful in amending the original agreement. The women's lobby, for example, managed to secure section 28 (2), and Aboriginal groups were able to secure extended constitutional negotiations through the provisions of section 37 (3). In short, the Accord was open to change through passioned argument. In 1987, however, the prospect of any change was immediately ruled out by the First Ministers. The Accord, they maintained, was a seamless web; while it might be debated in Parliament and the provincial legislatures, and in some provinces even exposed to public hearings, it was not to be changed. Effective debate was precluded; a deal had been struck and the die was cast.

Thus unease over the Meech Lake Accord springs less from the private nature of the First Ministers' process than it does from the lack of a preceding public debate, the intergovernmental content of the Accord, and the fact that effective debate on the Accord was shut down by the seamless web analogy. I would argue, however, that the sense of unease extends back even further into our political psyche to touch our basic conceptions of political community.

The Loss of Dynamic Tension

In the prolonged debate leading up to the Constitution Act of 1982 there was a vital dynamic tension that was unfortunately absent in 1987. The former debate featured dramatically different visions of the Canadian political community championed with great vigor by articulate men such as Pierre Trudeau, René Levesque, Bill Bennett, Allan Blakeney, Richard Hatfield, Peter Lougheed and Brian Peckford. Outside the arena of executive federalism Canadian academics, journalists, public servants, novelists, lobbyists, poets and advertising agencies also wrestled with competing visions of the national community.

In this debate, Pierre Trudeau and his supporters played a critically important role. Their importance stemmed not from the fact that they were right, although they may have been, but rather from the fact that they presented a vigorous defence of the national community, a defence of the centre against the more provincially-oriented visions of most premiers. They maintained the essential dynamic tension in the constitutional debate, the tension between nation-building and province-building, the tension between a view of Canada as a distinct society and a view of Canada as a country composed of distinct provincial communities, a tension most dramatically expressed in the competing national visions of Pierre Trudeau and René Levesque. This tension finds appropriate reflection in the Constitution Act of 1982 which opts exclusively for neither nation-building nor province-building, but which recognizes, sustains, and constitutionally entrenches the inherent and healthy tension between the two.

This dynamic tension does not appear to have been present in the political process leading up to the Meech Lake Accord, and as a consequence does not find reflection in the Accord. Its absence in both cases can be traced to Prime Minister Brian Mulroney. Although Mr. Mulroney has many assets as a party leader and prime minister, these do not include a well-articulated national vision. While Mr. Mulroney has been legitimately preoccupied with national reconciliation following the tumultuous years of the Trudeau governments, a belief in national reconciliation cannot replace a clearly articulated sense of the national community, **and of the role that the federal government must play in nurturing that community**. At least it cannot do so within the context of the First Ministers' Conference when the Prime Minister comes face to face with the more province-centered visions of the country's ten premiers.

The concern here goes back to the political process that produced Meech Lake. In the First Ministers Conference, ten premiers can be expected to defend and promote the interests of their provincial governments and, perhaps to a lesser extent, of their provincial communities. The premiers necessarily have a view of Canada in which provincial governments play a central and increasingly important role. This is not to say that the premiers lack any sense of national vision extending beyond their own provincial boundaries, that they are small men with only a parochial grasp of the Canadian political community. Rather it is to say that they need a foil, they need a champion of the national community and national government against which their own visions can be tested.

In 1987, Mr. Mulroney failed to provide that foil, or at least failed to provide it as effectively as Mr. Trudeau did earlier.[4] As a consequence the Meech Lake Accord fails to reflect the essential tension between nation-building and province-building, a tension that all Canadians incorporate to a degree in their political psyches. It is the constitutional product of ten premiers drawing up a constitution in the absence of a strong, vigorous and effective defence of the national community and government. The premiers alone, however, do not speak for Canada; the whole in this case is greater than the sum of parts.

All of this is not to say that the Meech Lake Accord dramatically changes Canada's constitutional fabric. With the possible exception of its recognition of Quebec as a distinct society, the changes embodied in the Accord are largely incremental ones. Yet in a cumulative sense, they nudge Canada down a constitutional path in which provincial governments are increasingly important players, and in which the role of the national government is diminished. If this change of direction reflected the sociological reality of Canada, if indeed Canadians are withdrawing from the national community and are strengthening their identification with narrower provincial communities, we should have no cause for complaint. I would argue, however, that the Meech Lake Accord does not reflect the sociological reality of Canada. Rather it reflects the political reality of a constitutional process in which First Ministers are the principal and, in the case of Meech Lake, virtually the only constitutional players. It reflects the political reality of ten provincial premiers going head-to-head with a prime minister whose national vision fails to extend beyond an understandable search for national reconciliation. The Accord gives constitutional recognition to the wrong reality; it serves the governments of Canada better than it serves the people.

The Impact of Free Trade

Although the public's unease with the Meech Lake Accord stems largely from the interplay of constitutional process and constitutional product, it may also have been sharpened by the federal government's concurrent search for a free trade agreement with the United States. Many although by no means all Canadians have been concerned that in the search for a free trade agreement, the Canadian government may give up too much to the United States. They seek reassurance that the government will stand up for Canadian interests, that there is a point beyond which the government will not go, that the Government of Canada has a vision of the national community that it will not sacrifice on the alter of free trade.

For such people, the Meech Lake Accord provides little reassurance. If it had provided public demonstration of a national government committed to the national community, of a government with a clear national vision, then I suspect Canadians would be more confident about the pending free trade agreement with the United States. In crude terms, however, there is a fear that a national government unable or unwilling to stand up to the provinces at Meech Lake will be unable or unwilling to stand up to the Americans. Conversely, Canadians who perceive any weakness in Canada's negotiating position on free trade may project that weakness back onto the Meech Lake Accord; if the federal government appears to have given up too much for free trade, then ipso facto it must also have given up too much for the Meech Lake Accord.

In this subtle and not altogether fair fashion, the two major issues on the country's political agenda become entangled. At a time when Canada stands poised on the brink of major changes in its economic and cultural relationship with the United States, Canadians want reassurance that the national government will not surrender too much, that it will retain sufficient legislative power and authority to defend the national community. The Meech Lake Accord fails to offer such assurance, and thus it too becomes subjected to the national uncertainties brought into play by free trade. Canadians who have difficulty seeing their vision of Canada reflected in the free trade agreement have similar difficulty finding its reflection in Meech Lake.

Conclusions

Constitutions should be built upon the rock of political reality if they are to endure, and in this respect the Meech Lake Accord may serve Canada well. It does provide constitutional recognition for the distinct character of Quebec, and for the increasingly prominent role that provincial governments have come to play in Canadian political life. It constitutionalizes the existing realities of executive federalism by providing for an annual First Ministers' Conference on the state of the economy 'and such other matters as may be appropriate.' Constitutions, however, should do more than simply reflect current realities. They should also provide a foundation upon which we can construct our political future. It is in this sense that the Accord fails Canadians for it reflects the realities of a particular political process, one dominated by provincial governments, more than it reflects the realities of the country at large.

In framing the Meech Lake Accord the First Ministers returned, consciously or not, to the debate in the early 1970s over special status for Quebec. At that time special status was rejected as a constitutional option in part because of the opposition of the federal Liberal government, and in part because other provincial governments were not prepared to bestow upon Quebec a status which they themselves did not enjoy. The Meech Lake solution was to bestow special or 'distinctive' status on Quebec, or at least to provide the Quebec government with the powers special status implied, and then to extend those powers to the other nine provincial governments. In effect, all provinces have won the powers that were denied Quebec alone in the 1970s. Special status has been universalized.

My fundamental concern, however is not with what the Meech Lake Accord says about the provinces, but what it fails to say about Canada, about the national community of which provinces were once seen as constituent parts. My unease, and it may be an unease that western Canadians feel most acutely, springs from the fact that the Accord fails to embody any vision of the national community, of Canada. It appears to be a document drawn up by provincial governments for provincial governments, the result of a constitutional contest in which the federal government was a referee but not a player aggressively pursuing its own interests and vision. Thus while the Accord may provide a vehicle through which we can construct stronger provincial communities, it does not hold out the same promise for the national community. The Accord may serve us well as Albertans or Nova Scotians or Quebecois, but it is less clear that it will serve us well as Canadians.

Notes

1 Alan C. Cairns, 'The Politics of Constitutional Conservatism' in Keith Banting and Richard Simeon, eds., *And No One Cheered: Federalism, Democracy & the Constitution Act* (Toronto: Methuen 1983) 55.

2 For a discussion, see Chaviva Hosek, 'Women and the Constitutional Process' in Banting and Simeon, *And No One Cheered*, 280-300.

3 For a discussion, see Douglas Sanders, 'The Indian Lobby', ibid., 301-332.

4 Mr. Mulroney's failure can only be speculation on my or anybody else's part. It may well be that behind closed doors Mr. Mulroney was a powerful and effective spokesman for the national government, that he was able to articulate and defend a compelling vision of the national community. But because we could not observe the process and have only the text of the Accord to rely upon, it is difficult to accept this image of the Prime Minister.

An Economic Perspective

Malcolm C. Brown

Deciding on an appropriate focus for this paper has been a particularly difficult task. In part, this is because the issues and problems raised by the Meech Lake Accord are more appropriate domains of analysis for political scientists and constitutional experts than for economists. But it is also in part because my views on the Accord have been rapidly evolving; my concerns have shifted from a vague sense of unease to a definite sense of alarm.

Initially, I found it incredible that anyone could consider consensus among the Prime Minister and the ten premiers to be an appropriate condition for initiating constitutional change. Where such consensus emerges the condition is redundant, since it is virtually impossible to identify circumstances where the change in question would not occur in any event. On the other hand, where such consensus does not emerge, it is easy to identify circumstances where the will of the majority of Canadians could be thwarted, however large that majority might be.

If the technical deficiencies inherent in the Meech Lake Accord are troublesome, the spirit of the Accord is repugnant. Its unspoken premise is that there is no Canadian community of interest, but only a set of provincial interests which are to be coordinated as much as can be agreed upon, through a procedure of unanimity among a small number of individuals who, history teaches us, often function in very parochial ways. The fact that Canadians will be constrained to press for the type of national community that they want mainly through the regional politician they elect as premier is disturbing enough. The fact that the group of eleven first ministers may become the most important political decision-making body in the country, without having a populist and democratic basis of support, is absolutely frightening.

Having stated my original criticisms of the Accord, I will confess that they did not make me as concerned about the ramifications of the Accord as many other analysts were. Like many economists, I have a tendency to think of the Constitution and its interpretations as a reflection of the political realities of a country, and not as a determinant of them. Thus, Meech Lake primarily served to make me sad that Canada had moved so far in the direction of provincial and elitist political decision-making, and did not indicate to me that a sudden shift in the power structure had been orchestrated.

In case my basic perspective on the relationship between political realities and the constitution strike the reader as hopelessly naive, let me hasten to point out that it is quite consistent with the way that Canada's political arrangements have evolved. Consider, for example, the shifting balance of fiscal powers between federal and provincial governments in light of the constraints imposed by the British North America Act, 1867. The 1867 Act allocated public expenditures of a national concern to the Federal government, and public expenditure of local and private concerns to provincial governments. It also gave unlimited taxation power to the Federal government but constrained provincial governments to direct, and preferably benefit-based, types of taxes. Subsequent judicial interpretations of the BNA Act broadened the scope of provincial government expenditure responsibilities by concentrating on the examples of activities of merely local or private concern given in section 92 of the Act – examples which were reasonable in 1867 but which became unreasonable as the economy evolved. Subsequent interpretations of the BNA Act also changed the definitions of direct and indirect taxes in completely arbitrary ways, so that provincial governments now rely on indirect taxes more than does the Federal government.

A more recent example of how the Constitution Acts are interpreted to suit political needs occurred in 1981, when it looked like the Federal government might repatriate the Constitution unilaterally (i.e., without the support of the provincial governments). The Supreme Court was asked to make a decision whether unilateral repatriation would have been constitutional and legal. A literal reading of the Constitution Acts compelled the Court to conclude that unilateral repatriation was indeed constitutional, but it also stated the desirability of having provincial government consent – a reasonably clear example of the Court deferring to the political realities of the time.

My point is that the evolution of Canadian political and fiscal powers has not been brought about by politicians and judges unable to understand what was in the Constitution Acts, but by individuals responding to the political and economic pressures in their society. Insofar as these pressures have been accurately perceived, one can even make a plausible argument that the evolving interpretation of the Constitution has been a good thing. But in any event one must conclude that the Constitution Acts are not the constraints on governments' economic powers, and the determinants of individuals' rights and freedoms, that they are often considered to be.

Of course, in considering the relationship between the political and economic realities of a society and the wording and interpretation of its Constitution, it must be admitted that the line of causation is rarely entirely in one direction. This perhaps explains why I have become increasingly concerned about the ramifications of the Meech Lake Accord. In effect, I have been worrying more about the lines of influence running from the Accord to Canadian society than I did initially. By formally identifying Canada as little more than a collection of communities, and by downplaying the rights of individuals (women, French-speaking Canadians outside Quebec, etc.) unless these rights are integral to the survival of a provincially powerful political group, the Accord fosters a society which is at odds with individual human dignity. It also fosters a political arrangement where the imbalance of powers favouring centrifugal forces is such that the nation-state may not be able to survive.

The Economic Model of Federalism

The fact that the Meech Lake Accord may foster a distribution of political powers inimical to the long-run survival of Canada brings me to the core of what an economist might hope to bring to any discussion about a nation's constitution. It tends to be a surprise to many people that, within economic theory, there is, in fact, a model of an optimal federal state. This model is based on the premise that the optimal federal state must achieve three major objectives. First, it must create, and maintain, fiscal equity among all citizens of the state; and never just equity among sub-components of the population. Second, it must be conducive to economic efficiency, by allowing both people and capital complete freedom to locate in those parts of the country where their contributions to national output are greatest. Third, it must strike an appropriate balance between the centripetal and centrifugal political and economic forces in the state such that the assigned fiscal responsibilities among national and regional governments represent a stable equilibrium arrangement.

This optimal federal state has a number of important features, the first being that the national government should control all stabilization policies (bearing on employment, inflation, etc.), all income redistribution programs and policies, and all allocation policies where the market failure problem is at a national level. In this context, market failure alludes to a situation where the features of a good are such that consumption must occur on a collective, rather than an individual, basis. For example, national defence represents a good which must be purchased collectively by all Canadians, and which cannot be efficiently purchased by Canadians separately, or even in sub-groups. Accordingly, national defence represents an allocation policy which, according to the economic theory of an optimal federal state, should be assigned to the national government.

The second feature of the optimal federal state is that regional governments should engage only in allocation policies designed to resolve market failures occurring at the regional and local level. Police and fire protection, and maintenance of local parks, are reasonably good examples of goods where regional and/or local government provision would be considered optimal by most analysts (as of 1987).

The third feature concerns the assignment of taxation powers. For optimal economic results, the national government should have unlimited taxation power, and regional governments should preferably be restricted to benefit-based taxes. If regional governments cannot be restricted to only benefit-based taxes, because of the constraint on total taxation capacity that this would imply, then they at least should be restricted to direct taxation (as defined in economic theory).

The implication of the economic model for an optimal federal state is that a regional government is simply a geographically large local government; and that both regional and local governments have roles that are complimentary with, and never competitive with, the roles of a national government. In considering this implication, one must be impressed with how close the BNA Act, 1867, came to describing the optimal federal state, in economic terms. Moreover, if one accepts the economic model, one must be concerned with how far the Canadian federal state has strayed from the original guidelines. Canada's current constitutional arrangements, even before Meech Lake, make the provincial governments geographically small national governments, and thus competitive with the Federal government in almost every sense imaginable.

It is important to consider what the ramifications of 'Meech Lake' federalism are, assuming that the economic model of a federal state has validity. First, it could be expected that current Canadian federal arrangements will lead to greater inequities among Canadians. Second, it could be expected that Canadian production efficiency will be lowered, as citizens are encouraged to remain in the province of their birth and of their cultural orientation. Third, it could be predicted that the Canadian federal state will eventually dissolve as the centrifugal forces in the constitutional arrangements become increasingly dominant. Hence the predictions from the economic model have rather disturbing implications for the future of Canadian federalism.

The Meech Lake Accord promotes the above ramifications by changing the relative costs of making constitutional, and even political, adjustments to the Canadian system. It reduces the cost of making adjustments which cater to provincial interests but increases the cost of adjustments which have the potential for increasing the sense of national community.

For example, suppose that at some time in the future, the Yukon formally applies to become a province, and that this does not threaten the rights or privileges of any existing province. Nevertheless, it is not difficult to imagine a scenario where the Premier of Alberta might offer his support conditional on a wanted change in energy policy, or the Premier of Quebec might make his support conditional on some change in language rights. In other words, every constitutional change of this nature will require that regional politicians be bought off by concessions which may have no objective other than getting these individuals re-elected locally.

Consider another example, related to Canada's health financing policies, where the potential for 'undemocratic' log-rolling is more complex but no less real. Since the beginning national health insurance has been a program which the vast majority of Canadians in all provinces have supported. Yet a number of provincial governments have remained opposed. In the absence of the Canada Health Act, 1984, there is no doubt in my mind that some of these provincial governments would relatively quickly phase down medicare to make it look more like the American system of health care finance. In the process, they would do everything possible to avoid making the policy a focus of a provincial election, and certainly would never let it become a matter of a provincial plebiscite. In other words, in these provincial governments' collective minds, their electorates are either ignorant or wrong concerning the matter of how health care should be financed.

The Canada Health Act thus represents a policy favoured by the majority of Canadians in all provinces, but yet is a policy which could never get unanimous support from all provincial premiers. Under the Meech Lake Accord, there will be no future analogue to the Canada Health Act in relationship to any social change which might be of concern to Canadians. Moreover, even the Canada Health Act itself may be subject to a gradual phasing down as the log-rolling agendas among the premiers and the Prime Minister evolve.

If I had my 'druthers' I would like to see the Accord forced back to the drawing board, because it would indicate in a symbolic way that the centripetal forces favouring Canadian identity are still a reality, if not all that strong. But even with a re-working of the Accord, I have little doubt that the concept of Canada is in for a rough political ride over the foreseeable future. About the only bright spot on this horizon is that Canada may become the first geographic entity in the world to establish definitively whether there can be a political unit somewhere between a federal state and a common market!

The 1987 Constitutional Accord and Federal-Provincial Relations

Claude Rocan

The purpose of this paper is to discuss the impact of the 1987 Constitutional Accord on federal-provincial relations in Canada. The basic argument is that the 1987 Constitutional Accord is consistent with Canadian federalism as it has developed over the past 120 years, and will give our federal system the flexibility needed to adapt to the exigencies of the future.

Let us begin by looking at some trends in Canadian federalism. It seems clear that federalism operates today in a way not anticipated by the drafters of the B.N.A. Act, 1867, now called the Constitution Act, 1867. In dividing up areas of federal and provincial jurisdiction in sections 91 and 92 respectively, the Fathers of Confederation may have thought that they were dividing the roles and responsibilities of the two orders of government in neatly divided categories. As we know, however, the 'watertight compartments' concept is no longer a realistic way to look at Canadian federalism.

The complexity of issues with which modern governments must deal has led to a great deal of overlap in the roles and responsibilities of the two orders of government in a number of areas. The area of post-secondary education is one that involves both levels of government, and will do so to an increasing extent as adjustment mechanisms become more and more important in dealing with the shifts in labour market trends. The areas of health, social assistance, and housing provide other examples where federal and provincial powers intersect.

One can also point to the 'Trade and Commerce' power which appears to give sweeping powers over the economy to the federal government, but which, in effect, leaves some very significant gaps. The regulation of strictly local, intra-provincial business activity falls to provincial governments. The area of provincial purchasing power alone has a massive effect on economic activity in Canada. In this light, it is significant to note that the federal government now accounts for less than 50% of public sector procurement in Canada.

One final example comes from public policy-making as it applies to aboriginal people in Canada. Again, at first glance it seems that this matter would fall under federal jurisdiction because section 91(24) of the Constitution Act, 1867 gives the federal government the power to legislate in matters relating to Indians and Indian lands. Federal legislative jurisdiction over this area would seem to be confirmed by the passage of the Indian Act by Parliament.

However, the apparent straight-forward nature of this case is purely illusory for several reasons. First, in many areas of Canada the federal government has adopted the policy that it is not responsible to provide services for registered Indians living off-reserve. Moreover, while section 91(24) clearly applies to Indians, and the courts have determined that it also applies to Inuit, the federal government has taken the position that it does not apply to Metis, or to Non-Status Indians. Even in the case of on-reserve status Indians, the matter is not as simple as it may appear. Section 88 of the Indian Act states that where the federal government chooses not to enact special legislation for Indians, provincial laws of general application will apply. This has led to a situation in which provinces are involved on reserves in important ways, in some cases assuming as much as 50% of on-reserve costs.

What makes the 1987 Constitutional Accord so significant – and, in my view, so beneficial – is that it will adjust federal-provincial mechanisms in keeping with changes to modern federalism, changes including but by no means restricted to the matter of over-lapping jurisdictions discussed above. To be more specific, the Accord increases the ability of provinces to participate in national policy-making in certain specific areas, as well as in some more general areas. Furthermore, the Accord allows provinces to tailor some national policies so that they better reflect the needs and circumstances of those provinces. Given the way federalism has evolved in Canada, this development is quite important, and perhaps even necessary.

Critics of the Accord often charge that it decentralizes Canada because it increases the powers of the provinces. This argument is misleading because it overlooks the fact that the powers of the provinces are not being increased in the sense that provinces will be better able to operate autonomously within their own field of jurisdiction, insulated from the federal government. Rather, the Accord provides mechanisms by which provincial governments can more effectively participate in discussions that affect all of Canada. This is accomplished in a variety of ways.

First, the Accord provides for an increased role for the provinces in the selection of members to two important central institutions: the Supreme Court of Canada and the Senate. To be clear, the provinces will not be in a position to dictate to the federal government who should sit on the Supreme Court. When a vacancy occurs, the provinces will submit names of candidates to the federal government, which will then be in a position to select from the names put forward. Except in the case of judges from Quebec, the federal government will be able to 'shop' from the lists submitted by the provinces. I see nothing insidious about provinces participating in this way in Court appointments. After all, a part of the role of the Supreme Court is to act as an umpire between the two orders of government. Since this role is becoming increasingly important, the legitimacy of this institution will be enhanced if provinces play some role in the appointment of its members. Until the Senate is reformed, provinces will also have a role – in this case, a more direct role – in making appointments to that body.

Second, in relation to immigration, provincial governments will be allowed to participate in setting immigration policy as it affects their specific province. An opportunity will exist for provinces to negotiate an immigration agreement with the federal government which will reflect their specific needs and circumstances.

Third, the amending formula has been changed to include more items requiring the unanimous consent of the federal government and all ten provinces before change can be effectuated. These new items relate to central institutions in Canada, in which all provinces have a major stake.

Fourth, the Accord's spending power provision will allow provinces to opt out, with compensation, from new shared-cost programs in areas of exclusive provincial jurisdiction. (Compensation will require that provinces establish their own programs compatible with the national objectives of the federal program.) This will have the effect of increasing the level of consultation and negotiation between the federal government and the provinces before such programs are put into place. This is because the federal government will want to avoid initiating programs in which the majority of provinces will want to opt out.

Finally, one aspect of the Accord which has received an insufficient amount of attention is the creation of two new central institutions in Canada; the annual First Ministers' Conference on the Economy and the annual First Ministers' Conference on the Constitution. Of course, First Ministers' Conferences on the Economy have been held on an annual basis since 1985, but this Conference will now be constitutionally entrenched, as will the annual Conference on the Constitution. The creation of these institutions is important because it will establish important new structures for both orders of government to address issues of national importance.

Given all of these changes, the question can be fairly asked whether we have, in creating these new avenues for provincial participation in national policy-making, set the scene for a good deal more discord between governments than has been the case in the past? Admittedly, there is no way of answering this question definitively, and to an extent we may well have increased the potential for conflict between the two orders of government in Canada. But some level of discord, after all, is inevitable in a democratic system, and I believe that a part of our belief in federal structures is based in our belief in democratic principles. Moreover, I do not think that the discord arising from the new structures introduced by the Accord will have a destructive effect on the Canadian federation.

The new provisions for Supreme Court appointments as well as for the negotiation of bi-lateral arrangements on immigration do not seem likely to trigger major battles, assuming a certain amount of good faith on all sides, which it is not unreasonable to assume. Although it is not difficult to recall those times when the federal government and one or more provinces have clashed, we must not overlook the general spirit of good-will and accommodation which has sustained the Canadian federation since its inception.

In terms of the spending power section, there will no doubt be more intensive consultation and negotiation which may prolong the early stages of establishing such programs, but should not preclude the establishment of new programs. It is worth remembering, too, that the application of this measure is relatively narrow. It is intended to cover only **new, shared-cost** programs in areas of **exclusive provincial jurisdiction**.

The introduction of the new central institutions also contains the potential of increasing the amount of discord in the Canadian political system. However, as a result of these reforms First Ministers will become increasingly sensitive to the importance of achieving the objectives of their governments through co-ordinated action with other governments. This in turn will lead to a more intensive, but not at all sinister, level of intergovernmental diplomacy. Eventually, this is likely to spawn less regionalism in Canada rather than more, because leaders of all governments will gain, through more intensive contact with other jurisdictions, a broader appreciation of the realities in other parts of Canada. Similarly, while changes to the amending formula have the potential of producing considerable conflict, the recent constitutional exercise itself shows that unanimity is not an unrealistic objective, provided that a certain amount of good-will exists among the participants.

In conclusion, I would like to make one final point which is entirely speculative in nature. Critics of the Accord have expressed concern that many of its features tend to elevate executive federalism to new levels. However, I suspect that as the two First Ministers'Conferences evolve there will be greater pressure to enlarge the circle of participants. Perhaps First Ministers will decide to set up committees of ministers to report to them on certain issues. In the case of the First Ministers' Conference on the Economy, this tendency has already begun to manifest itself. Nor is it inconceivable that some groups of Canadians might be invited to participate in discussions which pertain to a particular issue. In a way, the precedent was set for this during the process on aboriginal constitutional affairs.

Clearly there is no way of knowing precisely how the new Meech Lake arrangements will work in practice. In any exercise of constitutional reform, a certain amount of risk is inevitable. However, given the trends in the evolution of Canadian federalism, there is an undeniable need to reshape our federal institutions. What is often forgotten by critics of the Accord is that there is also a very substantial risk in maintaining the status quo, which is the risk of adhering to outdated institutional structures which could frustrate future progress and which, in the long run, could put into question the very legitimacy of these structures. Moreover, the fact that the status quo does not include Quebec's participation in many issues of vital interest to Canada makes this risk unacceptably high.

The Accord introduces the opportunity for a positive new dynamic in federal-provincial relations. It will take some good will, and some creativity, on the part of Canadians to rise to the challenge. I hope and expect that these will be forthcoming. Certainly, the inclusion of the Province of Quebec as a full and active participant in the Canadian federation will add considerably to our chances of success in this endeavour.

Who Spoke For Canada?

Doreen Barrie

There are a number of substantive problems with Meech Lake which other authors in this collection have discussed. My concern is with the process by which such immensely important constitutional changes are made. The question to be addressed is whether it is time to re-evaluate the process of constitutional change in Canada. What the Meech Lake Accord shows, I will argue, is that the present method is flawed because it is too secretive, too hasty, too flexible and too politicized. As a result of these weaknesses, the interests of Canadians as a whole appear to have been forgotten in the Accord, making 'Who Spoke for Canada?' a very valid question.

Secrecy

One of the advantages of a parliamentary system is its efficiency. Strong executives can do what they deem necessary even in the face of fierce opposition. Conventions surrounding confidentiality of cabinet discussions and cabinet solidarity ensure that a majority government can proceed with its agenda with little hindrance. But an undesirable side effect of the parliamentary system is that the secrecy may become habitual, causing a passivity among the population and permitting the government to shield even the most innocuous information from the public eye. The lack of scrutiny of day-to-day decisions, no matter how important, may be acceptable. However, binding decisions which change the nature of the country, which will have far-reaching consequences for future generations are surely of a different order.

Clearly such matters should only be decided after canvassing the views of the people whose lives will be affected. The Meech Lake Accord was signed with no public input. Even though public hearings were held in some provinces, participants were fully aware that no suggestions for change would be entertained.

Haste

Because amending a constitution is such a serious business, proposed changes must be very carefully considered. Many ordinary pieces of legislation, which can be repealed at any time, receive a good deal of consideration before they reach the House of Commons. Interest groups are consulted, public hearings are held and the matter receives an airing **before** the bill is introduced in the House. Yet, the Meech Lake Accord demonstrates that sweeping constitutional changes can take place with greater haste and less input than revisions to the Income Tax Act.

The Accord was sprung on an unsuspecting population as a *fait accompli*. Federal officials had apparently spent months visiting provincial capitals laying the groundwork, but the final document was hammered out over a very short period of time.

The picture of a handful of people confined to a room until they could reach an agreement is somewhat distressing. Is this the way something so important should come about? Can a group of individuals be expected to take the long view, to examine all the implications of an agreement when they are numbed by fatigue? More important, is it desirable to let eleven men (because it was ultimately eleven **men**) make such momentous decisions?

Flexibility

Federal constitutions are designed to be enduring documents, not exactly straitjackets but having a fair degree of rigidity to ensure they are not revised too easily. If the Canadian constitution can be changed drastically as a result of two meetings between the First Ministers (since ratification by Parliament and the legislatures is a mere formality), then it is too flexible. It signals the possibility of swift and frequent change in the future precluding the sort of careful consideration that such an exercise merits. It also trivializes what should be an extremely important document.

Politicization

It should not be possible to use the constitution as a tool in partisan warfare, yet the present method of constitutional amendment lends itself precisely to such use.

In the present instance, Brian Mulroney could have been motivated either by a genuine desire to usher Quebec into the constitutional fold or to stem the erosion of Conservative support in Quebec. No matter how high-minded his intentions, it is very easy to put the wrong construction on his actions as the federal government bargained away some of its own powers in what appears to be a desperate bid for provincial support. Naturally provincial premiers will zealously guard provincial interests but it isn't clear that in the latest round of constitutional talks anyone was guarding the national interest. It is as if the representative for Canada was absent from the table.

There is an unfortunate tendency for the Prime Minister to be regarded as just another participant at First Ministers' Conferences — at times a weak one, because ten others are often aligned against him. If he appears to accept this perception, he legitimizes it. While each premier has a concrete constituency, the Prime Minister's is more nebulous. The situation is delicate because while acknowledging a premier's right to speak for his slice of Canada, the Prime Minister has to make clear that the whole is more than the sum of its parts. As provincial populations have such vigorous champions, another voice raised on their behalf may seem redundant and perhaps this is why some Canadian Prime Ministers have appeared almost apologetic in their appeals to the national community. Nevertheless, the onus is on the Prime Minister to protect the national interest — conceived more broadly than what suits the current government's electoral interests.

In fairness to the governments involved, it must be pointed out that because of the way the present amendment process works, it is not surprising that short-term considerations should predominate. Given their high profile, First Ministers' Conferences are not the most appropriate arena for constitutional change. With the media quick to assess winners and losers, with participants anxious to look good, it is unrealistic to expect politicians to court certain defeat by taking an unpopular stand. To leave this undertaking solely in the hands of politicians is an intolerable burden because no matter how well intentioned some are, there are no incentives for a statesmanlike stance. In fact, there may be penalties.

Ideally, the amendment process should be an objective, nonpartisan exercise detached from the hurly burly of everyday politics, for what is at stake is not just the here-and-now but the very framework within which all parties must work.

Conclusion

As the weaknesses of the present amending procedure have been brought into sharp focus by the Meech Lake Accord, perhaps it is time to re-evaluate it. The procedure for change must be such that it is beyond the reach of dictator and visionary alike and the only way to ensure this is to draw the people into the debate. It is for experts in constitutional law to devise the precise mechanism, but if the only participants are governments, then the situation is ripe for manipulation. If the First Ministers are reluctant to relinquish this important responsibility, then proposed changes should at least be discussed openly with built-in provisions for public input **before** the final document is drawn up. The ensuing debate would put a much-needed brake on proceedings, giving sufficient time for different points of view to be heard and for the ramifications of the revisions to be well understood.

At the moment, most Canadians consider constitution-making an arcane exercise understood only by constitutional lawyers and political scientists. This is hardly surprising since they have never been called upon to play a role. Yet as more Charter of Rights cases come before the courts, the constitution will become an instrument for a growing body of people and I suspect, they will no longer accept it as the special preserve of governments. But a constitution is more than an **instrument**, it is also a reflection of a nation's soul, a potent **symbol** of the values that a nation upholds. Since it expresses their aspirations and epitomizes what they stand for, it is only fitting that the people should have a say in changing it. In this way it will be difficult to ignore national considerations or to fear that Canada will be absent from the bargaining table.

Meech Mumbles...

William F. Gold

Has a nation that professes attachment to the rule of law ever contemplated major constitutional change in such a state of conversational vacuum?

If the Meech Lake Accord fails to secure the consent necessary by 1990 — and the possibility is by no means remote — it will have fallen victim to a unique political confluence of misunderstanding, fear, special pleading and, above all, a lack of sustained, clarifying, national debate. Founded on a popular misconception that Quebec was somehow not part of Canada thanks to its refusal to sign the 1982 constitutional arrangements, Meech Lake seems to be foundering on a simple lack of national discussion.

There is talk, of course. The reference to Quebec as a distinct society, and the promises of on-going negotiations about the Senate and the fisheries, have fuelled the 'me, too' syndrome. Groups not specifically referred to in the document fear that such exclusion constitutes an anticipatory denial of rights. Thus women's groups and others fight for specific inclusion. The Territorial governments of the North, meanwhile, feel dreams of provincehood are jeopardized by Meech's re-adoption of the principle of unanimity for any future constitutional change required to create new provinces. So they're off to court. In the meantime, Prime Minister Brian Mulroney in his capacity as chief architect of the project, betrays no interest in initiating a direct reference to the Supreme Court of Canada in search of clarification of such phrases as 'distinct society.'

Quebec, Saskatchewan and Alberta were the swiftest ratifiers of the Accord. For those pains, they promptly found themselves embroiled in ancient questions of linguistic rights, with all sorts of people claiming 'see, that's what Meech will do' when in fact the particulars of current problems are all pre-Meech. Other provinces are wavering as the ranks of the original signing premiers are inexorably thinned by the passage of time and the will of the voters. Pro-Meechers now crowd the ante-room of Premier Frank McKennas's New Brunswick office. Soon they must repair to Manitoba to placate Liberal leader Sharon Carstairs whose opposition is clearly a hazard.

So, in point of fact there is Meech all around us. It's in the political air. Yet the debate is particularized, localized, diffuse and spotty. Why? The federal opposition parties have utterly failed in their duty to the country. They have not opposed. They have pandered. The New Democrats under Ed Broadbent and the Liberals under John Turner took the course of expediency from the very first day. The rest of us have since had cause to regret that bizarre process of personal opting out. Those two leaders may have future cause for regret as well.

What a contrast with this decade's earlier history. When Pierre Trudeau unveiled his then constitutional package just after the 1980 election, Opposition Leader Joe Clark was on national television within minutes with a cogent analysis of the deal that approved some and opposed much. Eventually he and his party had real influence in the shaping of the final package. Throughout the two-year process, Clark's opposition made possible a genuine national debate flowing from the cockpit of Parliament. All Canadians could listen in. An issue that otherwise would surely have been fragmented into the half-submerged dialogue of the premiers (and was at the very end) was left open to the people.

Contrast that with Meech Lake. Before they opted out of the most fundamental of their political responsibilities, the duty to oppose, Turner and Broadbent satisfied themselves on only one point. Did Quebec want Meech? Yes, they answered themselves, Quebec did want Meech. Goodbye, loyal opposition.

Grit and NDPer alike were trolling then and are trolling now for Quebec's indispensable support. Thus there is no national debate. Despite obvious tension within both opposition parties, there will be no national debate. Talk of the Accord will continue to take place at the special-interest margins of the major issues involved. In such an environment political initiatives can die for want of nourishment, and sometimes it is best that they do die even at a price.

The major challenges nationally have been raised from outside the mainstream. Former Prime Minister Trudeau, and former Liberal cabinet minister Don Johnston have objected. They have not been so much answered as brushed aside. Yet their objections are fundamental. If, as they claim, Meech changes the bilingual thrust and focus of Canada from a federal mission to one of provincial enclaves, then the country is changing profoundly. Perhaps history dictates such change, Meech or no Meech, but shouldn't the possibility be at least discussed?

Any examination of Meech can result in a vision of a much different Canada. It will consist of two parts. One will be French and named Quebec. The other will be English and have nine names. On both sides of the language divide these critters will be able to peel off from the others and go their own way in social policy matters. Federal MPs will find themselves voting on programs that are not in fact operative in their own jurisdictions.

The institutionalization of First Ministers' meetings on the Senate and the fisheries further establishes the permanency of this extra-Parliamentary and singularly undemocratic apparatus. The very Meech Lake process itself has already shown how deals cooked up among premiers and a prime minister can somehow slip through the cracks of the national consciousness. In some policy areas formal policy ratification won't even be necessary in the parliamentary sense. Even when it is, the event and the deed can be widely separated in time.

The additional federal-provincial machinery thus required will sooner or later lead to the establishment of a formal First Ministers' secretariat. The worst fears of those who have long warned of creation of yet another level of quasi-government, and a nearly-unaccountable one at that, will be that much closer to fruition.

As the Meech Lake scenario unfolds something else is taking place in Canada. Underneath the special pleadings of the specific Meech claimants, and helped along by the airless hollow of a central national debate that simply isn't happening, the national mood of Canada is disturbing.

Don't look for it in the polls, in the legislatures, or the houses of Parliament. It's not surfacing there. It is to be found instead among friends and neighbours, children and parents, fellow workers and business associates. It is a sense of rootlessness. An erosion of the Canadian Fact is slowly taking place. Our sense of home is drifting. Where, now, do we live? Is it Canada? Or is it Alberta, Ontario or wherever? Will one distinct society give inadvertent birth to nine more?

When we can't even talk about Meech Lake, questions like that have to be asked.

Human Rights

You can be certain that there is nothing in the Meech Lake Accord that diminishes in any way the rights of women or anyone else...[A] lot of people are using that as a Trojan horse because they don't want a distinct society and the Meech Lake Accord. Brian Mulroney.

I can summarize my concerns with the Accord in short order. First, it completely ignores aboriginal peoples and their place in the existing constitutional order. In that sense, it totally misstates Canada as it is. It takes us back to a myth of 120 years ago that the fundamental character of Canada is of the French and English. Smokey Bruyere.[1]

When you sit and listen and read [commentary on the accord] you have the awful feeling that the First Ministers forgot women, forgot minorities, forgot the aboriginal peoples and never even thought about the Yukon and Northwest Territories coming in as provinces. Pauline Jewett.[2]

INTRODUCTION:
HUMAN RIGHTS

One of the most significant developments in the public response to the Meech Lake Accord has been the opposition from a variety of minority groups,[3] who have been concerned about its implications for the protection of human rights in general, and their rights in particular. The Mulroney government has argued that the Meech Lake process is the 'Quebec round' of constitutional negotiations, and that other issues should be postponed until the question of Quebec's place in confederation is settled. But women, natives, and ethnic groups have, in the last two decades, fought their way onto the center of the Canadian national consciousness and political agenda, and they refuse to be forgotten in any attempt to define the essence of Canada. Many of these groups feel that the Meech Lake Accord jeopardizes their current rights. They are unwilling to accept government reassurances about future constitutional talks or future measures to ensure their hard-won rights since they have felt betrayed so many times in the past.

Paradoxically, the efforts which have been made via the Accord to help Québécois feel secure have heightened the insecurity of others. Many minority groups feel betrayed by the country's being redefined and dramatically altered without their having any say in the matter. This frustration was heightened by the unwillingness of the key political actors in the ratification process to entertain **any** amendments to the Accord, on the ground that if any amendments were entertained the whole process might unravel. The minorities feel that all Canadians are equal, and that making some more distinct, or possibly more equal than others, is unacceptable.

Minority group concerns about the Meech Lake Accord run deep. Women's groups argue that the distinct society clause of the Accord, along with the mention of multicultural and aboriginal rights without mention of gender rights in section 16 of the Accord, threatens the equality provisions of the Charter of Rights. In her article in this chapter, Kathleen Mahoney discusses the wide range of concerns women have with the legal implications of the Accord. Ethnic groups (as noted by Anthony Parel in this section) argue that the interpretive framework of the Accord, with its emphasis on English and French speaking Canadians, takes Canada back to the notion of two founding peoples and a bicultural vision of the country which undermines the legitimacy of multiculturalism. Both women's and native groups also fear the weakening of federal responsibility for social programs since in their experience the provinces are less sympathetic to their needs than the federal government.

Native leaders such as George Erasmus, (whose testimony before the Joint Committee of the Senate and the House of Commons is included in this chapter) wonder why it was possible for the First Ministers to so quickly come to an Accord based on concepts such as 'distinct society,' which are vague and will be left to the courts to decide, when the very same politicians told them just months earlier that aboriginal rights could not be entrenched in the constitution because they were too vague and would have to be decided by the courts. Native groups also see the provision for the unanimity of all provinces in future constitutional change and in the creation of new provinces as effectively blocking both future constitutional talks on aboriginal rights, and the potential for the northern territories to ever become provinces. A measure of natives' concerns in Alberta on these issues was that in November, 1987, the Indian Association of Alberta organized the largest public protest in the province against the Meech Lake Accord.

Some francophones outside Quebec also expressed misgivings that the Accord, with its provisions that provincial governments simply 'preserve' rather than 'promote' the linguistic duality of Canada, provided them very weak linguistic assurances. Government language policy in Alberta and Saskatchewan in 1987 and in the spring of 1988 highlighted these fears. The Alberta government's demand that New Democrat MLA Leo Piquette apologize to the legislature for speaking in French without the permission of the speaker, seemed wildly inconsistent with the generous spirit of tolerance that supposedly underlay the spirit of the Accord. The language policies of the Saskatchewan government, (announced in April 1988) and of the Alberta government, (introduced in June, 1988) in response to a Supreme Court decision concerning language guarantees that went back to the Northwest Territories government of the 1890s, reinforced the arguments of those who felt that the Accord offered little or no protection to French-speaking minorities outside Quebec. Saskatchewan had been the first province outside Quebec to ratify the Accord, supposedly to make French-Canadians feel at home in Canada, but then shortly thereafter introduced legislation which appeared to provide only the minimum in language rights. The government policy seemed geared to not offending the sensitivities of those opposed to the French-language rather than a response to the needs of French-Canadians in Saskatchewan.

Premier Bourassa's refusal to stand up for the French-speaking minorities in Alberta and Saskatchewan during his western tour in April, 1988 confirmed the views of the critics who felt that the Accord would simply give Bourassa a free hand to do what he wanted with the English-speaking minority in Quebec. As noted by Karen Taylor-Browne in her article, as Bourassa abandoned the role of defender of French-Canadian minorities outside Quebec, francophones in Alberta and Saskatchewan felt betrayed.

Similarly, many anglophones in Quebec see the Accord as a betrayal of their rights. They argue that the Accord will allow further erosion of their rights and provide constitutional justification to legislation such as the Quebec language law, Bill 101, which many of them find offensive.

The Meech Lake Accord, under the banner of re-uniting the Canadian 'family,' has simply heightened the frustration of those who have felt traditionally left out of the 'family.' Women, official language minorities, natives, and other ethnic groups, have often seen provincial governments as the agents of their oppression, and yet the Meech Lake Accord gives these governments significantly new powers. As pointed out to the Joint Committee on the Constitution by human rights groups such as the Human Rights Institute of Canada,[4] provincial governments (such as the Aberhart government in Alberta or the Duplessis government in Quebec) have historically been more inclined than the federal government to respond to hostile public opinion and restrict minority rights. Many groups fear that under the Accord, their rights could be eroded and the capacity of the federal government to protect them severely diminished. Many of them have only recently won recognition, and they have a strong sense of insecurity.

The articles in this section all explore and express the feelings and frustrations of groups who feel ignored by the white, male dominated, dualistic or Quebec-centered vision of Canada they see reflected in the Accord. As noted in the final section of this book, these concerns had by the summer of 1988, played a key role in bringing the Accord to the brink of collapse. These minority group concerns have been central to the opposition to the Accord in New Brunswick and Manitoba.

One of the less noted but nonetheless contentious elements of the Accord relates to the provisions concerning immigration and the integration of immigrants. The immigration provisions have direct bearing on the rights of immigrants, but as Kruhlak notes in his wide-ranging assessment, they also have broader implications for Canada's economic growth and national unity. Under the Accord, Quebec will be constitutionally guaranteed a given number of immigrants in relationship to its population and will play a role in selecting immigrants. In addition, the Canadian government will withdraw services for the reception and integration of immigrants in Quebec and the federal government will pay for some provincial integration services. These measures have been taken in response to Quebec's longstanding concern over immigration, given the traditional choice by new immigrants of the English over the French language and the demographic importance of immigration in Quebec where the birth-rate of French-Canadians has declined significantly.[5]

Kruhlak and others have pointed to the troubling aspects of provincial governments playing an aggressive role in immigration policy. They note that conceivably, Canada could eventually have several different immigration policies. In addition, it is possible that the federal multicultural policy could be threatened by the Accord.

Constitutional change in Canada has always been a delicate and complex process given the strong regional and linguistic cleavages in the country. The debate over the Accord has shown that the process of constitutional change is becoming more complex. Relatively new actors on the political stage — organized, and articulate groups — will not be as easily ignored as they were in the past. The framers of the Meech Lake Accord largely ignored women, natives, and other groups. They did so at the Accord's peril.

Notes

1 President, Native Council of Canada. Minutes of the Special Joint Committee on the 1987 Constitutional Accord, August 25, 1987, 12:96.

2 MP, New Westminister-Coquitlam. Minutes of the Special Joint Committee on the 1987 Constitutional Accord, August 20, 1987, 10:55.

3 The term minority is used here in its sociological sense, applying to socially disadvantaged groups who are singled out for differential and unequal treatment, rather than to a mathematical minority. Thus women, though a majority of the

population, are referred to here as a minority group. For a definition of minority group, see Evelyn Kallen, *Ethnicity and Human Rights in Canada* (Toronto: Gage, 1982) Chapter 5.

4 Minutes of Proceedings and Evidence of the Special Joint Committee of the Senate and of the House of Commons on the 1987 Constitutional Accord, 21 Aug. 1987, 11A:9.

5 For background on these concerns, see the articles by Richard Jones and William Coleman reprinted in the section 'The Politics of Language,' in Michael Behiels ed. *Quebec Since 1945: Selected Readings* (Toronto: Copp Clark, 1987)

Women's Rights

Kathleen Mahoney

Mr. Speaker, there is absolutely nothing in the Meech Lake Accord that would diminish or in any way affect equality rights for women and minorities. (Hansard, June 26, 1987, Prime Minister Brian Mulroney)

This statement indicates one of two things: either the Prime Minister is completely incorrect in his assessment of the Meech Lake Accord or many words in it mean absolutely nothing. While neither of the alternatives may seem plausible, I attempt to make a case for the former. In this paper, I examine and evaluate what the proposed 1987 amendments to the Constitution could do to women's equality guarantees in the Canadian Charter of Rights and Freedoms. My argument is premised on the understanding that the Charter of Rights and Freedoms represented a major step forward in the evolution of rights, particularly for women and minority groups. Since 1985, women have achieved remarkable advances largely due to Charter guarantees of equality before and under the law and the right to equal protection and equal benefit of the law without discrimination.[1] The Charter made it clear that equality for women was not a right to be acquired, but a state that exists. Understandably, women are now most apprehensive about any constitutional amendment which could take away or threaten what it has taken centuries to achieve. Even the slightest risk to women's equality rights is considered a serious problem. I suggest the risks to women's rights in the 1987 Constitutional Amendments are not slight. Rather, it is my opinion that the Accord, if passed, will likely diminish constitutional rights that Canadian women currently enjoy.

The paper is divided into three sections, the first addressing the wording of certain key sections of the Accord which create a constitutional inequality among rights; the second, a discussion of recent case law suggesting the Meech Lake Accord could be immune from Charter review; and third, the adverse impact the spending provisions in the Accord may have on women's rights, benefits and protections. The provisions which are the subject of this discussion are s.2, the linguistic duality and distinct society clause; s.16, the exclusion clause; s.95B(3), the section relating to immigration; and s.106A, the Federal spending power provision.

The Affect of the Proposed Amendments on the Charter

The Accord provides that the Constitution Act 1987 would amend the Constitution Act 1867 by adding the following:

> 2(1) The Constitution of Canada shall be interpreted in a manner consistent with
> (a) the recognition that the existence of French-speaking Canadians, centered in Quebec but also present elsewhere in Canada, and English-speaking Canadians, concentrated outside Quebec but also present in Quebec, constitutes a fundamental characteristic of Canada; and
> (b) the recognition that Quebec constitutes within Canada a distinct society.

> (2) The role of the Parliament of Canada and the provincial legislatures to preserve the fundamental characteristic of Canada referred to in paragraph 1(a) is affirmed.

> (3) The role of the Legislature and Government of Quebec to preserve and promote the distinct identity of Quebec referred to in paragraph 1(b) is affirmed.

> (4) Nothing in this section derogates from the powers, rights or privileges of Parliament or the Government of Canada, or of the legislatures or governments of the provinces, including any powers, rights or privileges relating to language.

Section 2 must be read with s.16 of the Accord which states:

> 16. Nothing in section 2 of the Constitution Act, 1867, affects section 25 or 27 of the Canadian Charter of Rights and Freedoms, section 35 of the Constitution Act, 1982, or Class 24 of section 92 of the Constitution Act, 1867.

It is posited that these sections of the Meech Lake Accord affect the equality rights protected in sections 15 and 28 of Charter of Rights. Those sections read as follows:

> 15(1) Every individual is equal before and under the law and has the right to the equal protection and equal benefit of the law without discrimination and, in particular, without discrimination based on race, national or ethnic origin, colour, religion, sex, age or mental or physical disability.

> (2) Subsection (1) does not preclude any law, program or activity that has as its object the amelioration of conditions of disadvantaged individuals or groups in-

cluding those that are disadvantaged because of race, national or ethnic origin, colour, religion, sex, age or mental or physical disability.

28. Notwithstanding anything in this Charter, the rights and freedoms referred to in it are guaranteed equally to male and female persons.

The first indication that the Meech Lake Accord affects equality rights is found in the words of the linguistic duality and distinct society clauses and in s.16 of the Accord. The opening words of s.2(a) state that the Constitution of Canada **shall** be interpreted in a manner consistent with its provisions. What this means is that in any constitutional dispute involving linguistic duality or the Quebec distinct society, the Courts will have no choice but to apply s.2 in the process of arriving at a decision, unless the rights involved are in the exclusion provided by s.16. Section 16 says the distinct society and linguistic duality interpretation cannot apply to cases where aboriginal rights or rights affecting the multicultural heritage of Canada are involved. However, at the same time aboriginal rights and multicultural rights are insulated from the effects of s.2 of the Accord, s.16 makes it clear by implication that women's rights guaranteed by the Charter will be interpreted in the context of s.2. This conclusion is well supported in law by the rule of interpretation which says that the expression of one idea means any other idea is excluded.

By treating women's equality rights in the Charter of Rights and Freedoms differently from cultural rights, s.16 will establish two new categories of rights — those affected by the Meech Lake Accord, and those immune from it. This will create an imbalance among equality rights which will inevitably have adverse affects on sex equality rights. The affects will manifest themselves in equality jurisprudence generally, but particularly in the application of s.1 of the Charter.

At the present time, women's rights and other equality rights have the same weight.[2] If any equality right is breached, the burden of proof shifts to the infringing party to justify the infringement based on s.1 requirements. Section 1 states:

1. The Canadian Charter of Rights and Freedoms guarantees the rights and freedoms set out in it subject only to such **reasonable limits prescribed by law as can be demonstrably justified in a free and democratic society**. (emphasis added)

The distinct society and linguistic duality clauses will add new limiting factors applicable when women's rights are breached but not when aboriginal or multicultural rights are breached. This will undermine women's rights in at least three respects. First, as the words 'distinct society' are undefined in the Accord and their scope is unknown, it could be argued that s.2 could permit limits even though they may not be justified in a free and democratic society. It is unlikely this argument would succeed in a Canadian Court, but it certainly could be made.

Second, even if 'distinct society' is interpreted to mean a free and democratic one, the differential weighting of rights will upset the s.1 balancing process. At the present time, standards used in a s.1 review differ in individual cases, depending on the evidence before the Court as to the invidiousness of the classification upon which discrimination is based and the importance of the individual interest which is adversely affected.[3] The Accord will create new standards of review based not just on evidence in each individual case, but also on the **type** of right infringed. If and when women's rights come into conflict with promotion of the Quebec distinct society or linguistic rights, the standard of review will be different than when aboriginal or multicultural rights are in the balance.

Third, women's rights could be affected in all subsequent constitutional disputes involving cultural claims. If such a spill-over affect occurs, rights of all women in Canada will be jeopardized.

This argument is consistent with established principles of constitutional interpretation. When the Court is called upon to decide between competing rights, the general constitutional environment within which the rights exist is an important factor. The Court looks at the history of the right, whether or not it was protected at common law and its relationship to other constitutional rights. As women's equality rights have never enjoyed protection at common law, and have a very short history of protection under the Charter,[4] their status within the Charter becomes crucial. It is quite likely that the weighting given to cultural rights in the 1987 amendments would be enough to tip the balance away from women's rights in the overall constitutional environment. This is why women both inside and outside Quebec are justifiably concerned about the elevation of cultural rights to a high constitutional plane integral to Canadian federalism without any concomitant elevation or protection of their rights.

A related cause for concern is the fact that most discrimination against women is culturally based. Cultural norms are often responsible for stereotyping women on the basis of outdated or unfair presumptions and generalizations, preventing their individual pursuit of goals and aspirations. Both the Lavell[5] and Lovelace[6] cases are examples of sex equality rights being sacrificed by government and the Courts to preserve a cultural norm of male dominance. In the Lovelace case, it was only after the United Nations Human Rights Committee found Canada in violation of its international obligations, that the offensive Indian Act provisions were amended.

Two other provisions in the Meech Lake Accord could give rise to adverse affects on women's rights. They are subsection (4) of s.2 and s.95b(3). Subsection (4) of s.2 states:

> (4) Nothing in this section derogates from the powers, rights or privileges of Parliament or the Government of Canada, or of the legislatures or governments of the provinces, including any powers, rights or privileges relating to language.

This section clearly disregards individual Charter rights, while protecting the constitutional status of federal and provincial governments. By doing so, it ignores the constitutional status of individual Canadians who joined the constitutional family in 1982. By omission, it permits derogation from individual rights, and when read with the s.16 exclusion clause, it is clear that women's rights in particular will be vulnerable to derogation.

Section 95b(3) exacerbates the vulnerability. It states that the Charter applies to immigration agreements entered into under the Accord.[7] According to established rules of interpretation, this special incorporation of the Charter into only one section of the Accord must mean that the Charter was not intended to, and does not apply to the whole Accord. If this is the case, in a post-Accord Quebec there would be nothing upon which to even base a constitutional complaint when rights collide. Women are justifiably concerned at this prospect remembering the extent to which their equality rights were not protected in the pre-Charter era. The Supreme Court's decisions in Edwards[8], Bliss[9], Murdoch[10] and Lavell[11] show that women cannot assume their interests will be treated fairly and equitably without Charter protection. In a paper entitled 'The Meech Lake Accord and the Federal Spending Power: A Good Maximin Solution,' Pierre Fortin states:

> ...if our present extremely low fertility rate persists we will soon be losing 30 percent of our population every 30 years through natural decline. It is not obvious that immigration alone can replace demographic losses of such magnitude without creating social chaos. Of course, no constitutional amendment can offer protection against the collective suicide that would result from our distaste for child rearing. But at any rate Quebec will clearly want to influence its demographic future through policies affecting marriage, divorce, the family and the workplace, and not only through immigration policy. There will be important consequences for taxation, family allowances, child care programs, and labour and manpower policy.[12]

Without some assurances that equality rights would be constitutionally protected in the scenario Professor Fortin describes, women in Quebec will be very vulnerable to the winds of political change and the high value placed on cultural preservation.

In summary, the Meech Lake Accord weakens constitutional equality guarantees for women both inside and outside the distinct society of Quebec by creating an inequality among equality rights. The persuasive argument has been made that the weakening effect will extend to areas of private law as well. Professor McKinnon says once rights are denigrated in the constitutional sense, they lose their legitimacy and value in the broadest, societal sense.[13] Perceptions of what is and is not fundamental to the values of society are very much affected by constitutional law. She says equality perceptions and outcomes in the family law courts, human rights tribunals, rape trials as well as in the boardrooms and at the bargaining table are shaped by constitutional law and processes.

> A political act like the Accord supports or detracts from a climate of concern in a way that affects the results of particular cases, shifts the ground beneath legal arguments, determines what becomes persuasive. It gives life to law. On this level, constitutional process begins as politics but ends as law. The status of sex equality itself as a fundamental commitment of society is thus as much constituted by such documents as it is reflected in them.[14]

Confederation Compromise

In addition to the arguments based on the language of the Accord, case law suggests women's equality rights could be jeopardized unless Charter protections are specifically incorporated into the proposed 1987 amendments. The Supreme Court of Canada in the Reference re Roman Catholic Separate High Schools Funding case[15] held in 1987 that the Charter cannot be used to invalidate an inequitable provision in the 1867 Constitution. The Court said provincial legislation enacted to benefit Catholic schools in Ontario was immune from a Charter attack even though all parties agreed that the legislation infringed equality guarantees and freedom of religion. The Court reasoned that section 93 of the Constitution Act, 1867 which expressly permitted special treatment to denominational, separate or dissentient schools, could not be invalidated by the Charter because s.93 represented a 'fundamental part of the Confederation compromise.' The Court also held that the inapplicability of s.15 of the Charter was not dependent on s.29 of the Charter. Section 29 reads:

> 29. Nothing in this Charter abrogates or derogates from any rights or privileges guaranteed by or under the Constitution of Canada in respect of denominational, separate or dissentient schools.

The Court ruled that although this section emphasized the special treatment guaranteed by the 1867 Constitution, its existence was not essential to insulating s.93 from Charter review. Justice Wilson, writing for the majority said:

> I believe it (section 29) was put there simply to emphasize that the special treatment guaranteed by the Constitution to denominational, separate or dissentient schools, **even if it sits uncomfortably with the concept of equality embodied in the Charter** because not available to other schools is nevertheless not impaired by the Charter.[16](emphasis added)

She added that the protection came from the power granted by s.93 to the provinces rather than from the nature of the right. She states at p. 295:

> But they [rights and privileges] are insulated from Charter attack as legislation enacted pursuant to the plenary power in relation to education granted to the provincial legislatures as part of the confederation compromise. Their protection from Charter review lies not in the guaranteed nature of the rights and privileges conferred by the legislation but in the guaranteed nature of the provinces plenary power to enact that legislation.[17]

Justice Estey, writing for two members of the Court came to the same conclusions, but by way of different reasons. He stated:

> Action taken under the Constitution Act 1867, is of course subject to Charter review. That is a far different thing from saying that a specific power to legislate as existing prior to April 1982 has been entirely removed by the simple advent of the Charter. It is one thing to supervise and on a proper occasion to curtail the exercise of a power to legislate; it is quite another thing to say that an entire power to legislate has been removed from the Constitution by the introduction of this judicial power of supervision.[18]

Even though Justice Estey's reasoning is narrower than that of Justice Wilson, neither of the judges disagrees that some legislative powers granted as part of the confederation compromise are immune from Charter review.

On the basis of the Supreme Court's decision, a strong argument can be made that provincial legislation passed to further the objectives of the distinct society/linguistic duality provision in s.2 would be immune from Charter review. There is no doubt the Accord was drafted with constitutional compromises in mind and an analogy to the Reference case will be irresistible if the courts interpret subsection 3 of s.2 of the Accord as granting legislative power to Quebec 'to preserve and promote the distinct identity of Quebec.' If so, s.2 would assume a place of primary importance, much like s.93 of the Constitution Act 1867.

It would not only override competing equality claims it would do so unimpaired by the Charter.

Even though the Special Committee in its Report[19] very strongly asserted that the Reference re Roman Catholic Separate High School Funding could have only a very narrow and specific application, the case is already being used to meet a Charter challenge to the Accord. The federal government has argued in the case of Penikett and the Yukon Territorial Government v. The Queen et al[20] that the Bill 30 Reference is authority for the proposition that constitutional amendments are not subject to review by the Charter. They argue that the Meech Lake Accord provisions relating to the appointment of judges and senators, the veto regarding creation of new provinces and the exclusion of Yukon representatives from future constitutional conferences cannot be challenged because one part of the constitution cannot be used to invalidate another part.[21] Whatever way the Courts choose to interpret the Meech Lake Accord and the Bill 30 Reference decision, it is nevertheless seems clear that the principle of sex equality will be secondary to principles of dualism in Canada and the promotion of the 'distinct society' in Quebec.

Federal Spending Powers

The third way the Meech Lake Accord will affect women's equality rights is through the proposed amendments to federal spending powers. Equality issues arise because the amendments will likely affect standards and access to social programs fundamentally linked to equality of opportunity. Women in Canada are disproportionately poorer than men and must rely more heavily on social programs and services in order to compete and survive in a male dominated society. If access to social programs such as health care, social assistance, pensions, postsecondary education, job education and training, legal aid, public housing, compensation to victims of violent crime and young offender programs is diminished or delivery standards are lowered, women will suffer more than men.[22]

The Meech Lake proposals will affect access because they take away the federal government's ability to maintain and initiate social programs. Giving power to the provinces to create their own programs will most likely result in differential access depending on place of residence.[23] Standards will be affected because of the extreme vagueness in the working of s.106A of the Accord which states:

> The Government of Canada shall provide reasonable compensation to the government of a province that chooses not to participate in a national shared-cost pro-

gram that is established by the Government of Canada after the coming into force of this section in an area of exclusive provincial jurisdiction, if the province carries on a program or initiative that is compatible with the national objectives.

None of the key words in s.106A are defined. The term 'national shared-cost program' is open-ended. It is not clear if an amendment to, or renegotiation of an existing program such as the medicare program under the Canada Health Act[24] would be considered to be 'established...after the coming into force of this section,' or if the section would just apply to new programs such as daycare, community health or dental care.[25] The danger of losing universal access and standards is increased by use of the words 'national objectives' which are also undefined. The complete failure to include minimum standards in the Accord such as portability, universality, accessibility and comprehensiveness could lead provinces to cut programs, limit access and develop a system of provincial standards.

Problems inherent in the lack of definition of 'national objectives' are further magnified by the requirement that the provincial programs be 'compatible with' the national objectives. This term too, permits of subjective interpretation. It could mean that an inferior, less accessible provincial replacement of a federal social program would comply as long as it did not go against the spirit of the federal initiative.

Probably most of the definitional problems created by s.106A will end up before the courts, inappropriate fora for decisions regarding spending, because they are not accountable to the electorate, and their decisions will more likely than not result in a patchwork quilt of services, standards and accessibility across the country.[26]

In summary, if the goals of social programs are to promote greater social justice and a fairer, more compassionate society, then the Meech Lake Amendments go a long way to undermining them. Section 106A undermines women's equality rights because national standards and conditions are essential to the achievement of equal opportunities and the reduction of disparities. The goal of equality will not be advanced if women can be differentially treated in the receipt of essential social programs and services on the basis of province of residence.

Conclusions

In 1928, women became legal persons in Canada.[27] In 1982 their personhood became constitutionally equal to that of men. These milestones were achieved after centuries of legal and political battles which often left women ostracized, marginalized and disillusioned with the democratic and judicial processes. In 1987, five years after the ultimate battle had apparently been won by the inclusion of equality guarantees for women in sections 15 and 28 of the Charter, ten provincial premiers and the prime minister of Canada re-negotiated women's rights without their notice, consent or participation. Women were subsequently told they had nothing to worry about because there was 'absolutely nothing in the Meech Lake Accord that would diminish or in any way affect' their constitutional rights to equality. I have argued that these assurances are not true, that the proposed amendments will profoundly affect the status of equality rights and outcomes in legal disputes because of the hierarchy of rights they create. I have also argued that the amendments denigrate the entire Charter by expressly applying it to only one section of the Accord, impliedly excluding it from the rest. In light of case law which appears to rank constitutional documents by insulating the 1867 Constitution from Charter review, the threat to women's equality rights created by the Accord is compounded. Finally, I have argued that the Accord interferes with social and economic programs women must have, on a standardized basis, in order to ensure progress in their aspirations toward equality. I conclude that if the 1987 amendments to the constitution are ratified and become law, women's rights will be seriously undermined.

Notes

1 The equality provisions of the Charter did not become effective until April 17, 1985, a full three years after the Charter came into force. The purpose of the delay was to enable Parliament and the legislatures to repeal or amend discriminatory legislation. Numerous Acts were changed during that period and subsequently, as a result of Charter challenges. The equality jurisprudence beginning to develop under the Charter also indicates positive new developments for women's rights in the Courts.

2 The Ontario Court of Appeal in McKinney v. University of Guelph (1987) 24 OAC 241 addressing the issues as to whether or not there was a difference in the degree of protection accorded to any of the rights guaranteed under s. 15 found there was none and warned against finding any differences in the future.(p.276)

3 Ibid, 276.

4 The Charter came into effect in 1982 but it wasn't until 1985 that the equality provisions became effective.

5 Section 12(1)(b) of the Indian Act was challenged in the case of A.G. Can. v Lavell; Issac v. Bedard (1973), 38 DLR (3d) 481, 11 RFL 333, 23 CRNS 197 SCC. It provided that Indian women who married non-status Indians lost their Indian status,

yet Indian men who married non-Indians retained their status under the Act. The challenge was taken under the Bill of Rights and was unsuccessful. The Supreme Court of Canada held that as long as all Indian women were treated the same, no discrimination existed.

6 Sandra Lovelace had the same complaint as Ms. Lavall, but pursued her case to the United Nations Human Rights Committee where Canada was found in violation of Article 27 of the International Covenant on Civil and Political Rights. The Committee said the obligations on Canada to protect minorities need not be carried out in a manner that conflicts with other rights in the Covenant. UN Human Rights Committee — G/50 215/51 CANA (8) R.6/24.

7 The section states: 95b(3) The Canadian Charter of Rights and Freedoms applies in respect of any agreement that has the force of law under subsection(1) and in respect of anything done by Parliament or the Government of Canada, or the legislature or government of a province, pursuant to any such agreement.

8 Edwards v. A.G.Can. [1930] A.C. 124, [1930] 1 D.L.R. 98 (D.C. 1929), rev'g [1929] S.C.R. 276, [1928] 4 D.L.R. 98 (1929). This case is better known as the 'Persons' case whereby the Privy Council in England overruled the Supreme Court of Canada, holding that women were legal persons in Canada and could be eligible for positions that required applicants to be persons, such as the requirements for appointment to the Senate of Canada.

9 Bliss v A.G. Can [1979] 1 SCR 183, [1978] 6 WWR 711, 78 C.L.L.C. 14, 175, 92 D.L.R. (3d) 417, 23 N.R. 527. In this case, the Supreme Court of Canada ruled that discrimination on the basis of pregnancy was not discrimination on the basis of sex and that a pregnant woman could not complain about provisions in the Unemployment Insurance Act, 1971 which denied regular benefits to pregnant women who did not qualify for maternity benefits.

10 Murdoch v. Murdoch [1975] 1 S.C.R. 423, [1974] 1 WWR 361, 13 R.F.L. 185, 41 DLR (3d) 367. In Murdoch, the Supreme Court refused to give a wife a proprietary share of the family farm notwithstanding her contribution of 15 years of hard labour doing farming tasks.

11 Supra, note 5.

12 Pierre Fortin, 'The Meech Lake Accord and the Federal Spending Power: A Good Maximin Solution,' unpublished, prepared for the Conference on the Meech Lake Accord, Faculty of Law, University of Toronto, Oct. 30, 1987.

13 Catherine McKinnon, testimony before the Ontario Special Committee Hearing on the Meech Lake Accord, March 31, 1988.

14 Ibid, 11.

15 77 N.R. 241.

16 Ibid, 295.

17 Ibid.

18 Ibid, 306.

19 The Report of the Special Joint Committee of the Senate and the House of Commons, The 1987 Constitutional Accord, Queen's Printer, 57-60.

20 [1987] 5 WWR 691.

21 Court did not accept this argument, saying that the issue of whether the Charter can never limit a constitutional amendment was not before the Supreme Court in the Bill 30 Reference case. The decision is being appealed.

22 Canada, Special Joint Committee of the Senate and the House of Commons on the 1987 Constitutional Accord, Minutes of Proceedings and Evidence (Ottawa: Queen's Printer, 1987) 20 August 1987, 10:82-10:106, Canadian Advisory Council on the Status of Women.

23 Ibid, 5 August 1987, 3:110-3:137, Legal Education and Action Fund. The Legal Education and Action Fund Brief (LEAF) to the Special Joint Committee pointed out many equality cases involving access to social programs and Charter equality guarantees.

24 S.C. 1984 C.6.

25 Supra, note 22, 18 August 1987, 8:31 Canadian Nurses Association, Testimony of Ginette Rodger.

26 Deborah Coyne, 'The Meech Lake Accord and the Spending Power Proposals: Fundamentally Flawed,' unpublished, prepared for the Conference on the Meech Lake Accord, Faculty of Law, University of Toronto, Oct. 30, 1987.

27 Supra, note 8.

The Meech Lake Accord
and Multiculturalism

Anthony Parel

The manner in which the Meech Lake Accord dealt with multiculturalism has upset many ethnic communities in Canada. They argue that
the Accord has failed to recognize the rightful place of multiculturalism in the Canadian mosaic. Its rightful place, they claim, is one of
parity with bilingualism and the distinct society principle applied to
Quebec.

The question of multiculturalism entered into the Meech Lake Accord only as a political afterthought. Initially Meech Lake had only one
aim in view, and that was to secure the assent of the Government of
Quebec to the new constitution. Naturally, therefore, there was no
mention of multiculturalism in the original Meech Lake documents.
As Thor Broda of the Ukrainian Committee remarked to the Special
Joint Committee of the Senate and of the House of Commons, 'the premiers and Prime Minister forgot about the multicultural reality when
they were talking at Meech Lake.'[1] Multiculturalism was introduced
into the Accord only after the Langevin Block debates, and in anticipation of criticisms from Canadian ethnic communities. Section 16 of
the Accord, accordingly, was added. It was hoped that it would satisfy the ethnic communities. In the rather dramatic language of the Report of the Special Joint Committee of the Senate and the House of
Commons, Section 16 was added 'on the road between Meech Lake
and the Langevin Block.'[2]

That multiculturalism should make its entrance into Canada's latest
constitutional document as an afterthought should not be surprising:
for it is in keeping with the way multiculturalism had always entered

the Canadian political debates of the last quarter century. I need only mention two well known instances. The first is the Royal Commission on Biculturalism and Bilingualism. As the Commission progressed in its deliberations, it was soon discovered that it was focusing almost exclusively on the French and the British cultures and that it had forgotten nearly one-third of Canadians who were neither French nor British by descent. Book IV of the report of this Commission, entitled 'Cultural Contributions of the Other Ethnic Groups,' attempted to correct this situation, and enlarged the focus of enquiry. A new formula of 'multiculturalism within the framework of bilingualism' was subsequently developed to accommodate the interests of Canadian ethnic communities.

The second instance where multiculturalism was obviously an afterthought was the Constitutional debate of the 1980s. The first draft of the Canadian Charter of Rights and Freedoms did not contain any reference to multiculturalism. Over one-hundred submissions critical of this omission were made by various ethnic communities to the Hays-Joyal Joint Committee on the Constitution. The outcome of these criticisms was the introduction of Section 27 into the Charter of Rights and Freedoms: 'This charter shall be interpreted in a manner consistent with the preservation and enhancement of the multicultural heritage of Canadians.'

It is true that Section 27 of the Charter did not create any new rights for multicultural communities; it merely provided an interpretative norm for the whole Charter according to which the rights of ethnic groups as groups could be protected and guaranteed. As Gordon Fairweather, Chief Commissioner of Canadian Human Rights Commission has pointed out, Section 27, though only interpretive norm, has already, in its short history, contributed greatly to the protection of the group rights of ethnic minorities in Canada. It was successfully invoked in several cases, for example, the Keegstra case, the Big M Drug Mart case, and in the R. v. Videoflicks case.[3]

Section 27 of the Charter, in other words, constitutionalized multiculturalism for the first time. It gave ethnic or ethno-cultural groups a constitutional recognition, though not on par with the British and the French cultures. Even when it was affirmed that French culture and British culture were fundamental to Canada, the cultures of other ethnic groups were also recognized as being worthy of preservation and enhancement. However, it would appear that the intent of the framers of the 1982 Constitution Act was that multiculturalism should remain subordinate to biculturalism.

What, in comparison, was the intent of the framers of the Meech Lake Accord concerning multiculturalism? Their dominant intent was of course to secure the assent of the Government of Quebec to the 1982

Constitution Act. The minimum condition for realizing this goal was the acceptance of section 2 of the Accord. And section 16 which deals with multiculturalism, was added to it as an afterthought to calm the fears of the multicultural groups and the native communities of Canada. A brief analysis of sections 2 and 16 of the Accord would be necessary to clarify the emerging relationships in the Meech Lake Accord of multiculturalism to bilingualism, biculturalism and to Quebec's distinctive character. As everyone knows by now, both sections 2 and 16 are meant to be interpretative norms. Section 16 reads as follows: 'Nothing in section 2 of the Constitution Act, 1867 affects section 25 or 27 of the Canadian Charter of Rights and Freedoms, section 35 of the Constitutions Act, 1982 or class 24 of section 91 of the Constitution Act, 1867.' We are not concerned here with the effects of this section on the interpretation of aboriginal rights; we limit our concern to multiculturalism alone.

Section 2 in part reads as follows:

> 2.(1) The Constitution of Canada shall be interpreted in a manner consistent with (a) the recognition that the existence of French-speaking Canadians, centered in Quebec but also present elsewhere in Canada, and English-speaking Canadians, concentrated outside Quebec but also present in Quebec, constitutes a fundamental characteristic of Canada; and (b) the recognition that Quebec constitutes within Canada a distinct society. (2) The role of the parliament of Canada and the provincial legislatures to preserve the fundamental characteristic of Canada referred to in paragraph (1) (a) is affirmed. (3) The role of the legislature and Government of Quebec to preserve and promote the distinct identity of Quebec referred to in paragraph (1) (b) is affirmed.

Though both sections 2 and 16 are interpretative norms, the former applies to the entire Constitution, whereas the latter applies only to the Charter. This gives section 2 a preponderance over section 16. As far as multiculturalism is concerned, the Meech Lake Accord marks no constitutional advance. On the other hand, the Accord does mark an advance as far as biculturalism, i.e., linguistic duality and Quebec's special identity are concerned. This advance consists in the fact that linguistic duality has now the backing of the legislative power of all the eleven legislatures of the land. Likewise Quebec identity clause has the backing not only of the legislative arm of Quebec Government but also of its executive arm. In other words, according to the Meech Lake Accord linguistic duality and Quebec's identity have gained the upper hand over multiculturalism.

The fear of the critics from ethno-cultural communities is that section 2 as it stands now would adversely affect the future of multiculturalism in Canada. Speaker after speaker from ethnic groups appearing before the Special Parliamentary Committee made this point.

Mr. George Corn, President of Canadian Ethnocultural Council, stated that his council's first recommendation was that multiculturalism and linguistic duality be given parity. According to him Canada 'is fundamentally bilingual and multicultural.' He wanted section 2 of the Accord to include an additional paragraph which would read: 'the multicultural heritage of Canadians also constitute a fundamental characteristic of Canada.'[4]

Emilio Binavince of the United Council of Philippino-Canadians argued that, 'to put it very bluntly,' there was no protection of multiculturalism in the Charter. He implied that in case of a conflict between multiculturalism and Quebec's distinct identity clause or linguistic duality, the latter would win.[5]

Dr. Lilian Ma of the Chinese Canadian National Council was also critical of section 2: bilingualism, she argued, did not embrace all Canadians; 'it may officially, but may not in fact, whereas culturalism does.'[6] She wanted to entrench multiculturalism in section 2: 'only in this way can we feel that the concept of multiculturalism can be protected.'[7] Multiculturalism, according to her, was not just for the so-called ethnic Canadians; it was an all encompassing concept that embraced all Canadians, including English-speaking Canadians as well as French-speaking Canadians.

Mr. Dieter Kiesewalter of the German-Canadian Congress also wanted an amendment to section 2. He felt that as it stood now, it did not reflect 'the social reality of Canada in the 1980s.'[8] He recommended that the clause 'the multicultural nature of Canadian society constitutes fundamental characteristics of Canada' be added to section 2.[9] In his view section 16 was not adequate to protect the interests of multiculturalism. It would not be able to meet court action taken on behalf of linguistic duality or Quebec's special identity. 'As a result, failure to include a statement of the multicultural nature of Canadian society could lead to an emasculation of section 27 of the Charter and indeed of multiculturalism in Canada.'[10]

Mr. M.J.S. Grewal, of the National Association of Canadians of Origins in India felt the same. He said, *inter alia*, that if 'the French in Quebec must be recognized as a distinct society, then it should appear as part of Canada's multicultural mosaic, in concert with other distinct elements.'[11]

Mr. Thor Broda of the Ukrainian Canadian Committee was perhaps the most emphatic opponent of section 2. He wanted section 2 to place 'equal emphasis on multiculturalism and linguistic duality.' He would rather see English-speaking Canadians and French-speaking Canadians as part of a larger multicultural mosaic. As for section 16, it was, according to him, quite insufficient to give equality to multiculturalism and linguistic duality. 'We cannot support a Constitution,' he stated, 'that ignores the multicultural reality of Canada, one whose underlying rationale is the outdated and discredited concept of two founding nations.'[12] He was in favour of an amended section 2 which would enshrine the principle of equality of multiculturalism with biculturalism and the distinct society principle. He would agree to the recognition of Quebec's distinct identity only in exchange for Canada's recognition of multiculturalism as one of the nation's fundamental features.[13]

The ethnocultural groups were not the only ones to criticize section 2 for its omission of any reference to multiculturalism. The two opposition parties were in basic agreement on the need to include multiculturalism in that section, the Liberal Party being more emphatic and more precise in its recommendation than was the New Democratic Party. Sergio Marchi, the Liberal M.P., told the Special Joint Committee of the Senate and the House of Commons that if section 2 meant to define Canadians, it was necessary that the definition be 'predicated on four cornerstones: the French dimension, the English dimension, the multicultural dimension, and the aboriginal dimension.'[14] To leave the last two dimensions out of such a definition, he felt, had the implication of their being considered 'second class' and expendable.[15]

The Liberal Party proposed a detailed amendment to section 2, and wanted 'the recognition of the multicultural nature of Canadian society, and in particular respect for the many origins, creeds and cultures as well as the differing regional identities that helped shape Canadian society,' be included as part of that section.[16] According to 'The Report,' the New Democratic Party did not propose any change in the present text of the Accord. It merely urged First Ministers to give 'early consideration' to the fact that multiculturalism was a fundamental characteristic of Canada.[17]

One of the disappointing features of the Meech Lake Accord was that given the finality of the way it was presented, it prevented any meaningful public debate on such crucial sections as section 2. The criticism I recounted above were all made before a Special Joint Committee of the Parliament, the majority of which had already made up its mind on the outcome of the hearing. The public played no effective role in defii ing the fundamental characteristics of Canada. In this respect the parliamentary hearings had the character of a political charade. As far as multiculturalism was concerned, the final Report of the Committee could do nothing more than include a few platitudes, explain the significance of section 16, and promise future study of multiculturalism by First Ministers. Thus it 'fully agreed' that the multicultural heritage was of 'vital importance' to Canada, but not important enough to be included in section 2.[18] The excuses for this stand were hardly convincing: Meech Lake Accord did not pretend to give a 'comprehensive' definition of Canada; had it attempted to do, it would have gone beyond its agenda!

Instead of opening up section 2, the First Ministers were content with adding another section, section 16. The intent of this section was to allay the fears that section 2 would 'affect' the constitutional provisions relating to multiculturalism and aboriginal rights. As an interpretative clause it was 'designed to preserve certain constitutional values in the face of the 'distinctive society' and 'linguistic duality' interpretative clauses. Its function is thus to 'interpret the interpreters'.'[19] In other words, it was meant to shield certain constitutional provisions from the effects of the linguistic duality/distinct society clauses; to make sure that section 2 of the Accord did not derogate anything from section 27 of the Charter. But shielding does not mean that there would not be conflicts between sections 2 and 16 of the Accord. As Professor Wayne MacKay has noted, 'the courts are going to have to make some difficult value choices in many cases between promoting a distinct society in Quebec and in doing so, limiting the rights of certain ethnic groups or multiculturalism in Canada.'[20]

As for the present, 'The Report' did not take seriously the concerns of the multicultural groups: all it could do was to say that it did not see any reason why First Ministers would not address the issue of multiculturalism in the future. It expressed the hope that multiculturalism 'may one day achieve' the prominence it now seeks.[21]

I conclude this brief analysis of the impact of the Meech Lake Accord on multiculturalism with three observations. The first is that section 2 of the Accord has made the multicultural communities of Canada more aware of their political importance to Canada. As a result they now want multiculturalism to have parity with bilingualism and the distinct society principle. Whether this is a reasonable demand or not, is not the question; the point is that they are making it. Secondly, the refusal of the First Ministers to accommodate their wishes by amending section 2, has engendered a sense of grievance among some ethnic communities. Thirdly, this sense of grievance could pit ethnic communities against the official linguistic minorities. This is a distinct, though regrettable, possibility in provinces where such communities far outnumber the official linguistic minority. From the multicultural perspective, then, the losers of the Meech Lake Accord might well be Francophones outside Quebec.

Notes

1 'Minutes of Proceedings and Evidence of the Special Joint Committee of the Senate and of the House of Commons on the 1987 Constitutional Accord,' (hereafter 'Minutes'), no. 7, 108.

2 'The 1987 Constitutional Accord: The Report of the Special Joint Committee of the Senate and the House of Commons,' (hereafter 'The Report') (Ottawa 1987) 61.

3 For a brief analysis of these cases see Gordon Fairweather, 'Multicultural Canada: The Impact of the Charter of Rights and Freedoms,' a lecture delivered at The University of Calgary, September 18, 1987, *Notes for Remarks* by R.G.L. Fairweather, Chief Commissioner, Canadian Human Rights Commission, Ottawa, 1987. In the course of his decision on the Keegstra case, Mr. Justice Quigley of Alberta referred to section 27 as a guide to his understanding of the 'freedom of expression' guarantee in section 2(b) of the Charter. In the Big M Drug Mart case, Chief Justice Dickson cited section 27 to argue that the prohibition of Sunday commerce in the Lord's Day Act violated section 2(a) of the Charter. In the R. v. Videoflicks case, several retailers challenged the validity of the day of rest provision in the Ontario Retail Business Holidays Act as a violation of section 2(a) of the Charter. The Ontario Court of Appeal supported the challenge. See Gordon Fairweather, op. cit., 9-11.

4 'Minutes,' no. 7, 42.

5 Ibid., 52.

6 Ibid., 62.

7 Ibid., 63.

8 Ibid., 70.

9 Ibid., 72.

10 Ibid., 72-73.

11 Ibid., 82.

12 Ibid., 110.

13 Ibid., 111.

14 Ibid., 47.

15 Ibid.

16 'The Report,' 151.

17 Ibid., 157.

18 Ibid., 52.

19 Ibid., 61.

20 Ibid., 63.

21 Ibid., 52-53.

Native Rights

Chief Georges Erasmus

Minutes of Proceedings and Evidence of the Special Joint Committee of the Senate and of the House of Commons on The 1987 Constitutional Accord, Wednesday, August 19, 1987, pp. 9:49 — 9:53.

Chief Georges Erasmus (National Chief of the Assembly of First Nations): Thank you, Mr. Chairman. On May 27 of this year I signed a letter, along with leaders of the Inuit Committee on National Issues, the Native Council of Canada, and the Metis National Council, to the Prime Minister, expressing our concerns about the Meech Lake accord. When the June Langevin text emerged, we found the First Ministers had dealt with aboriginal concerns simply by inserting a general clause, clause 16, intended to protect the interests of aboriginal people from the proposed section 2 of the Constitutional Act 1867 — i.e., the Quebec distinct society interpretation clause.

This was the barest minimum that the aboriginal leaders had advocated, and the fact that we got the bare minimum seems to reflect the attitude of First Ministers to do the bare minimum in dealing with the rights of aboriginal peoples. For five years we were engaged in constitutional discussions, and it is this bare-minimum attitude that prevailed throughout the process.

On June 1 I was instructed by a resolution passed unanimously by the chiefs at our eighth annual assembly to convey in every possible form the concerns that we have with the Meech Lake accord and possible amendments. Before dealing with those concerns, I must remind you that the Assembly of First Nations is on record as stating its support for Quebec's aspirations to be a functioning partner in Confederation. However, two points must be made with regard to our support. First, the circle of Confederation is not complete simply with the entry or re-entry of Quebec alone into the Canadian family. The circle will only be complete when the rights of aboriginal peoples in Canada are unequivocally expressed and protected in the Constitution, and when that relationship between the First Nations and the rest of Canada is respected.

Secondly, it is our strongly held position that any arrangements or agreements struck by the federal and provincial governments must not implicitly or intentionally diminish or prejudice the rights or status of the First Nations of Canada, and I cannot stress that strongly enough.

Mr. Chairman, it is not my intention to enter into a debate about legal terms or theory. We of the First Nations are concerned with the practical facts of the expressed recognition of Quebec as a distinct society for several reasons. First, it perpetuates the idea of a duality in Canada, and strengthens the myth that the French and the English peoples are the foundation of Canada. It neglects the original inhabitants and distorts history. It is as if the peoples of the First Nations never existed.

It suggests that historically, and presently as well, the French peoples in Quebec formed the only distinct society in Canada. The amendment fails to give explicit constitutional recognition to the existence of First Nations as distinct societies that also form a fundamental characteristic of Canada. If anyone is more distinct, surely it is the peoples of the First Nations.

In the province of Quebec, how will the interpretation of Quebec as a distinct society affect the aboriginal and treaty rights of the peoples of the First Nations living in that province? Will this create a checkerboard across Canada as to how rights may be exercised in various provinces? Does clause 16 provide sufficient protection to prevent the possible override of Quebec's aspirations over aboriginal rights?

We were told for five years that governments are reluctant to entrench undefined self-government of aboriginal people in the Constitution, yet here is an equally vague idea of distinct society, unanimously agreed to and allowed to be left to the courts for interpretation.

Let us turn now to spending powers. If national programs are established in the future, in areas of exclusive provincial jurisdiction, uneven standards could result in different parts of Canada if one or more provinces opt out. An opting-out province does not have to meet national criteria or standards in its own programs, but only has to undertake its own initiative or program compatible with national objectives.

Now, Mr. Chairman, I do not have to tell you or the hon. members that appropriate socio-economic programs are vital to aboriginal communities. Our experience shows us that when provincial governments choose to deliver services or programs to First Nations, be they national or provincial programs, they fall far short of what we need. And what if we want to run our own programs, consistent with self-government? We have no constitutional assurance that the federal government would exercise its power under section 91.24 to facilitate a particular program for First Nations which do not wish to take part in a provincial program and which may want to administer their own program. Nor is there any guarantee that all of the reasonable compensation received by an opting-out province from the federal government would in fact be used for the same overall program as the national program.

What about the proposals on immigration? Under these proposals any province and the federal government can get together and decide on the level of immigration into a province. What happens if hundreds or thousands of immigrants are directed into areas where there are unsettled land claims by aboriginal peoples? Suppose, for instance, the Government of British Columbia and the federal government decided to settle thousands of immigrants into the Nass Valley while the Nishga land claim and title are yet unresolved or the Queen Charlotte Islands.

Another major concern, Mr. Chairman, is the proposed amending formula. According to the Meech Lake accord the creation of new provinces will in the future require the unanimous consent of Parliament and the provincial legislatures. Aboriginal peoples and others in the territories will not be able to determine their own political destiny. This is a denial of self-determination. Any single province will have the power to veto the establishment of new provinces for any reason, any reason, especially if you look at the situation in the context of the possible extension of existing provinces into the territories.

We are concerned that the concept of unanimity under the guise of cooperative federalism or, as it has been called, executive federalism, is slowly becoming a constitutional convention. Over the past five years we have not been able to achieve even majority support for our constitutional aspirations using the section 38 formula, never mind unanimous consent. If the concept of unanimity were to apply to any future amendments to clarify aboriginal and treaty rights, or provide for the explicit recognition of aboriginal self-government, our experience shows that amendments would be impossible. We might as well forget trying to achieve one.

Coming back to the proposed amendment, Mr. Chairman, do you know that repeal of the formula for creating new provinces, paragraph 42.1(f) of the Constitution Act, 1982, is an item on the agenda of the 1983 Accord on Aboriginal Rights? And this item was never discussed. Yet at Meech Lake, First Ministers had no difficulty reaching an agreement on this matter, to the detriment of aboriginal peoples and others in the territories, in our absence.

Mr. Chairman, the next items on any First Ministers' agenda should be aboriginal and treaty rights. The longer the process goes on dealing with other matters, the more our rights are being compromised. The 1983 Constitutional Accord agenda on aboriginal matters must still be completed.

The Prime Minister repeatedly suggested that a First Ministers' meeting on aboriginal matters would be convened if it could be shown that the necessary consensus for a constitutional amendment on self-government could be attained. Yet no similar condition has been imposed on First Ministers who wish to discuss provincial concerns at future First Ministers' meetings, despite the lack of agreement on some of those concerns in the past. Why is there this double standard?

It is vital that aboriginal people participate in all matters affecting them at future First Ministers' meetings, or else risk the very possibility that aboriginal rights, interests, status, and aspirations are further undermined. It is incredible that the First Ministers are planning to discuss fisheries in the absence of aboriginal people, when everyone in Canada knows that fishing is an aboriginal right, confirmed in many treaties, and is an industry in which several first nations earned their livelihood. The Court of Appeal of British Columbia recently affirmed this aboriginal right.

Mr. Chairman, many constitutional experts and lawyers have made it clear that from the terms of the Meech Lake accord there will be a major shift towards increased provincial power and control. This significant move towards greater decentralization within Canada will continue when the second round of First Ministers' conferences takes place. Why else would Newfoundland put fisheries on the agenda?

If federal powers are to be increasingly weakened in favour of the provinces, without including aboriginal protections, we believe the ability of the federal government to exercise its moral and legal responsibility in practical terms under section 91.24 of the Constitution Act, 1867, will be significantly eroded, whatever the Constitution says.

Mr. Chairman, for the reasons I have stated, the Assembly of First Nations would like to make some proposals in relation to these amendments:

First, there must be explicit recognition of aboriginal peoples as distinct societies which constitute another fundamental characteristic of Canada.

Second, there must be a renewed constitutional process, specifically dealing with treaty and aboriginal rights. Our agenda is unfinished. The process should continue until the agenda is complete.

Third, there must be participation of aboriginal peoples in other First Ministers' meetings on the Constitution on matters that directly affect us.

Fourth, there must be a guarantee that opting-out provisions in the proposed amendments will not in any way prevent First Nations from access to any national program, or prejudice our right to administer such programs ourselves. Subsection 106A.(1) should not be allowed to affect 25 or 35 of the Constitution Act, 1982, or 91.24. Similarly, those sections should be protected from the immigration proposals in paragraph 95(a).

Fifth, subsection 45(1) in article 9 in the accord should be removed. There is no valid reason which justifies unanimity in the establishment of new provinces. If that were to become the rule, it would be almost impossible for new provinces to be created. The creation of new provinces should be a matter of exclusive federal approval. Thank you.

The Francophone Minority

Karen Taylor-Browne

Canadian census figures collected over the past forty-five years show that since World War II the size of the French-speaking population in Canada has decreased relative to both the English-speaking and total populations of Canada. During the same period the population of Quebec has also diminished relative to the total population of Canada (see p. 186, Table I).

These statistics are of great concern to all Canadian francophones and francophiles who are aware of them. They are also at the root of many of the language policies which the governments of Canada and Quebec have attempted to implement over the past twenty-five years.

The Government of Canada's approach to reform has been motivated by a vision of Canada which was articulated in the mandate of the Royal Commission on Bilingualism and Biculturalism. The Commission was asked:

> to inquire into and report upon the existing state of bilingualism and bicultural-ism in Canada and to recommend what steps should be taken to develop the Cana-dian Confederation on the basis of an equal partnership between the two founding races, taking into account the contribution made by the other ethnic groups to the cultural enrichment of Canada and the measures that should be taken to safe-guard that contribution...(Privy Council document 1963, 1106)

In their efforts to implement the Commission's recommendations, the Federal government has received little cooperation from most of the English dominant provinces. This provincial intransigence has been, and continues to be, disastrous for francophones living outside Quebec.

TABLE 1

Proportions of Anglophones, Francophones and Quebecers
in Canada: 1941 - 1986**

Year	Total Population	English Mother Tongue	%	French Mother Tongue	%	Quebec Population	%
1986*	25,309,340	15,709,650	62.1	6,354,840	25,.1	6,532,460	25.8
1981	24,343,180	14,918,460	61.3	6,249,095	25.7	6,438,400	26.5
1971	21,568,310	12,973,810	60.2	5,793,650	26.9	6,027,765	28.0
1961	18,238,247	10,660,534	58.5	5,123,151	28.1	5,259,211	28.8
1951	14,009,429	8,280,809	59.1	4,068,850	29.0	4,055,681	28.9
1941*	11,506,655	6,488,190	56.4	3,354,753	29.2	3,331,882	29.0

** Based on 100% figures.
* Recording method changed in this year relative to the preceding years.

From the fully cross-tabulated results of the 1981 census, one can calculate rates of assimilation of people of French origin as high as 95%. Even using assimilation figures based on comparisons of mother tongue and home language, the rates are as high as 72% (see pp. 188-9, Table 2). Since the manner of recording language related questions on the 1986 census was substantially different from that of preceding years, it is difficult to say whether these rates of assimilation are slowing. Calculations based on single language responses suggest that they are not.

Close to 27% of Canadians outside Quebec whose unique mother tongue was French speak only English in their homes. In Newfoundland, Saskatchewan, Alberta and British Columbia this figure exceeds 50 or even 60%. Only 6.25% of Quebecers who list English as their only mother tongue now use French as their exclusive home language.

Given that the other provinces do not support francophone minorities in a way which could slow assimilation, it should surprise no one that various Quebec governments have decided that they must act alone to prevent the ultimate demise of French in North America. Instead, many people interpret Quebec's efforts to protect the French language as an attack on English. There has been strong condemnation of the kinds of language legislation Quebec has proposed since 1974 when the then government of Robert Bourassa introduced Bill 22, a precursor of Bill 101 which shows remarkable similarities to its infamous successor. The courts have also been unsympathetic. Parts of all the Bills have been ruled unconstitutional.

Being unable to work within the Canadian constitutional system, Quebec has been prepared to adopt more radical solutions. The most destructive of these was, of course, complete separation from Canada.

While the threat of separation retreated when the Parti Quebecois lost the referendum on sovereignty association, Quebec has not been prepared to become a full participant in the Canadian constitutional system unless they are given the power to implement their language policies. The 1987 meeting of First Ministers at Meech Lake demonstrated the Government of Canada's willingness to accede to Quebec's demands. Sadly, the document which was the product of that meeting not only threatens the rights of individual Canadians, it encourages national disunity. Furthermore, it is unlikely to ensure the survival of the French language in Canada because it virtually ignores the needs of the close to one million French-speaking Canadians who live outside Quebec.

This paper will attempt to demonstrate the validity of the last proposition. It will also propose a change in the Accord which would help resolve this problem.

TABLE 2
Assimilation Rate Calculated from 1981 Census Figures**

	Total Population	French Ethnic Background	French Mother Tongue	French Home Language	French Mother Tongue who use French Home Lang.	French Mother Tongue now speak only English	Assimilation based on French origin	Assimilation based on French Mother Tongue*	Anglophone assimilation to French*	Unofficial language speakers adopting French*	Unofficial language speakers adopting English*
Canada	24,083,495	7,101,380	6,176,215	5,923,010	5,748,490	44,410	1,352,890	410,990	122,520	161,065	1,496,145
%	100.00	29.49	25.65	24.59	93.08	0.72	19.05	6.65	0.83	5.10	47.40
Newfoundland	563,745	26,450	2,690	1,810	1,155	310	25,300	1,540	635	25	1,885
%	2.34	4.69	0.48	0.32	42.94	11.52	95.65	57.25	0.11	0.61	45.81
P.E.I.	121,220	20,445	5,915	3,725	3,425	585	17,025	2,495	295	10	915
%	0.5	16.87	4.88	3.07	57.95	9.90	83.27	41.18	0.25	0.76	69.58
Nova Scotia	839,800	107,305	35,690	24,450	22,420	1,880	84,885	13,270	1,960	70	10,330
%	3.49	12.78	4.25	2.91	62.81	5.27	79.11	37.18	0.25	0.39	57.13
New Brunswick	689,370	277,910	231,940	216,585	209,325	2,035	68,585	22,615	7,080	180	4,775
%	2.86	40.31	33.65	31.42	90.25	0.88	24.68	9.75	1.58	2.22	55.85

Quebec	6,369,070	5,196,845	5,248,440	5,256,830	5,128,140	4,065	68,705	120,300	82,130	46,560	106,370
%	26.45	81.60	82.41	82.54	97.71	0.07	1.32	2.29	11.82	10.94	23.87
Ontario	8,534,260	949,570	467,885	332,940	307,290	17,955	616,630	134,945	21,975	3,675	706,575
%	35.44	11.13	5.48	3.90	65.68	3.84	64.94	28.84	0.33	0.25	48.29
Manitoba	1,013,700	99,580	51,990	31,045	28,980	3,465	70,600	23,010	1,795	207	129,775
%	4.21	9.82	5.13	3.06	55.74	6.66	70.90	44.26	0.02	0.12	55.33
Saskatchewan	956,440	68,765	25,325	10,090	9,180	2,765	59,585	16,145	790	120	86,235
%	3.97	7.19	2.65	1.05	36.25	10.92	86.65	63.75	0.10	0.01	51.04
Alberta	2,213,650	181,625	60,900	29,550	25,820	5,680	155,805	35,080	3,205	525	215,440
%	9.19	8.20	2.75	1.33	42.40	0.93	85.78	57.60	0.17	0.15	60.21
B.C.	2,713,615	168,020	43,695	15,125	12,060	5,445	155,960	31,635	2,525	540	252,510
%	11.27	6.19	1.61	0.56	27.60	12.46	92.82	72.40	0.11	0.12	56.35
N.W.Territories	45,740	2,890	1,235	630	535	125	2,355	700	70	25	4,035
%	0.19	6.32	2.70	1.38	43.32	10.12	81.49	56.68	0.28	0.13	20.53
Yukon Territories	23,150	2,080	520	225	160	50	1,920	360	55	10	1,775
%	0.10	8.98	2.25	0.97	30.77	9.62	92.31	69.23	0.27	0.42	74.42

** Based on the 20% sample.
* Calculated by comparing home language and mother tongue figures.

Undermining the Minority

The government of Quebec is well aware that there are three factors which contribute to the proportionate decline in the francophone population: the high assimilation rate of minority francophones, the very low birthrate in Quebec (1.4 children per family compared to the national average of 1.7 and the 2.1 needed to maintain population levels), and the overwhelming propensity of new immigrants to adopt English rather than French as their dominant official language (see the two right hand columns in Table II of the Appendix). It is obvious from the text of the Meech Lake Accord and from the lack of support that Robert Bourassa has given francophones in Saskatchewan and Alberta who are fighting to restore the French language rights they had when those areas were first annexed to Canada, that Quebec has decided to secure the position of the French language in Canada by concentrating on changing the last of these causes and ignoring the first.

Quebec's plan requires them to recruit enough immigrants to maintain the province's relative numerical strength. They must then have sufficient power to ensure that all new immigrants are acculturated into Quebec society. The linguistic duality and distinct society clauses in the Meech Lake Accord plus the changes to section 95 of the Constitution dealing with immigration reflect these objectives. Control over appointment of Supreme Court judges and Senators allows Quebec to assure that its interests will be given a sympathetic hearing in the Senate and in the Supreme Court.

The most obvious problem with this scheme is that the other provinces get exactly the same powers, except for those accruing from the distinct society clause. The result will certainly undermine the position of French-speaking Canadians who live outside Quebec. The most obvious reason for this involves the question of immigration.

Quebec already has a bilateral agreement with Ottawa to recruit and receive the number of immigrants proportionate to the size of its population, plus 5% as required. By giving all provinces the same option, the 1987 Constitutional Accord virtually guarantees that the francophone minorities will become proportionately smaller since it is extremely unlikely that any province other than Quebec would consider a potential immigrant's ability to speak French as a reason for extending preferential treatment to them. As the sources of the majority of French-speaking immigrants are very poor developing countries it is unlikely that any substantial number of people from such places would be considered suitable immigrants unless their ability to speak French is considered an asset. By being diluted in number it is even less likely that the francophone minority outside Quebec would gain the support they need to survive linguistically.

Proponents of the Meech Lake Accord argue that the clause of the Accord requiring preservation of our linguistic duality will assure the minority of the assistance they require. This belief in the Accord is misplaced.

While many people have been prepared to condemn Quebec for the treatment it gives its anglophone minority, few stop to consider that the position of the English-speaking community in Quebec continues to be far superior to that of any francophone minority. People do not know that the number of children receiving education in English in Quebec exceeds that of the anglophone school age population in the province.[1] They are also unaware that Quebec's Bill 142 guarantees health and social services in English.

With the doubtful exception of officially bilingual New Brunswick, no other province provides such breadth of service. In some provinces the only right francophones have is for education in French. That is guaranteed by section 23 of the Canadian Charter of Rights and Freedoms.

Many groups have suggested that the explicit and exclusive reference to sections 25 and 27 of the Charter made in section 16 of the Meech Lake Accord will mean that the provisions of the Accord will supersede the Charter in all other areas besides multicultural and aboriginal rights. However, compared to other sections of the Charter, section 23 is already in a tenuous position.

To begin with, it falls in a jurisdiction which is indisputably controlled by the provinces: education. Furthermore, sub-section 23(1)a has never been ratified by Quebec: a fact recognized by section 59 of the Constitution proper.[2] This being the case, one must assume that the Accord contains a mechanism by which Quebec's objection to sub-section 23(1)a, or any other section for that matter, will be accommodated. The 'distinct society' clause obviously fills this role.

Women and minority groups have all been concerned about the effects of the distinct society clause in Quebec. However, its inclusion in the Accord also poses a threat to the francophone minorities outside Quebec.

The problem is created by the juxtaposition of the phrases 'preserve' and 'preserve and promote' that would appear in section 2 of the Constitution. By saying that both the government **and the legislature** of Quebec are 'to preserve and promote' the distinct society, the Accord clearly diminishes the force of the obligation given to the Parliament of Canada and the legislatures of the provinces **only** 'to preserve...the existence of French-speaking Canadians, centred in Quebec but also present elsewhere in Canada, and English-speaking Canadians concentrated outside Quebec but also present in Quebec.' Furthermore, the reaffirmation of federal and provincial powers contained in section

2(4) of the Accord would seem to give the provinces the exclusive right to determine what actions would be required to fulfil the obligation to 'preserve' the minority in areas over which they have sole jurisdiction. Quebec obviously wishes this exclusive right if it is to acculturate all new immigrants. For the francophone minorities this could be ruinous.

Ever since the proclamation of the Charter of Rights and Freedoms, francophone groups across the country have been attempting to use section 23 to establish rights to schools or school boards which would provide their children with appropriate French language education. Some governments, such as Alberta's and Nova Scotia's, have refused to intervene in disputes between local boards of education and francophone organizations in cases where the francophones believe the provisions for their children's educations are inadequate. These governments are not willing to concede that section 23(3)b) implies that the francophones themselves should have any rights to determine what types of educational programmes or facilities are appropriate for their children. The francophone associations have asked the courts to decide.

By reinforcing the provinces' powers over language issues, particularly in an area like education, the Meech Lake Accord virtually guarantees the assimilation of francophone children whose only access to their mother tongue outside the family circle is education. It might also prevent the federal government from intervening on the minority's behalf.

One of the principal means by which the federal government has helped the minorities has been through the Federal/Provincial Shared-cost Programme for Bilingualism in Education. Without the establishment of this programme in 1970, it is unlikely that the minority and bilingual education programmes which now exist would ever had been established. Even now, when the federal government can request accountability for the funds, provincial governments do not always ensure that local boards of education which receive the monies actually spend them on the programmes they are meant to support. It is unlikely that the provinces' performance in this regard would improve if they choose to create their own programmes and then ask for compensation from the federal government as the changes to section 106 of the Constitution proposed in the Meech Lake Accord would allow them to do.

Without federal money being directed to them, local boards across the country would undoubtedly demand programme and transportation fees from parents of French immersion pupils. Some are attempting to do so already. Such actions would bring the phenomenal growth in French immersion programme enrollments across the country to a halt and make access to high levels of bilingualism a function of the size of a family's budget.[3] Efforts to raise levels of non-francophone bilingualism in Canada could be severely diminished and the francophone population could suffer as a result.

International Perspectives on Language Retention

Research in the areas of language contact, shift and loss demonstrates that when two language groups are in close contact, the linguistic survival of both groups will depend on a variety of demographic and psychological factors including the total and proportionate size of the groups, the geographic concentration of the two language communities, the national and/or international currency and prestige of the languages, and the level of institutional support each group enjoys. In some cases a minority can be more linguistically powerful than the majority because their language is more prestigious or useful, or because they are the ones who control the institutions of the country and can thus ensure that their own population is provided with more extensive services than the larger but less powerful group. Just such a situation existed with regard to the English-speaking minority in Quebec until the early 1970s.

While French is one of the most prestigious and widely spoken languages in the world, its position in North America is very fragile indeed. That is, of course, because Canada shares a common border with the most powerful country in the western world. The official and only working language of the United States' close to 250 million inhabitants is English. Given the closeness of the economic ties between our two countries, any Canadian who wishes to succeed in trade and commerce must speak English. Even those who have no desire to work in large businesses have difficulty escaping the influence of English in science, technology and electronically mediated information and entertainment channels.

Canadian census figures demonstrate the results of the imbalance in the strength of the two languages. In spite of general increases in individual bilingualism in both groups over the past forty years, rates of bilingualism among francophones is still four times greater than that of anglophones (see p. 194, Table 3).[4]

It is generally recognized in language acquisition research that the development and maintenance of high levels of competence in a language will depend on an individual being able to use the language in a wide range of personal, social, cultural, economic and even political domains. If minority francophones do not have services available to them in French in these domains they will be forced to use English in most situations. Through this process they become more proficient in English than in French: a situation which gradually leads them to

TABLE 3

Levels of Bilingualism by Mother Tongue*

		NUMBERS		
Year	Total	French Mother Tongue	English Mother Tongue	Other Mother Tongues
1981	3,681,960	2,236,145	1,114,250	331,565
1971	2,900,155	1,958,745	510,995	430,415
1961	2,231,172	1,665,979	318,463	246,730
1951	1,727,447	1,339,118	253,262	135,067
1941	1,474,009	1,100,423	246,551	127,035
1931	1,322,370	1,044,388	189,516	88,466

		PROPORTIONS		
Year	Total	French Mother Tongue	English Mother Tongue	Other Mother Tongues
1981	15.3	37.2	7.5	10.5
1971	13.4	31.7	5.3	15.4
1961	12.2	30.1	4.0	10.1
1951	12.3	31.0	3.8	8.1
1941	12.8	33.1	3.8	7.6
1931	12.7	36.9	3.5	5.4

* Based on 20% data.

lose the ability to speak French. However, unless some of the services can be provided by non-francophone bilinguals, the number of people who would be required to leave Quebec to provide the services would be such that the entire francophone population would become diluted and the monolingual population would continue to shrink.[5] That could lead to community language death since full bilingualism is redundant.

Since rates of non-francophone bilingualism in Canada are currently so low, there is a decided need to promote French language learning in this group. Unfortunately, through the juxtaposition of the 'preserve' and 'preserve and promote' phrases, the Meech Lake Accord makes it very clear that no level of government has the right to **promote** the use of a language which is in a minority in any province.

Given the kinds of restrictions which Quebec would need to place on English in order to assure the acculturation of new immigrants and to prevent the native francophone population from attaining the high levels of bilingualism which would enable them to leave Quebec, it is quite possible that the Quebec government would want to restrict Federal government promotion of bilingualism in Quebec.[6] Under the Accord they might be able to claim it was unconstitutional. This would undoubtedly lead the English-speaking provinces to believe that their treatment of French was generous by comparison and perfectly consistent with the terms of the Accord. There is already evidence that governments in Western Canada do not feel they need to improve opportunities for the use of French, or indeed respect the status of French as an official language, to satisfy the provisions of the Accord.

Evidence of Post-Meech Lake Events

Three weeks before the Meech Lake text of the Accord was signed, a francophone member of the Alberta legislature, M. Léo Piquette, attempted to ask a question in French in the assembly. Although court cases were proceeding which challenge the legality of the 1892 vote of the Legislative Council of the Northwest Territories to abolish the use of French in the assembly and courts of the region now divided into the provinces of Alberta and Saskatchewan, the Speaker of the legislature stopped M. Piquette. He subsequently asked M. Piquette to apologize for his use of French. M. Piquette refused to do so, citing his constitutional right to use his native language.[7] The committee that was struck to investigate the matter established a policy which places French in the same category as any unofficial minority language. They announced their decision on the same day Premier Getty put forward the motion to ratify the 1987 Constitutional Accord. This is, unfortunately, not the only Government of Alberta action which demonstrates the limits of the obligation Alberta feels it has to **preserve** its francophone minority.

On June 17, 1987, just days after the signing of the Langevin text of the Accord, the Alberta Government tabled a new School Act. Although the Act stated that children of people who qualify under Section 23 of the Charter of Rights and Freedoms are entitled to be educated in French, it did not define the manner in which the Section 23 provisions were to be implemented. All details were left to future ministerial regulation.

Regulations, because they are statements of policy, not law, provide little assurance to the minority that their children's educational needs will be appropriately met. The current situation would strongly indicate that they will not.

In 1987-88, only 1,750 of the estimated 12,000 francophone children in Alberta of school age were enrolled in francophone programmes: the worst record of any province in Canada in spite of the fact that Alberta has the country's fourth largest francophone population.[8] Only two of these programmes were located in separate francophone schools. All others were in schools where English programmes simultaneously operate. There were no separate francophone high schools. Efforts of francophones in Edmonton to get such a school resulted in francophone and French immersion parents and children being pitted against one another because neither the Board involved nor the Minister of Education would agree to fully accommodate the different needs of the two groups. Given that Alberta's Minister of Advanced Education has stated publicly that he feels monies currently being used to fund French language education would be better spent on the teaching of Japanese, it is quite possible that these kinds of confrontations over the provision of appropriate schooling in French could well undermine the understanding and cooperation which has developed between French-speaking and English-speaking Albertans over the past twenty years: an understanding which is essential if the francophones are to receive the services they need to retain their language.[9] The situation will certainly be worse if the Federal government can no longer promote bilingualism by providing funds for non-francophones to be educated in French: something which could happen if Quebec were to claim that promotion of bilingualism is unconstitutional according to the Accord.

While the situation described above may be worse in Alberta than elsewhere, Alberta is certainly not the only province reluctant to recognize minority francophone rights. Cases based on section 23 of the Canadian Charter of Rights and Freedoms have been brought before courts in almost every province. A number of governments also refuse to ratify Part XIV(1) of the Criminal Code of Canada which provides for the right of an accused to have a criminal trial in the official language of his or her choice. Furthermore, following the Supreme Court of Canada's decision that the French language rights of section 110 of the North-West Territories Act, 1891, were still in force, the Government of Saskatchewan decided to use an option the court gave them, to declare English the only language in which legislation would need to be enacted. Cabinet would decide what, if any, legislation was important for the minority and needed to be translated into French.

Conclusion

These examples clearly demonstrate that many English-speaking politicians do not realize that if the French language is to survive in Canada its status must be respected and a form of bilingualism which allows as many French-speaking citizens as possible to have access to a full range of services in their language must be put in place. Interestingly enough, however, it would appear that average Canadians do support this view.

A Canadian Facts Survey commissioned by the Commissioner of Official Languages in 1985 demonstrated that a majority of both English and French speaking Canadians believed that the official linguistic minorities in their provinces should have access to educational, medical and federal government services in their own language. A majority of both anglophones and francophones under 25 believed that services provided by provincial governments, businesses and even department stores should be offered in both official languages. There was overwhelming support across age groups and linguistic backgrounds for the proposition: 'It would be a good thing if all Canadians could speak both English and French.'[10]

While the literature on language loss would indicate that full bilingualism is not a good thing for Quebec, these opinion poll results appear to indicate that Canadians have come to accept the vision of Canada as an equal partnership between French and English which was present in the mandate of the Royal Commission on Bilingualism and Biculturalism. The men who met at Meech Lake on April 30th, 1987 might well have considered this and modelled their description of the 'fundamental characteristic of Canada' on the statement in the Commission's mandate.

Unlike the linguistic duality clause of the Meech Lake Accord which places the same restrictions on the promotion of French as it does on English, such a definition would have no such limitation. Furthermore, if they were to augment the statement with a reference to our aboriginal peoples as well as the 'other ethnic groups,' the resulting description of Canada overcomes a major problem of the 1987 Constitutional Accord: the subordination of the Canadian Charter of Rights and Freedoms caused by the specific and exclusive mention of Sections 25 and 27 in Section 16 of the Accord.

Notes

1 Quebec is extremely liberal in its treatment of qualifying members of the English minority. They will go as far as subsidizing residential schooling for any child who cannot attend an English language day school. In addition, the fact that there were no restrictions on access to English schooling in Quebec until 1974 meant that there were many children in Quebec who were not English-speaking who received English language schooling. Bill 101 allows the children of such people to also receive their education in English.

2 Beginning with Bill 22 in 1974, Quebec tried a variety of methods for determining who would qualify for English language schooling. The use of parental mother tongue as a qualification was considered too broad a category to determine with accuracy. Linguistic competence tests were also considered too inaccurate and very difficult to administer.

3 Since the first publicly funded French immersion programme began in Montreal in 1963, the enrollments in this programme have increased to over 200,000 in 1987. An annual registry of these programmes compiled by Canadian Parents for French shows that in 1987 the programme was available in close to 200 communities across Canada.

4 The statistics for 1986 have not been included in this table because they have not been fully cross-tabulated as yet. Comparisons with previous years will be made considerably more difficult because in 1986 multiple responses to all language related questions were recorded. In previous years this had not been done.

5 The limitation of post-secondary educational opportunities in French outside Quebec has lead to a situation in which there is a dearth of minority francophones who have received training in French in the professions and skilled trades. In fact, Statistics Canada figures demonstrate that the level of educational attainment of minority francophones is below national norms. Until facilities are available for their education, therefore, it is necessary to have trained non-francophones to provide French language services. When and if there are appropriate educational opportunities, it would still be necessary that some non-francophones be bilingual because the minority francophone population is too dispersed to allow a full range of services to be provided internally by the minority itself.

6 At the present time more than half of the Secretary of State's funds for bilingualism in education actually go to supporting English language educational programmes in Quebec. Half of the remaining amount supports French language education for non-francophones outside Quebec. As a result, only a very tiny amount is available for minority francophones.

This agreement is up for renegotiation in 1988 and if the statements of the Commissioner of Official languages and reports of the Federal government are any indication the rules for funding will change. Unfortunately, some of the changes are likely to be negative ones for bilingual education programmes since the Nielsen White Paper on Government spending suggested that only programmes for the minority should continue to receive Federal monies. While he has stated that he would not like to discontinue support for non-francophone bilingualism outside Quebec the Commissioner of Official languages has recognized that the budget for supporting language education programmes has been consistently eroded and that unless there is some expansion to the funds he would have no alternative but to restrict funding to the minority. An independent evaluation of the Official Languages in Education Programme prepared by Peat, Marwick and Partners in association with Dr. Stacy Churchill (May 1987) suggested that such a move would have serious negative effects on bilingual programmes.

7 The Supreme Court ruling in the case of Mercure vs. The Government of Saskatchewan (mentioned briefly below) vindicated M. Piquette. However, the Government of Saskatchewan's decision to rescind the French language rights which the Court had recognized clearly demonstrated to the francophone associations across Canada that the Meech Lake Accord would not help their cause. Any vacillation in their position on the Accord ended. Premier Bourassa was labelled a traitor for not supporting their position.

8 There is an unknown number of francophone children among the close to 25,000 children in Alberta who attend French-immersion programmes. However, immersion programmes are meant for children who have little or no exposure to French outside of school. They are thus neither socially nor psycholinguistically suitable for children whose first language is French.

   In 1969 the B. & B. Commission recommended that minority schools be established wherever possible and that no more than a very small number of non-minority children be allowed to attend such schools. In spite of this, the Alberta government did not recognize a difference between immersion and francophone schooling until 1984. Even then, it was only after court action based on Section 23 of the Charter of Rights and Freedoms that two schools were founded: one in Edmonton and one in Calgary. All other provinces besides Alberta and B.C. had made some type of legal or administrative distinction between immersion and francophone schools as long ago as 1970. B.C. made an administrative distinction in 1976.

9 The provisions for French immersion schooling under the proposed Alberta School Act would give these programmes exactly the same status as un-official language schools, religious or philosophically oriented alternative programmes or programmes where a particular teaching method or philosophy would be used. All would be 'alternative programmes' whose implementation would be at the exclusive discretion of local boards of education who could, if they decide to implement the programmes, charge both tuition fees and transportation fees to any family whose child attends. Without a church or ethnic association to subsidize such fees the children of virtually all ethnic backgrounds who attend French immersion programmes in order to become fluent in Canada's two official languages could be excluded for financial reasons. Such a situation is bound to create resentment between non-francophones who wish a bilingual education for their children but must pay extra fees for it and francophones who, by virtue of Section 23 of the Charter should be able to receive a fully funded French language education.

10 Discussions of this survey are to be found in the Commissioner of Official Languages Report for 1985 and in S. Churchill and A. Smith, 'The Emerging Consensus,' *Language and Society* 18 (September 1986) 5-11. The latter is a publication of the Office of the Commissioner of Official Languages.

Constitutional Reform and Immigration

Orest M. Kruhlak

The implications of the Constitutional Amendment, 1987 on immigration and on policies such as multiculturalism are profound. These implications have not been adequately addressed by either the academic community or the media. That there has not been much discussion of this section of the Accord is not unique, for most of the Accord has received approval without effective analysis or discussion. It is obvious, at least from examining the actions of the politicians, both federal and provincial, that getting the Accord was more important than what it says. I will restrict myself in this analysis to matters pertaining to the immigration provisions and the possible consequences from that Section of the Amendment proposal.

Immigration is one of the most important areas of public policy. It receives very little attention from Canada's political science community. Immigration has, and will continue to affect the make-up of Canada. If it is examined at all by those interested in the study of public policy, it is generally studied in relation to labour-market analysis. While this is important, immigration policy should be analyzed on a much broader basis, particularly in light of Meech Lake, for no other area of public policy so dramatically affects who we are as a people. Immigration affects Canada's political, social and economic life; consequently, important changes such as giving the provinces an enhanced role in immigration policy deserve greater consideration than they have received in the discussions on the Meech Lake Accord.

Immigration policy and practice is a shared responsibility under the existing Constitution with the provision that the federal power is paramount. While it is a shared power, not all of the provinces have at any one time indicated an equal interest in immigration matters. Only six have entered into agreements with Ottawa affording them a say in the types and numbers of immigrants they wish to see coming into their provinces. The other four provinces have left all aspects of immigration up to the federal government. Indeed, the Bennett government of British Columbia indicated, as late as 1983, that as far as they were concerned immigration was solely the responsibility of the federal government, though Premier Vander Zalm has recently stated that the province should play a more active role in immigration matters.

Under current immigration practices there are three principal components or categories of immigrants: the family re-unification component; the independent component; and the refugee component. These components or objectives are established in the Immigration Act of 1978 and are not subject to change in the proposed amendments in Bills C-55 or C-84 which are currently before Parliament. That is to say, the fundamental objectives remain untouched even though changes are being proposed which may profoundly affect the way the objectives are administered and realized. Meech Lake will not, apparently, affect this situation for the Amendment proposal states that the federal government '...will keep supreme authority over national standards and objectives like family reunification....' Needless to say the issue of national standards is one which has preoccupied many Canadians and is one which is central to the debate on the Meech Lake Accord not only with respect to immigration but to other sections of the proposed amendment.

It is submitted in the Meech Lake Accord that with respect to Quebec, Canada

> ...will, as soon as possible, conclude an agreement with the Government of Quebec that would (a) incorporate the principles of the Cullen-Couture agreement[1] on the selection abroad and in Canada of independent immigrants, visitors for medical treatment, students and temporary workers, and the selection of refugees abroad and economic criteria for family reunification and assisted relatives. (b) guarantee that Quebec will receive a number of immigrants, including refugees, within the annual total established by the federal government for all of Canada proportionate to its share of the population of Canada, with the right to exceed that figure by five percent for demographic reasons, and (c) provide an undertaking by Canada to withdraw services (except citizenship services) for the reception and integration (including linguistic and cultural) of all foreign nationals wishing to settle in Quebec where services are to be provided by Quebec, with such withdrawal to be accompanied by reasonable compensation, and the Government of Canada and the Government of Quebec will take the necessary steps to give the agreement the force of law under the proposed amendment relating to such agreements.

Moreover, 'Nothing in this Accord should be construed as preventing the negotiation of similar agreements with the other provinces relating to immigration and the temporary admission of aliens.'

My first concern with these proposals is that there has been very little discussion concerning the enhancement of the role of the provinces in matters concerning immigration policy and practices. Without any discussion, the Government of Canada has decided to increase the role provinces other than Quebec can play in the selection of immigrants and apportioning of the number of immigrants between provinces.

Protecting the provisions of the Cullen-Couture Agreement from change except by agreement between a province and the federal government is not, in itself, problematic. One could argue that this is simply giving greater force to a procedure which is just about 10 years old and that giving it constitutional authority is simply recognizing a political reality. However, where are the position papers that discuss the changes? Where is the Government of Canada's explanation of why it believes that Quebec and the other provinces should have an enhanced role in immigration policy? Do Canadians want the provinces playing a major role in immigration matters? Do we want to have two or five or ten different immigration policies operating in this country? Very clearly what the Government of Canada has agreed to in Meech Lake leaves the possibility of a proliferation of immigration policies. Reserving the right unto itself to set national standards, classes of immigrants or numbers does not change the reality that each province will, for all practical purposes, be able to establish its own immigration policy.

Moreover, the Meech Lake Accord does more than simply protect Cullen-Couture for there is an addition to that Agreement which gives, for the first time, Quebec and presumably the other provinces the right to select immigrants from within Canada. That has not been part of the process in the past and is, in fact, a significant departure from current practice. Applying for landed immigrant status from within Canada has been an exceptional practice, granted under Ministerial Permit for very special cases, and not a standard practice. One had to make application to immigrate to Canada from outside the country and this was required for reasons of equity. Now it is proposed to incorporate into Cullen-Couture and into an Agreement between Quebec and Canada the right of Quebec to select immigrants from within Canada. The implications of this change for possible conflict is extensive. Quebec will have the right to select immigrants from within Canada but the Government of Canada unless it changes its practices will not. Surely citizens will have some difficulty in understanding why Quebec should be able select immigrants in a manner in which the

Government of Canada cannot. Furthermore, if the Government of Canada were to change its practices and allow application for landed immigrant status to be routinely made from within the country it would be opening the borders to totally uncontrollable immigration. Canada already has significant problems in terms of bogus refugee claimants and to say to the world, 'come to Canada and make application for immigrant status from within Canada,' would present horrendous problems in terms of controlling the flow of immigrants. It would very likely play havoc with essential administrative practices such as security clearances and could potentially made a mockery of the practice of establishing annual immigration levels. But what if two or three other provinces choose to avail themselves of the Meech Lake Accord and enter into agreements similar to that negotiated with Quebec? Will it be possible to control immigration numbers? Will the Government of Canada be able to maintain the integrity of the objectives of the Immigration Act in regards to categories of immigrants? Perhaps it will be able to do so but documents are not available explaining how all of this would be accomplished.

Given the enhanced role for Quebec (and potentially for the other provinces) in the selection of immigrants and given the assertion that Quebec must attract its immigrants, will Quebec be required to have a complement of immigration offices everywhere that the Government of Canada maintains immigration offices? Or will it, as is the case today, simply open offices where it wishes to? The matter of where one maintains offices is not a simple administrative matter, but is critical to the type of immigration policy one practices. Given the enhanced role of the provinces in the selection of immigrants, where they choose to open offices has a direct bearing on the type of immigrants they will be able to select and that has important implications for Canada's immigration policies. What if Quebec and other provinces choose not to open offices in the Third World? Office location is a major policy matter that has caused a great deal of controversy. For while Canada has had, since at least 1967, an immigration policy that no longer discriminates on the basis of ethnicity, national origin and colour, we have had administrative procedures that, in effect, allowed for discriminatory policies to continue. Where you open an office determines, at least in part, what kinds of immigrants you are able to select. Thus, no office in Africa means very few if any immigrants from Africa. The law is not discriminatory but administrative practices could serve to ensure that the result would be the same as if the law continued to incorporate discriminatory features.

Thus, administrative arrangements are absolutely critical. Will Quebec be required to have immigration offices around the world where Canada currently has offices or will it be allowed to open offices in only selected locales? Will all applications from people who wish to reside in Quebec have to be funnelled through those offices? One does not, after all, apply for landed immigrant status in Canada through the mail. One must present oneself to an immigration officer for a face-to-face interview. If offices are opened in only limited locales then the capacity of individuals to make application for status in Quebec will be severely limited if they are unable to afford the expense of travelling from their home to the office.

A further question related to the matter of selection is: Does the Charter of Rights and Freedoms apply outside of Canada? If it does not then discriminatory features in the selection process could be utilized that would be unacceptable in Canada. (An interesting aside to this is whether one set of selection criteria would apply in the case where Quebec selects immigrants from within Canada pursuant to the provisions of the Accord and a different set when it selects immigrants abroad.) That some form of discrimination is practiced in the immigration process is not in and of itself unique. Every country which accepts immigrants practices some form of discrimination in the selection process. But does Meech Lake provide for something which in fact will be unique for Canada?

Since Quebec was given immigration rights in the Meech Lake agreement to provide it with means of protecting and enhancing the 'distinct society' provision of the Accord, surely Quebec has something in mind in terms of an immigration policy. It makes no sense to say that Quebec is a 'distinct society' if measures are not provided to ensure that it remains a distinct society.

At the domestic level, Bill 101 is directed at maintaining that distinct society and I would argue that the immigration provision of Meech Lake is of the same magnitude. It is there to enable Quebec to maintain its distinctiveness. But what constitutes a distinct Quebec society? The government's constitutional document *Strengthening the Canadian Federation* states that '...most French-speaking Canadians live in Quebec...and this is an important part of what makes Quebec a distinct society within Canada.' Canada's linguistic duality is of course not a matter of debate. Quebec certainly is the home of millions of French-speaking citizens, most of whom are unilingual French. That is a critical aspect of Canada's diversity. But while Canada is a bilingual country in law and, one hopes, increasingly in practice, does the right of Quebec to maintain a distinct society take precedence over Canada's bilingual character? Will Quebec, because of the distinct society clause, be able to select as potential immigrants only those applicants who have a command of the French language? We should be told if in fact this is the case before Meech Lake is approved. Moreover, if British Columbia, for example, should enter into a similar

immigration agreement with Canada as has Quebec, will British Columbia be able to screen out immigrants who speak no English even if they
have a knowledge of French? If in fact the above outlined scenario is
potentially accurate, what are we saying to the world about our much
heralded duality? Is that duality really one of two solitudes? Furthermore, what are we saying about the national government if in fact the
provinces will have a critical if not final say in the selection of immigrants to Canada? Will the Canadian government in fact be able to
ensure that national standards and objectives will be realized? What
evidence do we have that the political will will be exercised in matters
concerning immigration when we have seen a reluctance on the part
of the federal government to do so in other areas such as post-
secondary education?

A further concern about Quebec distinctiveness needs to be brought
out into the open for debate. If Quebec's distinctiveness is only a matter of language that is problematic enough, but do the authors of the
clause have something more in mind when they talk about Quebec's
distinctiveness? Quebec is today a basically white society with most
of its roots in Europe. Does Quebec's distinctiveness require that its
basic white, European and Christian antecedents be maintained? If the
answer is yes, then I would suggest that Canadians will be required
to engage in a lively debate as to the kind of country we will become,
a debate that will have far-reaching consequences in terms of what the
world thinks of Canada and Canadians. The reality of where Canada
gets immigrants has changed dramatically in the past two decades and
every indication is that immigration will continue to be from 'non-
traditional' countries. The traditional sources of Canada's immigrants,
first Northern Europe and the United States and then Europe in general, have for all practical purposes dried up. People in France have
shown little or no interest in immigrating to Canada and if that pattern continues and if Quebec wishes to maintain its distinctiveness in
terms of historical makeup then I would submit we are in for protracted debate about the kind of country Canada should or will be. If distinctiveness means more than a knowledge of the French language then
Canada and Quebec's immigration policies are going to undergo some
severe tests. The very essence of this country's human rights philosophy will be put on the table for what could well be a counter-productive
debate. Canada has, since the 1960s, pursued an immigration policy
which is non-discriminatory in terms of ethnicity, religion and race and
to put that policy at risk because of the need to maintain Quebec's distinctiveness will have far reaching consequences both domestically and
internationally.

Furthermore, if Quebec is able to utilize a knowledge of French or
other criteria in its selection criteria for immigrants, then the implica-

tions of further sections of the Accord become even more dangerous. The Accord states that Quebec '...will receive a number of immigrants including refugees, within the total established by the federal government for all of Canada proportionate to its share of the population of Canada, with the right to exceed that figure by five percent....' Currently Quebec's proportion of the Canadian population is approximately 26%. The Government of Canada announced on October 30, 1987 that the immigration level for 1988 is 125,000 immigrants. Thus, according to the Meech Lake Accord, Quebec must receive at least 32,500 of the prospective immigrants, assuming that we were able to reach the projected target, but could in fact if it so desired take 38,750 of the total. (That is assuming of course, that one applies the five percent factor to give Quebec 31% of the potential pool of immigrants. If one applies the 5% factor to the number of 32,500 Quebec would only be entitled to take an additional 1,625 from the potential pool. Once again, there is no supporting documentation to tell us which figure is intended.) What, for example, happens if Quebec is unable to attract 32,500 immigrants in 1988? This is not simply a hypothetical question because Quebec has had difficulty in attracting immigrants in recent years. Quebec's portion of the national total has dropped appreciably in the past ten years. Will the Agreement require Canada to reduce the number of immigrants it will take in total so as to keep the ratio in balance? While the Agreement guarantees that Quebec will receive a minimum number of immigrants, what happens if Quebec is able to attract more than 38,750 immigrants (I apply the 5% factor to Quebec's proportionate share of the immigrant pool for I believe that is in fact what is intended)? Must Canada automatically raise the immigration level so as to keep the ratio in balance?

If the answer is in fact yes, does it not make a mockery of the entire exercise of setting immigration levels based on a whole series of economic and demographic factors? Moreover, what if Quebec is unable to attract its requisite number of immigrants but the rest of the country has no trouble reaching its target and wishes to do so? What if the other provinces and the Government of Canada wish to exceed the immigration level for a whole series of economic reasons? Can Quebec reasonably expect to dictate the labour market needs of the other provinces in the country? Again, if the answers to these questions is yes then it is clear that the way in which we determine how many immigrants this country needs is in for a very profound change. We must bear in mind that Quebec's immigration requirements are based on more reasons than simply labour market needs. The requirements of maintaining a distinct society are more important than labour market considerations. The proportionate requirement in the Agreement is no accident. Quebec will not, it is my contention, agree to immigration levels staying at, for example, 125,000 immigrants if it is unable to attract its proportionate share. To agree to do so would be to ensure that Quebec's proportion of the Canadian population would decline with the result that in future years Quebec would be entitled to a lower share of the overall immigration pool. If this should prove to be the case over a number of years, with Quebec constantly becoming a smaller part of the overall Canadian population, the results for the 'distinct society' could be disastrous. From the time of the Quiet Revolution, Quebec's proportion of the overall Canadian population has dropped from approximately 31% in 1961 to approximately 26% today. Surely it stretches the imagination to believe that Quebec authorities would be content to see Quebec become an even smaller minority in Canada. Thus the right to determine the total number of immigrants coming to Canada is an essential element in Quebec's guaranteed share of the total immigration pool.

If Quebec applies, as a criterion of selection, knowledge of the French language, then it is unlikely that Quebec will be able to attract 32,500 immigrants in 1988. Certainly it is unlikely to be able to attract 32,500 immigrants that are culturally and racially similar to Quebec's population today.

Furthermore, if language becomes a principle criterion of selection what would happen to the fundamental objectives of the Immigration Act? Could the need to know French over-ride the family re-unification provisions? Would the knowledge of French be the only criterion for independent immigrants? Would having relevant job skills become irrelevant? There has not been, to my knowledge, any discussion of these fundamental issues. To protect constitutionally an Agreement which has many unanswered questions surrounding it is problematic at best.

The final portion of the immigration section of the Accord that is problematic pertains to the provision of reception and integration services to immigrants. The Accord provides that Canada will withdraw all services directed to receiving and integrating immigrants into Canada in Quebec and that the Government of Canada will compensate Quebec for the services in place of Canadian government services. Therefore, after the Accord becomes part of the Constitution, Quebec will have sole responsibility on all matters concerning the cultural and linguistic integration of immigrants who settle in Quebec. The people who negotiated this agreement had no idea what they were agreeing to. They have given constitutional force to the proposition that, in the future, immigrants who come to Quebec will not be integrated into Canada but only into Quebec. And if that sounds unreasonable I would only suggest that one check what has been transmitted in the COFI's (Orientation and Training Centres for Immigrants) in Quebec to immigrants about Canada. It is generally acknowledged by experts in the field that Quebec has done a superior job in immigrant integration, an integration, however, that is strictly concerned with Quebec and not Canada. The idea of handing over jurisdiction to the provinces for integration activities is certainly questionable from the point of view of nation-building and national unity.

Up until this agreement, the reception and integration of immigrants was not the sole responsibility of one level of government. Both the federal and provincial governments could and did play an essential role. Federal programs were designed to ensure that immigrants gained knowledge about Canada, not just about one province. The underlying assumption was that immigrants were coming to Canada and not just to a province. In fact, the entire citizenship process is predicated on the assumption that a prospective citizen has knowledge about the whole country. What provisions exist in the Accord to ensure that in the course of the linguistic and cultural integration of immigrants, the immigrant will be taught about Canada? There are none. On the basis of our knowledge of the integration process as it has operated in Quebec, the Canadian content is minimal. What other country in the world gives over an important political socialization activity to one of its constituent parts?

Perhaps if one believed in the concept of a 'community of communities,' then it might make sense to have the constituent members of the federation responsible for integrating newcomers but I do not believe in the concept if for no other reason than I have never seen it adequately defined. I believe that Canada is something more than a collection of ten provinces and two territories. Moreover, I do not believe that we will develop a sense of belonging to Canada if we have immigrants being integrated into ten different conceptions of what Canada is. I would point out that there is nothing in the Immigration Act which speaks about national standards in terms of linguistic and cultural integration and it would be entirely up to the provinces to determine what immigrants learned or did not learn in the integration process. Isn't some discussion warranted about whether or not this is a wise course for a country to follow?

In addition, just what does the cultural and linguistic integration of immigrants mean in the Accord as it pertains to Quebec? Again, there has been no debate. There have been no documents produced for public examination. There is simply a statement that Quebec will become solely responsible. That Quebec should want control over the process is not surprising for, from the point of view of Quebec nationalist, it is imperative that Quebec controls what the immigrants are told about their new country. Furthermore, and again this is not surprising nor is it in many ways unreasonable, Quebec wants all immigrants to learn the French language and to become Quebecois. I am concerned that

Quebec will attempt to gain control of the entire Federal Multicultural Program in that province. Quebec is unlikely to 'allow' the federal government to operate a series of program activities that orient people to Canada and not specifically to Quebec or any other province.

In sum, the Meech Lake Accord, in its immigration section, has far-reaching implications for national unity in Canada as well as for Canada's future economic prosperity. Canada is and has become culturally diverse over the years. The Accord can profoundly effect that diversity and that has overtones for the unity of this society. Furthermore, most demographic projections indicate that early in the next century Canada's population will peak at around 29 million people and thereafter begin to decline. To prevent a population decline, policy-makers only have two alternatives: to increase immigration or to increase Canada's fertility rate. The latter alternative, Jacques Parizeau to the contrary notwithstanding, is not a likely scenario because it is highly improbable that he or anyone else will be able to convince Canadians or Quebecers to have more children. Thus the only realistic option available to governments is to increase immigration. To increase our net immigration to sufficient levels to prevent a population decline will require immigration targets far in excess of the proposed 125,000 immigrants in 1988. Based on immigration patterns which demonstrate that Quebec has, over the past number of years, received a declining proportion of immigrants, one can obviously see the implications of the Accord. If Quebec cannot reach its proportionate targets then total immigration will have to be held down and if that is done Canada's population will decline and our future economic opportunities will be limited.

Finally, the Accord makes provisions, as mentioned above, for all other provinces to have similar agreements. This increases further the potential for economic and political confusion and disaster. To illustrate, the Atlantic region of Canada gets virtually no immigration. There is simply very little reason, for example, for an immigrant to go to Newfoundland where there is an unemployment rate of 17.5%. What if Newfoundland decides to enter into an agreement similar to Quebec's and demands a proportionate share of immigrants similar to its proportion of the Canadian population? The potential for severe economic dislocation is self-evident.

Before the provincial governments formally agree to the Constitutional Amendment, 1987 they would be well advised to understand what they are placing into the supreme law of this country. From an immigration perspective this Accord has serious shortcomings and the political leadership of the country can no longer continue, irrespective of how important Quebec's signature is, to abandon future generations, if not this one, to the implications of population stagnation or decline. Every economic, political and social indicator says that the Government of Canada must remain the paramount player in immigration matters or Canada will be faced with dangers which will endanger the very unity of this nation.

Notes

1 The Cullen-Couture Agreement was signed between the governments of Canada and Quebec pursuant to the Immigration Act of 1978. The new Act made provision to enhance the role played by provinces both in the establishment of immigration levels and the recruitment of immigrants abroad. The only province to take advantage of the potential of the legislation was Quebec and that province opened immigration offices in a number of locations abroad.

Meech Lake
and
The Media

"...WELL THEN... IF NOT A RATIFIED CONSTITUTIONAL ACCORD WHAT DO YOU FEEL FORMS THE HEART AND SOUL OF THE CANADIAN PSYCHE?..."

INTRODUCTION:
MEECH LAKE AND THE MEDIA

Alan Cairns may have posed the most important question about the Meech Lake Accord when he asked 'Whose constitution is it anyway?'[1] He meant that the constitution should not only be the product of governments, it also had to reflect the concerns and views of interest groups and the general public. Since all of the governments and political parties favoured the Accord and apparently, it is suspected, tried in at least some instances to suffocate political debate so as to nullify opposition, the mass media had a special responsibility. They were the source for basic information and analysis, the vital conduit between the events at Meech Lake and the public that would have to live with and under the Accord. Canadians viewed Meech Lake through the media's filter, but as this section points out the media had its own interests, agendas and codes of professional responsibility. The media's lens may have distorted the message.

An extensive literature now exists on the impact that mass media have had in shaping political values and behavior. The first wave of research findings conducted in the inter-war period tended to support the view that the media were powerful and pervasive and could dramatically alter the perceptions and beliefs of entire populations.[2] Sometimes called the magic bullet theory, the hypothesis was that media images could sharply and directly penetrate people's consciousness and even sub-consciousness.

A second body of research pointed to the opposite conclusion. In the immediate post-war period a number of studies contended that people watch or read selectively and in accordance with their previous views.[3] There is selective exposure and retention as the mask of pre-existing beliefs screens out uncomfortable new information. If anything, previous perceptions are hardened by exposure to the media. It was also argued that people are influenced by a series of relationships and experiences; family, peers, educational institutions, religious bonds, etc. with information from the mass media mediated through a number of other institutions. The consensus drawn in the 1950s and 1960s was that the effects of the magic bullet were blunted by heavy layers of social and psychological experiences.

A third stream of research which takes a middle position between the magic bullet theory and the selective attention school has emerged principally in the 1970s and 1980s although its roots can be traced to work done much earlier by Walter Lippmann and others. This view has been refered to at various points as signaling, agenda-setting, or framing. It was Walter Lippmann who first formulated the proposition that 'the function of news is to signalize an event.'[4] He meant by this that the mass media had the power to alert the public about which events were important. Bernard Cohen whose research was conducted in the 1960s argued that, 'The press is significantly more than a purveyor of information and opinion. It may not be successful much of the time in telling people what to think, but it is stunningly successful in telling its readers what to think about.'[5] Two influential studies, one by McCombs and Shaw in the 1970s and the other by Iyengar and Kinder, in the 1980s support this agenda-setting or framing hypothesis.[6] Stated simply by Iyengar and Kinder the central proposition is that 'those problems that receive prominent attention on the national news become the problems the viewing public regards as the nation's most important.'[7] The audience may not be influenced to abandon previously held beliefs but it can be swayed on the direction to fix its gaze.

This section includes three articles. David Taras' article contends that CBC television news was a participant in constitution-making because it failed to alert its viewers, the Canadian public, about the substance of the Accord or its potential consequences for the national community. The main argument is that current television formats are so truncated in length and geared to excitement that they are unable to deal with issues that are complex, detailed or legalistic. The public did not receive the coverage that it needed or deserved. The second is by Elly Alboim, Ottawa Bureau Chief for CBC television news. Alboim describes the political settings and the motivations of the key players in the Meech Lake drama. The portrait is of manipulation, cynicism and desperation. According to Alboim, the media's obligation consisted of recording the events that unfolded and providing as much analysis as possible. They had to refrain from participating in events; keeping the story alive unnaturally or stoking unfounded controversy. With all of the governments and political parties endorsing the Accord, the media could not go on a crusade of its own. They had to accept that the story, at least for the time being, had played itself out. The last article by Lorry Felske is a review of newspaper coverage and editorial opinions in English Canada. Felske argues that newspapers tended to reflect the interests of their particular region. They also tended to focus on personalities rather than on substance. The overall assessment in these three articles is that the media are imperfect but powerful mirrors.

Notes

1 Address to Second Thoughts on Meech Lake: A Conference on Political Process, University of Calgary, November, 1987.

2 Shearon Lowery and Melvin Defleur, *Milestones in Mass Communication Research: Media Effects* (New York: Longman 1983) chapters 2-5.

3 See Carl Hovland, Irving Janis and Harold Kelley, *Communication and Persuasion* (New Haven: Yale University Press 1953); Elihu Katz and Paul Lazarsfeld, *Personal Influence: The Part Played by People in the Flow of Mass Communication* (Glencoe, IL: The Free Press of Glencoe 1955) and Joseph Klapper, *The Effects of the Mass Media* (Glencoe, IL: The Free Press of Glencoe 1960).

4 Walter Lippmann, *Public Opinion* (New York: The Free Press, 1922).

5 Bernard Cohen, *The Press and Foreign Policy* (Princeton, N.J.: Princeton University Press 1963) 13.

6 Maxwell McCombs and Donald Shaw, *The Emergence of American Political Issues: The Agenda-Setting Function of the Press* (St. Paul: West Publishing 1977) and Shanto Iyengar and Donald Kinder, *News That Matters: Television and American Opinion* (Chicago: The University of Chicago Press 1987).

7 Iyengar and Kinder, 16.

Meech Lake
and Television News

David Taras

The power of television to mold public opinion is one of the essential realities of Canadian political life. Most Canadians view the political world only through television and have few other sources of contact or information. Canadians rely on television for news to a far greater degree than they do on any other medium.[1] What is most important is the sense of intimacy, of direct experience, of 'witnessing' that gives television its magnetic power. Television conveys the feeling to people that they are seeing things for themselves. As Reuven Frank wrote nearly a generation ago, 'The highest power of television journalism is not in the transmission of information but in the transmission of experience.'[2]

The main argument in this article is that CBC television's reporting of the 1987 Constitutional Accord primed its audience to see the historic agreement as a relatively insignificant event. Since the Accord is complex, untidy and abstract it did not have the attributes that are valued by media decision makers. Although it can be argued that Meech Lake fundamentally altered the basic propositions of national life and brought new rules, a new dynamic, a different vision of the country, CBC television news could not, given its current format, deal effectively with these developments. Coverage was scattered, vague and incoherent. Public reactions to Meech Lake were very much like the coverage of the issue on television. Public opinion was not mobilized because television had not signaled the event. CBC television news played a particularly critical role because it has the largest viewing audience and is the news outlet that most Canadians turn to when there are important developments. It is also governed by a public mandate which gives the corporation the prime responsibility among all media outlets to 'contribute to the development of national unity and provide for a continuing expression of Canadian identity.'[3]

The article is divided into three sections. The first describes the formats that are used in television news reporting. Whether or not an event becomes news and how much play it receives is dependent almost entirely on how well it fits the news format. A second section analyzes the transcripts of CBC television's *The National* from 30 April to 5 June 1987. This period encompassed the two most critical events; the dramatic meeting at Meech Lake when the Prime Minister and the ten provincial premiers first agreed to the Accord and the negotiating session at the Langevin Block in Ottawa when the constitutional deal was sealed. A concluding section argues that the news format severely distorted the public's view of Meech Lake. In doing so television played a key role in Canadian constitution-making.

The Television News Format

A significant scholarly literature now exists on television news reporting. There is widespread agreement in the scholarly community that television now operates according to a well-defined set of routines and formats. The driving force is entertainment, not journalism or public service. Indeed the current formats are so rigid, and news shaped so much to appeal to the consumer, that journalists however dedicated and skilled, and the CBC has some of the most dedicated and skilled, are forced to work under circumstances that drastically limit their discretion.

The structure of television news is dictated by a series of harsh external realities. The most basic of these is that news shows must sell the size and characteristics of their audiences to advertisers in order to survive. As the audience has become increasingly splintered in the 1980s because of the proliferation of new channels and services, networks are locked in a desperate battle to capture and maintain audiences and of course to keep their advertisers. Where in the 1950s the CBC had only to compete against the main U.S. networks, it now has to contend with over thirty other channels in the Toronto market and at least twenty in most other Canadian cities. The advent of VCRs has fragmented the audience even further. In addition, network news programs have come up against an unexpected rival; the expanding horizon of local television news. Local news programs, which are the flagships of their stations, increasingly carry national and international news segments traditionally the mandate of the network-wide broadcast and have largely adopted the American big city news model with its diet of 'happy news,' attention grabbing human interest stories and lively chit-chat. Audience surveys have left little doubt about what the audience expects from the news – high energy, a fast pace, an entertaining format and stories about personalities and celebrities. Reuven Frank of NBC News has described the essential difference between meeting the demands of a newspaper as against those of a television audience,

> A newspaper...can easily afford to print an item of conceivable interest to only a small percentage of its readers. A television news program must be put together with the assumption that each item will be of some interest to everyone that watches. Every time a newspaper includes a feature which will attract a specialized group it can assume it is adding at least a bit to its circulation. To the degree a television news program includes an item of this sort...it must assume its audience will diminish.[4]

While no advertising appears during CBC's *The National*, the network as a whole is increasingly dependent on advertising revenues since the government beginning in 1984 imposed several rounds of strenuous cutbacks. CBC management is deeply committed to winning the battle for the news watching audience because news is central to the CBC's mandate. Advertising does appear during *The Journal* and advertising on shows that appear before *The National* are dependent on audiences switching to CBC in anticipation of the news. Most important perhaps is that the formats and values that have triumphed throughout North America due to economic forces have forced CBC to change the character of its news reporting. According to producer Tony Burman, *The National* has to be 'sharper, faster, tougher...first and best.'[5]

Todd Gitlin, whose book, *The Whole World Is Watching*, has become something of a modern classic for students of politics and communications, has argued that television news is structured to fit precise 'frames.'[6] To Gitlin, 'Frames are principles of selection, emphasis and presentation composed of little tacit theories about what exists, what happens and what matters.'[7] The frame is 'clamped over the event' being reported so that only stories or elements of stories that fit the frame are likely to be selected.[8] Stories that fall outside the frame, that do not have certain inherent characteristics, are dispensed with or downplayed. They do not become part of television's depiction of reality. Other scholars use different terms to describe essentially the same phenomenon; Altheide refers to the news perspective while Ranney describes this as structural bias.[9]

While researchers have different views about the characteristics of news frames, what the news formula actually consists of, for the purposes of this article only some of the most obvious characteristics will be discussed. The first and most essential is that news has an 'instant' quality. News is what is happening now, or is about to happen, not what happened last week or even yesterday. News is in the 'continuous present tense.'[10] Like freshly baked bread it quickly grows stale. The events of last week or even yesterday regardless of how important they may have been, can be displaced by almost any new development regardless of how trivial. News is constantly turning over and the speed of modern communications has insured that the shelf-life of news stories is desperately short.

Drama is the prime ingredient of most news stories. Drama requires sensationalism, winners and losers, and an emotional human element but most of all it requires conflict. As a CBC news editor observed about the CBC news process, 'We look for conflict often to the exclusion of a story. It's overwhelmingly prevalent. It's the nature of journalism to be a storyteller. It needs drama.'[11] In television news, conflict is structured in a certain way. Largely because of demands for objectivity and fairness which have come from government regulators but also because of the development of standards of objectivity within journalism, almost all news stories have a point-counterpoint format. The best issues from the perspective of media decision-makers are issues that neatly divided individuals or groups into two clearly opposing sides. The pro-con model is so rigidly adhered to, so ironclad, that items are routinely dropped if spokespersons for opposing positions cannot be found. Moreover, the process is often carried to absurd lengths. When the Surgeon General in the United States recently announced more new and damning evidence against smoking, a spokesperson for the tobacco industry was given an equal place in the news story. During the trial of hate propogandist Ernst Zundel in 1985, the testimony of concentration camp survivors was juxtaposed with claims made by Zundel that the holocaust never occurred. To heighten the sense of conflict, persons espousing opposing viewpoints are often shot from different camera angles.[12] The problem with this format is that many issues lend themselves to a variety of opinions and many shades of argument and cannot be readily collapsed into a choice between pro and con. There may also be on a given issue only a single defensible position; smoking is in fact dangerous to people's health and the holocaust did take place. Odd or extreme positions can be legitimized or given inordinate attention. In addition, this format limits investigative journalism. Since journalists are there merely to present the two sides of any issue, there is no pressure on them to push the analysis further or discover the truth.

Another tenet of news reporting is what Tuchman calls 'the spatial anchoring of the news net at centralized institutions.'[13] When journalists cast their net for news, their catch is likely to be limited to political leaders or high ranking government officials. Stationed as they are at fixed listening posts, such as the House of Commons, and under sharp budgetary constraints and deadlines, journalists usually turn to a small number of 'knowns' for stories or comments.[14] It is tempting to argue that as a result there is a kind of Ottawa 'echo chamber' where the same people are always being interviewed, each reacting to statements made by others in the 'echo chamber.' Corporate executives or interest group leaders will almost never appear regularly in the news because they are situated outside the net. This is despite the fact that many of these individuals are far more powerful than MPs. Thus, news generally occurs at certain locations, and involves certain kinds of people, and not others.

Television news also thrives on personalities. Drama can be enhanced and issues simplified if the focus is on conflict between individuals. According to Gitlin,

> From the media point of view, news consists of events which can be recognized and interpreted as drama; and for the most part, news is what is made by individuals who are certifiably newsworthy...In the mass-mediated version of reality, organizations, bureaucracies, movements – in fact, all larger and more enduring social formations – are reduced to personifications.[15]

Indeed, news analysis rarely goes beyond a discussion of the ambitions and motivations of individuals. Television journalists almost invariably want to know who is to blame, who has won or lost, who is doing what to whom. The social and economic forces that propel events are seldom credited with being as important as the actions of powerful individuals. In fact, social and economic forces are rarely touched upon at all.

Stories that fit the needs of television are ones that can be easily labelled and condensed. Stories are described using catch words such as Iran Contra, Tunagate or Free Trade. This kind of shorthand helps to simplify issues but it insures as well that with each new development the story will not have to be reexplained to viewers. The most difficult problem is how to telescope a complex event or issue into the time frame required for television news. The average news story is roughly 90 seconds long containing no more than 150 to 250 words. In fact, a transcript of *The National* would take up only about one third of the front page of a newspaper. The ideal length of a clip of someone speaking or being interviewed is, according to one CBC producer, twelve seconds.[16] There is little journalistic rationale for coverage being so brutally truncated. The rationale is to be found in the perceived attention span of the viewers and the need to grab and hold the audience with sharp, fast-paced, action-oriented stories.

Another essential ingredient of a television news story is high impact visual material. Visuals account for some 14 to 17 minutes out of *The National's* on-air time of 22 minutes. A cynic would argue that the news process has become little more than packaging visuals. Story angles are often dictated by and wrapped around the visual material that is available. As Richard Ericson and his colleagues found during their intensive study of CBC station CBLT in Toronto,

> The importance of visuals was revealed when there were problems in obtaining them. If particular visuals could not be obtained, or if obtained were deemed to be lacking in drama, immediacy or exclusivity, then the entire story was sometimes dropped.[17]

Interestingly enough South Africa lost its place as a leading story almost as soon as the South African government imposed a ban on filming riots and demonstrations. Without visual material the situation in South Africa could not be sustained as a television news story. The best visual material captures action or emotion or conflict. It is often the case that stories will be shot and video-tape edited so that these elements are highlighted. Each news story that contains visual material will have undergone a series of technical changes: cuts, zooms, splicing, etc. to create the maximum effect.

By its nature, television news is predisposed towards covering certain kinds of stories and not others. Stories that do not involve conflict among political leaders, high drama, or have interesting visuals are likely to be outside the news frame. A particular problem is with stories that are complicated, diffuse or legalistic; stories that run against the grain of what television wants. Covering the political process seems particularly anathema to television because it is time-consuming, cumbersome, difficult to explain and involves meticulous detail. Moreover, surveys indicate that the public seems to be taking less and less of an interest in politics. When consumer demand overrides journalistic values and standards there is little place for reporting the slow relentless workings of government or constitutions. The reality as Todd Gitlin aptly points out is that '...news concerns the event, not the underlying condition; the person, not the group; conflict, not consensus; the fact that 'advances the story,' not the one that explains it.[18]

Covering Meech Lake

CBC television news' reporting of Meech Lake, the period from 30 April to 5 June, can be roughly divided into four waves. The first wave focussed on the events at Meech Lake and reactions to them, a second concentrated on the divisions within the Liberal Party that resulted from the Accord, Pierre Trudeau's re-emergence onto the constitutional stage brought another spate of coverage and the Langevin Block meeting was the subject of a last round of intensive reporting.

CBC television news' coverage of the 1987 constitutional round began dramatically on the night of 30 April with two reports, one by David Halton and the other by Mike Duffy, from Meech Lake itself. Members of CBC's Ottawa bureau had with other members of the media kept vigil as the Prime Minister and the ten premiers negotiated into the early morning. In some ways the first news reports delivered before the actual contents of the Accord became known set the tone for much of the reporting that would follow and for political reactions to the Accord. In his lead-in introducing the two reports Knowlton Nash told his viewers, 'The discussions are continuing tonight at Meech Lake outside Ottawa where the Prime Minister and the ten premiers are trying to bring Québec into the constitution.' In every instance where the Meech Lake agreement was described by a newsreader the same note was struck; the Accord would allow Québec to sign the constitution. While it was well understood that this was Québec's round in the constitutional negotiations, and that gaining Québec's signature was the main objective, those opposing the Accord have complained that the debate was pitched by the media in such a way that opponents found themselves accused of being insensitive to Québec's needs or anti-Québec. Had producers and editors decided to describe the Accord in a different way; taking the tack for instance that the Accord would bring a sweeping shift of power from Ottawa to the provinces, a vast decentralization, the nature of the public debate might have been different.

The first report by David Halton revealed another important characteristic of the CBC's coverage. Halton reports that Québec had set five conditions as the price for its re-entry into the constitutional framework. Of the five conditions only one was mentioned, Québec's demand for a veto on future constitutional change. Had Halton described all of Québec's demands, the full dimensions of the Meech Lake deal would have been more readily apparent. The report signified that routine reporting techniques including highly abreviated and brutally short descriptions of issues and events were to be used in covering this latest constitutional round. The constitution would not be treated differently from other news stories.

That constitutional change was not seen as an especially important issue, deserving greater explanation than is normally the case in news stories, became evident during the second day of coverage. The first television images presented to Canadians in the aftermath of the agreement was of the jubilant mood of the House of Commons as it gave

Brian Mulroney a standing ovation. Ed Broadbent and John Turner were shown offering their congratulations to Mulroney even before the Prime Minister rose to address the House. Halton's report also included clips of Broadbent and Turner each expressing some concern about the Accord and historian Ramsay Cook arguing that the Prime Minister had given away too much to the provinces. The main images, however, were of triumph and unanimity. It is critical to point out that Halton never explained in any detail what the Accord contained, what it would mean, or what consequences it would have. The only description of the agreement's provisions offered by Halton was the following:

> Constitutional experts were also mulling over the first ministers' agreement yesterday which not only recognizes Québec as a distinct society, but also gives all provinces increased powers. Those powers give the premiers a veto over changes to some federal institutions, and a big say in Supreme Court and Senate appointments.

This was the longest and most comprehensive description of the Accord presented. Although constitutional experts are refered to, their views were never described in a full report or given anything but passing mention.

The second day of coverage continued to stress that Québec's acceptance of the Accord was the key issue. Reactions within Québec to news of the agreement were the subject of a second report by Paul Workman. Knowlton Nash introduced Workman's piece using the pro-con model which is the format for most television news stories. As Nash put it '...across the province today, there was argument about whether the deal was a sell-out or a victory.' The most vivid and dramatic quote was from Parti Québécois leader Pierre Marc Johnson who charged that 'someone's selling the house'; the reference was to Premier Bourassa.

Following this first wave of reporting the Accord was to receive little attention until 8 May. Indeed, it is disquieting to note how quickly a historic political event can be displaced as a news story. A brief report on Bourassa's response to Johnson's comments was the eighth item on *The National* on 3 May. On the 5th, 6th and 7th of May there were no stories at all on the Accord. It was only on 8 May when Liberal MP Donald Johnston broke with John Turner over Meech Lake that the CBC again fastened onto the issue. Struggles within the Liberal Party and the threat that these divisions posed to John Turner's leadership proved to be an irresistible news story for much of the media, and it emerged as the major theme in the CBC news' treatment of Meech Lake. During the five weeks between the negotiations at Meech Lake and those held at the Langevin Block, strife within the Liberal Party was featured in 14 out of 39 news reports about the Accord.

Descriptions of Liberal in-fighting were presented in lurid and graphic detail. And indeed there was considerable justification for concentrating on the Liberal Party battlefield. As correspondent Jason Moscovitz pointed out at the end of his report on 8 May, 'For the Liberal Party, it's another major split — the latest in a series. This one is potentially the most serious, because this family fight involves something as fundamental as two different visions of the country.' During the panel discussion featured on the *Sunday Report* of 31 May, Peter Mansbridge asked whether the media had stifled a full national debate on the substance of Meech Lake by fixating to such a great extent on splits within Liberal ranks. In response, Jeffrey Simpson, the influential columnist for *The Globe and Mail*, reiterated the argument that had been made by Jason Moscovitz saying,

> ...I think you're half right. Maybe we didn't concentrate enough on the substance of the deal. The other half I don't agree with. I mean, the Liberal Party, for all of this century, has been the principal bridge between French and English Canadians, and the Constitution is an important element of that bridge.

An additional incentive to concentrate on developments within the Liberal Party was that members of the media had been speculating for months about whether John Turner would survive as leader in 1988. Nothing would be more dramatic, and would make a better news story, than to see a king toppled and Meech Lake seemed to leave Turner deeply exposed and vulnerable. It should be noted, however, that some members of the media did feel that prospects for a full-blown national debate had been blotted out by the excessive coverage given to Liberal Party bloodletting. Don Newman, a veteran CBC journalist and currently President of the Press Gallery, argued that

> The major issue that came out of the national press gallery in Ottawa was what does this mean for John Turner's leadership and for the Liberal Party. It seems to me that the importance of the Meech Lake Accord goes far beyond what happens to John Turner or the Liberal Party. Everything is now reduced to the politics of an issue and essentially the politics of it. And that's why Meech Lake was reported so badly.[19]

It can also be argued that the amount of attention given to strains within the Liberal Party had the effect of drastically limiting the reporting of the positions taken by other groups. There is after all only so much time in a news broadcast and only so much time within a news broadcast that is normally devoted to Ottawa stories. Criticisms of the agreement by women's groups and by Native Canadian organizations were each reported on only one occasion. The reactions of religious and ethnic groups including those of francophones outside of Québec were never reported on. Those constituencies that Alan Cairns refers to as 'rights bearers' because of rights given to them under the 1982 Charter of Rights, were not treated as significant players on television news.[20] It might be argued that groups were not offended by the Meech Lake text as much as by the one that emerged out of the Langevin meetings. They only became mobilized after Langevin. It may also be that the concerns that they were beginning to express about Meech Lake were not as newsworthy as the more visually exciting and emotionally compelling drama within John Turner's party.

By the middle of May, Meech Lake had faded from the news. There were only five news items on the agreement from 15 to 26 May and none of these were lead stories. This would change suddenly with the constitutional offensive launched by Pierre Trudeau. While the media had maintained a 'watch' on Trudeau from at least 14 May, sensing that he would inevitably emerge to defend the constitutional regime which he had built, whose foundations were now being destroyed, Trudeau insists that he was moved to action only because so many others had remained silent. He had also waited until the week before the meeting of First Ministers that was scheduled for 2 June at the Langevin Block in the hope no doubt that his intervention would unsettle the tenuous alliance that had formed at Meech Lake. Trudeau's first salvo was an article which appeared in *The Toronto Star* and *La Presse* on 27 May. That night *The National* ran three stories on Meech Lake. The lead item by David Halton highlighted the personal acrimony that had developed between Trudeau and Mulroney. Trudeau had called Mulroney 'a weakling' and characterized supporters of Meech Lake as 'snivellers' who had destined Canada to be governed by 'eunuchs.' Ironically, it was only in describing Trudeau's position that the main criticisms of the Accord were presented to viewers for the first time on CBC television news. Halton pointed out that what angered Trudeau was that 'the dream of a single bilingual Canada was being betrayed' and that the Accord would 'give significant new powers to the provinces, to nominate Supreme Court judges and Senators and to opt out of new shared cost programs.' These details had not been spelled out previously on *The National*. The second item in that night's newscast was about the possible impact of Trudeau's statement on John Turner's hold on the Liberal Party leadership.

Trudeau then continued his assault on the Accord with a series of media interviews which were to be broadcast the next day. *The National* set the stage for this coverage by running a report on the nature of the public debate on the constitution. Citing 'growing opposition to the deal' Halton's report contained brief comments by Native leaders and by leading constitutional experts. This was the only occasion when the substance of the Accord rather than the politics of the deal, the political manoeuverings of politicians, was analyzed.

The final episode in this choreographed drama came on 29 May when the interviews done the previous day were broadcast. *The National* focused on the interview done with Barbara Frum which was about to appear on *The Journal*. The substance of the Accord again received little attention as David Halton seized on that part of the interview where Trudeau was asked about his remark that Mulroney was a 'weakling.' Halton's report turned on the question of who had been the stronger leader. The longest clip was of Trudeau making the following remark:

> Let them say we disagree with John A. Macdonald's concept of Canada, we disagree with Laurier's, we disagree with Mackenzie King's, we disagree with M. St. Laurent's. We disagree with Pearson. And, of course, we disagree with Mr. Trudeau. Because all I'm doing is doing what every other Prime Minister did before me — saying no to the provinces when they wanted too much power.

The report ended with two clips of Mulroney's reaction; one, in which he characterized Trudeau's attack as 'a bit of low-level comedy' and a second, where he defended Meech Lake as '...a sign of maturity and skill and strong national leadership.' The newcast's second item was the by now obligatory discussion about how this latest development would affect John Turner's leadership. The theme of leadership now seemed to be the thread tying together the CBC's entire approach to Meech Lake.

The final wave of coverage focussed on the final negotiating round scheduled to take place at the Langevin Block in Ottawa. As part of CBC's 'run-up' to the Langevin negotiations, Jason Moscovitz did a report on 31 May which surveyed the political terrain and identified problems that could still emerge to block the deal. The report was the seventh item on the news that night. Moscovitz's report was followed by the usual Sunday night panel discussion where the politics of the Accord and Trudeau's dramatic re-appearance on the political stage were the main topics. Jeffrey Simpson seemed to accept much of Trudeau's argument and his scathing analysis. He observed that

> This would be the first time...that there's been bargaining of a conventional kind. Because what happened at Meech Lake was Québec had five demands, Ottawa pretty much accepted them. And then went around and sold the demands to others by expending their powers. I mean, Lisianne Gagnon, who's a brilliant columnist from *La Presse*, said the Prime Minister played bartender, not by filling up people's glasses, but by asking them all to belly up to the bar and fill up their own glasses. So this will be the first time that there's actually been give-and-take bargaining, as opposed to simply buying people off.

The main thrust of the discussion was whether Trudeau had shaken up the Meech Lake alliance enough to prevent a final agreement. That the deal could fall through was a continuing theme over the next few days of reporting. In Mike Duffy's report on 1 June, Deputy Prime Minister, Don Mazankowski was quoted as saying, 'We are not sure whether the agreement will be ratified' and Ontario Premier David Peterson was presented as being unwilling to wager a lot of money on a positive outcome. In a second report that evening David Halton predicted a clash between Manitoba Premier Howard Pawley and Québec's Robert Bourassa and argued that without a trade-off between the two, final agreement would be elusive. Halton noted that federal officials thought that 'the odds aren't much better than even on getting that trade-off.' As the Prime Minister and the premiers had invested a great deal of political capital and prestige, the media's search for cracks and dissent may have been unrealistic; a sensational angle that ignored the fact that there was a strong collective need to push the deal through. Indeed it can be argued that one effect of Trudeau's harsh attack was that it made it less likely that any of the first ministers would break ranks and admit that they had made a mistake.

The Langevin Block meeting was covered extensively. *The National* of 3 June carried four reports; one, on the comments of the participants as they emerged from the meeting, a second on Mulroney and Turner's reactions, the third described details of the all-night session stressing that negotiations had come close to collapse on several occasions, and the fourth was a conversation between Nash and Halton on the significance of the Accord. The Nash-Halton conversation was another opportunity to explain what was in the Accord and the vision of Canada that it contained. Again the opportunity was not seized. In responding to a question about whether the Accord would weaken the federal government, the central question for most of the Accord's critics, Halton could only muster this explanation,

> Certainly, the deal marks a tremendous departure from the old approach to federalism based on the assumption of conflict between Ottawa and the provinces, and between the provinces themselves. This approach is based very much on the assumption that you can build national unity through consensus and cooperation.

Halton would not elaborate. A more ambiguous answer is difficult to imagine. Apparently a report done for later editions of *The National* by Wendy Mesley carried a more detailed description of what was in the Langevin agreement.

On 4 June, *The National* carried a long report on the agreement's immediate repercussions. Attention was riveted again on reactions within the Liberal Party and on whether a rump group had formed to oppose John Turner on the constitution. The report conveyed the sense that full-scale rebellion was not far off. By 5 June, Meech Lake had again slipped from the screen as a news item. The critical season had passed and the 1987 Constitutional Accord would not be in the news again as a major story for some time.

Some at the CBC argue that the existence of *The Journal* relieves *The National* of the obligation to explain and analyze issues. *The National* presents the news while *The Journal* digests, elaborates and delves more deeply into events and problems. In the case of Meech Lake, *The Journal's* coverage seemed little more than a continuation of the formats and assumptions presented on *The National*. During the period under study the 1987 Constitutional Accord was featured on at least three programs of *The Journal*: Trudeau's interview with Barbara Frum was the focus of one show, another program analyzed the Accord in the wake of Trudeau's entry onto the Meech Lake stage, and a debate was the centre-piece of *The Journal* the night before the fateful last round of negotiations at the Langevin Block. The most thorough analysis of the agreement to be presented on television was a half hour documentary report by Terence McKenna which was shown on the second program. McKenna explained the difficulties surrounding the recognition of Québec as a distinct society and the problems that threatened to emerge because of the weakening of the federal spending power. McKenna could not resist couching his report in the 'there are only two positions' model which is so ingrained in television journalism. McKenna observed, for instance, that there have been 'two opposing visions of Canada' although they appear in different guises; 'centralization versus decentralization, federal power versus provincial power, one Canada versus two nations and one Canada versus a community of communities.' McKenna had thus crudely taken a whole series of diverse issues and conflicts and created but two alternatives for the viewer. Trudeau's vision and Mulroney's countervision were the only choices according to McKenna. *The Journal* program which preceded the Langevin meetings featured a debate between three 'ardent supporters' and three 'convinced opponents' of the Accord. Prior to the debate there was a brief report about the main issues but its principal focus was on public reactions to the agreement. The responses of aboriginal, ethnic, civil liberties and women's groups were not canvassed. The debate which followed was quite heated with shouting and interruptions and as television it seemed to succeed. The format of course had insured confrontation. Whether viewers were better informed as a result of what amounted to a verbal wrestling match is doubtful.

Conclusion

CBC television news coverage of the Meech lake constitutional agreements was conditioned by its rigid adherence to the contemporary news format. The greatest limitation was the severe time constraint on the length of individual reports. Because of the need to collapse information into 'bite size' segments the contents of the Accord were never fully explained to the audience. Indeed, if it had not been for Pierre Trudeau's constitutional offensive, which forced the CBC to describe what was contentious about the agreement, viewers would have been left with only the vaguest notion about what were sweeping and historic constitutional changes. Another characteristic was *The National's* fixation on conflict. Since all of the first ministers and party leaders were in agreement, presenting a united front, journalists had difficulty at first finding an angle. However,the widening cracks within the Liberal Party soon satisfied this thirst with coverage of Liberal Party struggles eventually consuming almost half of all Meech Lake coverage. Trudeau's appearance was also reported as a conflict story; Trudeau, the lion in winter, challenging Mulroney's ability to govern. The substance of Trudeau's remarks were almost extraneous to the portrayal of conflict and they were not covered in great detail.

Moreover, CBC television news never went beyond the length of its own news net. That is, it was satisfied to cover the story as it was played out among the elected politicians. Ethnic, aboriginal and women's groups, being positioned outside the news net, were not covered. Meech Lake also didn't provide the high impact visuals so necessary for television news stories. While there was some dramatic footage when Mulroney received the acclaim of the House of Commons, pictures of the first ministers sitting at the negotiating table or arriving at the Langevin Block did not make for exciting viewing. Because there was agreement among the three political parties, there were no bitter exchanges during Question Period and hence attention-grabbing pictures.

Although Meech Lake fundamentally challenged the accepted constitutional arrangements and the popular view of Canadian identity, it did not have the attributes needed to make it a first rate news story from the perspective of television journalism. Coverage was sporadic, incomplete and turned overwhelmingly on the politics of the issue rather than on the content of the Accord and the possible impact on Canada's future. Meech Lake was filtered through the lens of the contemporary news frame and viewers as a result received a distorted view of what was actually taking place. Television had in its own way played a decisive role in constitution-making because it failed to prime its audience, the Canadian public, about the consequences of the Accord.

Notes

1 Peter Desbarats, *Radio and Television News: The Roles of Public and Private Broadcasters, And Some Other Critical Issues*, A report on the history, current state and future prospects of radio and television news for the Task Force on Broadcasting Policy, (February 1986) 4-5.

2 Quoted in Edward Jay Epstein, *News From Nowhere: Television and the News* (New York: Vintage 1974) 39.

3 Canadian Broadcating Corporation, *Journalistic Policy*, 3.

4 Quoted in Epstein, 40.

5 Knowlton Nash, *Prime Time at Ten* (Toronto: McClelland and Stewart 1987) 238.

6 Todd Gitlin, *The Whole World is Watching* (Berkeley: The University of California Press 1980) 6-7.

7 Ibid., 6.

8 Ibid. 7.

9 David Altheide, *Creating Reality: How TV News Distorts Events* (Beverly Hills: Sage 1976) and Austin Ranney, *Channels of Power: The Impact of Television on American Politics* (New York: Basic Books 1983).

10 Michael Schudson, 'Deadlines, Datelines and History,' in Karl Manoff and Michael Schudson, eds., *Reading the News* (New York: Pantheon 1986) 89.

11 Interview conducted 21 May, 1986.

12 Richard Ericson, Patricia Baranek and Janet Chan, *Visualizing Deviance: A Study of News Organization* (Toronto: University of Toronto Press 1987) 273.

13 Gaye Tuchman, *Making News: A Study in the Construction of Reality* (New York: The Free Press 1978) 23.

14 Herbert Gans, *Deciding What's News* (New York: Vintage 1980) 9-13.

15 Gitlin, 146.

16 Ericson, Baranek and Chan, 237.

17 Ibid., 280.

18 Gitlin, 28.

19 Interview conducted 26 January 1988.

20 See article in this volume.

Inside the News Story: Meech Lake As Viewed By An Ottawa Bureau Chief

Elly Alboim

I must confess that as the national political editor of CBC Television News, the Ottawa Bureau Chief, and as someone who lives and breathes this stuff, I couldn't figure out why you wanted me to give you my views about Meech Lake. From my perspective this particular issue has been over for months. When we look for scapegoats or as we look to assign blame for the public's illiteracy on the issue, the blame can be fairly evenly spread and obviously we accept some of it. But I must say that as the Bureau Chief of a national television organization, I'm actually quite proud of the work we did on Meech Lake and I suggest to you that maybe we're not looking at it precisely in the same terms. I'd like to take some time and backtrack a little bit on the politics leading up to the Meech Lake Accord. I just want to go back to some basics because I think they're important in setting the environment. I guess at the end of it I'm perfectly willing to talk about entertainment value and anti-intellectualism in the news. They are both obviously very serious and substantial problems. I'm not so sure, however, that they apply to our handling of the Meech Lake issue.

Let me first establish a little bit of my bona fides on this. I've got, obviously, no academic credentials to discuss the content of Meech Lake but like many self-taught convicts, I've done hard time. I have been responsible for the coverage of every First Ministers' Conference on the Constitution since 1977. By my count that is somewhere in the neighbourhood of 23 federal-provincial conferences. I have been briefed and buffeted and stung by virtually every expert in the country one way or the other on the various issues. I am one of the few journalists who understand the difference between sections 40, 41 and 42 in the old constitution and now know what section 42 is in the new one. I have a fair understanding of the detail. Let me establish what I believe this latest round of constitution-making was about.

This was a highly political and highly cynical exercise that had very, very little to do with the re-constitutionalizing of Canada. It had very, very little to do with the final content of the document. The motivations were clear from the outset. Brian Mulroney needed, for his own purposes, to establish that he could do in Quebec what Pierre Trudeau could not. That was, to my mind, the sole motivation for the federal initiative. I have no illusion that there was any vision of Canada, or any deeply felt sense of loss about Quebec not signing the constitutional agreement in '82. I think that we were engaged in a highly political and partisan exercise by the Prime Minister. I think the motivations of many of the anglo-premiers were equally clear. They were dragged into a process that they did not want to participate in. They were blackmailed into a process they had difficulty staying out of and they were determined to capture as much as they could in exchange for their acceptance. There was no selflessness, the premiers walked in to it with an agenda, a very clear one and they knew what they could get and they got it. This wasn't a nation-building exercise.

If there is a failure on the part of the media, it was a failure to concentrate on the long term consequences that the Accord might bring. The national press corps regarded this as a political exercise and we brought to that reporting a fair amount of sophistication about the political process. Where we may, and I repeat, may, have lost the handle on this thing is that once the political exercise was over, many of us lost sight of the fact that there was a fundamental realignment of the country. We proceeded to cover the exercise as a continuing political management exercise where the first ministers, realizing the fragility of the Accord, rushed to nail it down because of the clearly articulated fear that any delay would mean its destruction. The view was that organized interest groups and groups of concerned citizens, given enough time, would tear the thing apart. Don't be under any illusions that they don't know what they did. They do. Don't be under any illusions that they don't understand the difficulty. They do. They entered into a political compromise, understanding its fragility very well, and through two major acts of will, pushed it through. We, as political journalists, were watching a naked exercise of power and were attracted to the reportage of the exercise of power more than we were attracted to covering some of the substance of the accord. Now we may be faulted but we made a conscious choice. This was not a question of entertainment value or the lack of patience with the political process.

I covered the constitutional exercise between 1978 and 1982 through hours of television. The day of the Supreme Court ruling on October 28, 1981 we linked South Korea, every provincial premier, the Supreme Court, and we did six hours of live television with not a moving picture in it. There are times, not many, but there are times when journalists in Canada understand that certain stories transcend commercial and audience considerations and they proceed with them. And they proceed to do them as best they can. I think we understood after the signature of this accord what we were dealing with, then made a series of conscious decisions on how to proceed.

Let me remind you of the context under which we as journalists were operating. At the time we had a government battered and on the defensive. Its opinion poll standing was lower than any government had ever reached in Canadian history and it was in free fall. We had just emerged from the Oerlikon affair, we had lost our sixth cabinet minister and the free trade negotiations were at best uncertain. Media organizations in this country smelled blood in a way that we have never smelled blood before. Some thought that we were in a situation similar to the American press in the early days of Watergate. We were focussed on the extraordinary story of what appeared to be the collapse of the government with the largest mandate in Canadian history. Meanwhile, what was going on was a fairly quiet and arcane discussion about constitutional renewal that, in our terms, had no focus. Remember what the genesis of this was. Robert Bourassa, in his now famous Mont Bleu pronouncement, came up with a five point program, his bottom lines for renegotiating the constitution. At the same time the Liberal party was torn asunder by an argument between its federal wing in Quebec and the national party on the appropriate response to Bourassa. In the fairly dramatic February policy conference that party sawed off its position on Quebec, short of Bourassa's, because Turner could not swallow the issue of federal spending power. Remember he had reached a decision to have five years' worth of constitutional conferences to examine the federal power and he had an alternative to the distinct society.

The premiers, meanwhile, had met in Edmonton at the annual premiers' meeting and had agreed in the Edmonton Accord to deal with Quebec and Quebec alone in round one. Mulroney had set off a process using Lowell Murray, the Minister of Federal-Provincial Relations, and Norman Spector, the Secretary to Cabinet for Federal-Provincial Relations, sending them around the country in a fourteen-month canvas using the Bourassa principles to establish what the parameters of compromise might be. At the same time, Gilles Remillard, Quebec's Intergovernmental Affairs Minister, was travelling around the country, on behalf of Bourassa, doing exactly the same thing. Both were operating under the same thesis: no first ministers' meeting unless there's a probability of success. There was almost no public discussion of these developments because they all agreed that the issue was too fragile, divisions in the country were still too fresh, the post-referendum survival syndrome was that nobody wanted a public discussion of Quebec's demands. They wanted to put it together quietly and present it as a fait accompli so that the country would not have to go through another divisive public debate on constitutional re-arrangement. That's not a media decision, that was a political decision. They deliberately withheld briefing, comment and answers to questions about this process. The only media tracking it in any depth were the Quebec media, for obvious reasons, and they encountered an enormous amount of difficulty. There has very seldom been an on-going public policy process that was as tightly controlled as this one was for fourteen months. We were obviously substantially distracted by the issues I discussed, Oerlikon, free trade, tax reform and everything else. Individually, all the premiers were convinced that they could not afford to raise expectations, the consequence of failure would be extremely damaging both to Bourassa and to the country. So they proceeded with this secret process.

Now, the process did not escape the press gallery but there was a degree of cynicism abroad in the gallery about the process. On Mulroney's side, we understood his need to do what Trudeau hadn't done. But remember his constitutional history: when asked in the 1984 campaign about his constitutional agenda, his response was, you don't write constitutions in the back of pick-up trucks. Three days later he wrote his constitutional proposals on the back of an air-sickness bag on a plane and listed ten points that formed the basis of a speech in Sept Iles about his vision of constitutional reform. *Where I Stand*, the collection of Brian Mulroney's policy positions says nothing about constitutional reform.

Similarly, there was a feeling among Quebec-based journalists that Bourassa was on a double track and would ultimately be as satisfied with a failure as a success; that Bourassa would have been as happy to say Canada is not ready to accept us, than to walk into yet another First Minister's Conference as he did in 1971, and have to pull the plug once again. The collective wisdom of the gallery and the Quebec press was that this deal was virtually undoable. We had another small problem, not insignificant, which was that after the 1984 election we had substantial turnover in the Ottawa Press Gallery. Because press gallery membership rotates between elections, many of us had come for the 1979 and 1980 elections, stayed into the referendum, for the National Energy Program and then the constitutional re-arrangement. None of the news organizations then wanted to move their journalists out because of the continuing political tension. A lot of people lasted through the 1984 election and then the big turn of the wheel came in the Fall of '84 when the gallery turnover rate was somewhere around sixty percent as people went off to other assignments. So we had a group of reporters who had little constitutional background.

Alright, so we got to Meech Lake on April 30th, on a very cold night. It was very difficult physically – we were segregated by about a mile from the main building. We were allowed to stand outside it, if we wanted to endure the walk over and the rain. We could walk around the building, signalling to people through the windows to come and talk to us. Officials who weren't allowed in the actual room where the negotiations were taking place, came out and told us that they didn't know anything. But, we were able to patch together bits and pieces, not very much. We had very little understanding of the issues at play and in fact, some of the elements in the final accord were never on the table going in. That included the ultimate compromises on Senate and Supreme Court nominations. Bourassa talked about them in vague terms but the freezing of nominations, the freezing of appointments, the provincial nomination question was arrived at right at the table.

They signed their deal, the flashbulbs started going off on the third floor, and they all had champagne glasses in their hands when they called the media in. We all trouped in with our cameras at about 11:00 that night Eastern Time. They grouped us into a set piece, all the first ministers standing in a semi-circle around the Prime Minister – you all remember the image – with glasses of champagne in their hands. The Prime Minister carefully walked around that semi-circle, shook hands and they all patted him on the back. He made a statement. Peterson and Bourassa made statements. There were a variety of interviews. But unfortunately, they said, we have no detailed document for you; it's not ready. We'll tell you tomorrow morning what's in the deal. They tried to reduce us that night to reporting the hand-shaking, the historic achievement of re-introducing Quebec to the Constitution, on the basis of giving us only the broadest of outlines. This was deliberate; the document was ready, the paper existed. After all, it is hard to do a deal when you're not working with drafts. Word processors and xerox machines were all up there in Wilson House. The decision to manage this process without a paper trail is an astonishing public policy decision. It is manipulative and cynical, and it began that night. Luckily some of us have sources within provincial delegations as a result of covering First Ministers' Conferences. We were able to piece together things during the day and that night on *The National*, we did 15 minutes, to this time zone, with all the details of the accord. The next morning, we arrived downtown for a news briefing on the deal. It was one of the roughest news briefings I've ever been to. Government officials were not prepared to deal with the traffic in detail. We ended up with a division within the gallery where the old folks, like me, immediately had our hackles raised about the re-ordering of federal-provincial power, particularly on spending power. Those of us who had watched the process now suspected that we had a new national cabinet made up of the First Ministers that had as much clout as the current cabinet. We understood there was a new dynamic in federal-provincial relations, the Prime Minister had created an alternate level of government. We were trying to deal with a core reality which we believed but which the federal government would not admit to. The French media immediately assessed the deal as historic and significant and began actively harassing and pursuing their English confrères at the news conference for negativism and destructive comment. There also seemed to be a generation gap. Younger anglo reporters thought that some of the older reporters were clinging to the Trudeau vision of Canada and not understanding that that world had been passed by. The gallery was divided on the content of the deal, both generationally and linguistically.

   We were confronted with a dilemma. What we had was a very technical and complex document, and little expertise to deal with it and certainly very little will to deal with it. The issues were extremely abstract. Obviously the reallocation of power, the Charter limitations, and the implications of the distinct society had to be dealt with as did the cynicism behind the politics of the deal. For instance, the senate compromise: we had watched Don Getty walk in, demanding a Triple E Senate and come out with only a thin hope that that could now be achieved. People began bemoaning the fact that you required unanimity to amend the Senate when we all knew that because of its special relationship and section 92, Quebec had a veto over Senate reform anyway. And Quebec, in fact, had played that card refusing to play on senate reform if the West did not play on distinct society. Political cynicism somehow become transmuted into a joyous Canadian celebration of the reintegration of the country.

   So we concentrated on process because we had difficulty with detail in the first early days. There was substantial concern about how you write a constitution in the middle of the night among exhausted people when the Prime Minister insists that no technically competent person be allowed in the room for the negotiations. How does that work? What was the linkage to other goodies? What did the billion dollar grain payout have to do with Grant Devine's acceptance of the deal? I don't want to be too cynical but journalists had questions about those kind of linkages. We, ourselves, misunderstood Mulroney's style of negotiation. We misunderstood what his bottom lines were. Most participants said the national argument was carried by three premiers, Pawley, Peterson and Ghiz. It was not carried by Mulroney.

When confronted with that sort of reality plus a clear understanding of the fragility of the deal and the rush to text and passage, we began a search for dissent. Not because we need drama and conflict though, nobody is going to be upset when it develops. And sure if you have people yelling at each other, you've got a better story. At a certain point, we had a whole group of people without any particular expertise in constitutional law being confronted with the eleven first ministers of the country plus the most senior government officials, all saying, we did a hell of a job. So you look for someone who will question the deal. I didn't find anybody, except for Jeffrey Simpson, for about a week. I kept pounding it with my Toronto desk and they kept saying what is your problem, we don't hear any dissent. Everybody is telling us this is a good deal. We went to Chrétien, we went to Romanow. We looked for constitutional experts. I looked around the country, searching for people who were going to say in that first week or two, boy, there's something wrong here. But what I got was, 'got to wait for text, not quite sure,' there may be lots of movement between the political accord and legal language. 'Okay,' I said, 'but time is running out.' The Trudeau watch started. Every day we sent a reporter down to Trudeau's office. Will he do it today? Because most of us knew, instinctively having covered him for ten years, exactly what his problems would have been, line by line in the text. It was no secret. People close to him said 'well, you know, he's not ready yet, he's working on it, maybe he will, maybe he won't. He really wants Chrétien to do it. Chrétien won't do it.' Finally, his response appeared in *Le Devoir* and the *Toronto Star*. But remember it appeared only a week or two before the Langevin meeting.

The Liberal caucus was horribly divided. But only Don Johnston was willing to dissent publicly. Don Johnston is an anglo-Quebecer. It is very hard to have an anglo-Quebecer carry the mail against Quebec's claim to be a distinct society. It is very hard to give him a whole lot of credibility. Turner had an out, a very clear one: 'my party has articulated what its view on constitutional reform is and this is not it.' But he rushed across the aisle the next morning to shake Mulroney's hand. Ed Broadbent rushed across the aisle to shake Mulroney's hand. As you all know, and I don't have to belabor the issue, there is not a political party that will take on a region of this country anymore on any single issue. It doesn't matter what the issue is. They will not attack the peculiar awarding to Quebec of a contract on the CF-18. They will not attack British Columbia or the federal government for a peculiar deal to prop up the Bank of B.C.. They will not attack a billion dollar grain payment that went to farmers who didn't need it and had no criteria for deciding who did. They will not attack any issue that is regionally based for fear of losing votes. The poverty of national leadership has a lot to do with the playing down of Meech Lake. And if you don't think that John Turner or Ed Broadbent have substantial reservations about Meech Lake, you're kidding yourself. I went to Stephen Langdon and I scrummed him for 15 minutes, Steven Langdon, the NDP representative from Windsor. And Steven Langdon started creating a thesis about how the CCF had begun moving to a vision of a decentralized country and that this was consistent with the intentions of the Regina Manifest. As he told this to me, I looked at him and I said, 'What are you doing?' And he says, 'That's the way it's playing down and I'm not saying anything else.'

At a certain point, the media have to reflect reality. We have no special role. We're unaccountable. Nobody has elected us. Nobody gives us any sort of special responsibility to go tilting at windmills when the collective leadership of this country is saying something has been done and it's okay. Despite all that, I must say, we tried our best. We tried our best not to tear it down but at least to illuminate it.

When dissent crystallized, it crystallized around Trudeau. There were other strains as well. *The Journal*, which some of you may or may not remember, did a magnificent week on Meech Lake. They had a forty minute detailed documentary, item by item, issue by issue with virtually every constitutional expert who would come forward. They staged a one hour debate between three leading proponents and three leading opponents. *The Journal*, almost by itself, carried the national debate into the Langevin block. *The National* devoted a good deal of its time for close to a month on the discussion of Meech Lake – political process and content though, I must say, much more on political process.

When opposition began crystallizing, it crystallized, I think reasonably well, around three issues: the distinct society, on spending powers, and on human rights issues. To my complete lack of comprehension, the women's rights issue was not extant in that month of May, not in the way that multi-culturalism was because the Italian community in Toronto was greatly disturbed, and the way Aboriginal rights were. The women's issue that we all expected to surface very quickly, really didn't surface until summer. The premiers themselves, as they began to get pushed around, both in reaction to Trudeau, and in reaction to the beginnings of the debate on human rights and spending powers, suddenly began to reinterpret the Meech Lake agreement. And as you remember, in that final week before the Langevin meeting, Mulroney had a horrible problem with Pawley, Peterson and Bourassa all saying diametrically opposed things on the interpretation of the Meech Lake document. They walked into Langevin in near disarray because the public pronouncements were opposed to each other, particularly, the discussion on whether the Accord should refer to national standards or national objectives. They finally saved it when Ed Broadbent in a secret phone call to Mulroney said that Howard Pawley would go with the insertion of the word 'the' before national objective because when you say 'the' national objective, you're clarifying 'the' national objective, not an abstract national objective. But Broadbent was acting as an intermediary with Pawley; Turner was dealing with Peterson. They realized they had a problem with different interpretations when they walked into Langevin for another all night session.

At one point during the all night vigil, there was a sense among the federal delegation that the deal could not hold together. In fact they were telling us out on the sidewalks somewhere around 4:00 in the morning that they thought it was just about over. Then came the acceptance of the non-derogation clauses for aboriginals and multicultural groups by Bourassa and the acceptance by Peterson of the distinct society in return for the non-derogation clauses. Pawley agreed to final wording on 'the' national objective. But don't forget that once again at Langevin, not a single technical advisor from the provinces was allowed in that room, at any point. Every time they broke for coffee, each premier would go to consult with his experts. Then they would go back in the room. Then all the experts would suddenly get together to try and find out what the other positions were. They tried to work out a consensus among themselves so when their guys came out the next time they could kind of massage their backs like boxers, and send them back in with the right line. The only point when they had experts in the room was in the first two and half hours or so. There are wonderful stories of premiers who shall be un-named, coming out and talking to their handlers and repeating texts 180 degrees from what reality was on the table, mixing up clauses and numbers, not understanding the relationships. It really was very, very difficult.

Anyway, they got their deal and then you know what they did? They spent twenty-five minutes working out the communications lines so they would all say exactly the same three phrases when they walked out the door, because they knew about the cacophony going in. When they came out, all repeating the same phrases the reporters knew that the deal had been salvaged. We knew that anybody objecting to the new constitutional order had gotten all they were going to get. When the eleven first ministers signed the second time in blood, they were not going to admit of error or amendment for fear of looking silly. They worked out their lines, they worked out their defenses and they walked out of that room. And no matter how much distaste anybody felt, that was the political reality. If you didn't get to them in that first month, you weren't going to get to them ever. They knew it and Norman Spector knew it and every competent federal-provincial relations office official in any province knew it. The time for change was the four week period between Meech and Langevin. After that, two signatures on the same document by the same eleven people would require dynamite to blow apart.

The journalistic community was not a player in the drama. When the political leadership of this country has made that kind of a commitment and expressed that kind of a will twice, the media has little recourse. We turned our attention to the extra-parliamentary opposition. Extra-parliamentary opposition had considerable influence in 1981 and 1982 when the process was more open to change and amendment. In this case, there was an attempt by the prime minister to get each premier to commit that he would not have parliamentary hearings, that the only parliamentary hearings would be national parliamentary hearings in the middle of the summer. That didn't fly. We then walked out of Meech Lake knowing, as the whole world knew, that we were going to have parliamentary hearings in the dead of summer and if extra parliamentary opposition was to form, that's when it had to form. Now I must say to their credit, the women, the anglo-women of Canada, came within two days of getting an amendment. I don't think people understand that. They had Peterson on the ropes in the middle of the Ontario election campaign and he was just about done. And they were working on the documentation to have Peterson break with the Accord because he didn't think he could sustain the pressure. And then there was a phone call to Quebec asking for help. There's a dispute about this and I must say that this version has been denied, but there's a suspicion Ontario asked for help. Quebec applied pressure and the Quebec women broke with their anglo counterparts. I'm not saying that they broke illicitly. But it did give Peterson an out. Once that one fell apart, there was literally no political reason for the national media to be pursuing this process because what we were covering was a cynical political exercise that was pre-determined.

What I am interested in is the effect of this document on the future of the country. While the purpose of journalism in a case like this is to explain implications, to explain net effect, after that's done we know that this process is not going to be altered, it's going ahead. To continually pound on the potential difficulties of some of these clauses is not relevant to most of our audiences. They don't understand why we're doing it. There's very little we can do about it and we have to, at a certain point, get on with business. Remember, while the parliamentary committee was sitting and going through its choreographed hearings, we had three federal byelections in which Mulroney and Turner did battle, we had Turner about to lose his leadership, or so it looked like at the time, and we had the free trade deal about to sputter to an end from all we saw. When you start looking at the relative weight of importance of a process that is politically over, albeit it tremendously important and three that are ongoing that may have tremendous effect, there's no choice. We go with the flow. My feeling is that there is tremendous anger and frustration among many groups about the closed nature of a political process that should not have been closed; about the imposition of a dramatic turn in Canadian history, without consultation. I understand that anger and frustration, but I'm not sure it's the media's fault. I'm not sure that we didn't try our best during that period of time when it was crucial to explain it. The extra-parliamentary opposition did not understand the urgency. And it did not understand the cynicism of the political process at work. There are points of attack, but whether it can be stopped, I don't know. But ultimately if the media is confronted with a lonely crusade on technical and complex issues with and knowledge that there's little chance of it being changed or amended, at a certain point it gives up. Media can only reflect the reality that most Canadians are accepting and dealing with. I have no responsibility for social change. I'm not a social engineer. I report as best I can. And, if the opposition can't get it together and the political leadership unites for whatever cynical reasons and we report the cynicism as well as we can, at a certain point the game is played. That is a problem that all of us now share because of the dynamic of this process. But it's not necessarily journalism's failure.

Fractured Mirror:
The Importance of Region and Personalities in English Language Newspaper Coverage of Meech Lake

Lorry Felske

The agreement reached by the Prime Minister and the Premiers in the six weeks following their meeting at Meech Lake presented several challenges to the news media. As former Premier Thatcher of Saskatchewan once noted, most people rank their interest in constitutional change at 101 on a list of 100. Newspapers responded by treating this important story in terms of regional concerns and the personalities involved.

English language newspaper coverage was pushed in these directions by a number of basic considerations. First of all the agreement was complex and explanations of it had to compete with news stories pandering to broader interests. During the period from the Meech Lake to Langevin meetings, April 30th to June 3rd, 1987, the constitutional story was often elbowed aside by Stanley Cup playoffs, and American dramas such as Irangate, and Gary Hart's confessions about Donna Rice. A more legitimately important issue, free trade negotiations, also took headline coverage away from Meech Lake debate.[1]

Also presenting problems for media coverage were the indefinite focal points of the story. Between Meech Lake and Langevin the participants shifted, reinforced and elaborated their positions. Explaining the nuances of such posturing was a difficult task for any journalist. Finally, the lack of visual material posed another major difficulty with the story, especially for television coverage. Scenes of Mulroney and the premiers arriving and departing from conference locales, or the equally thrilling spectacle of politicians shaking hands, were poor aids in explaining the evolution of complex issues over these weeks. As the *Halifax-Chronicle Herald* noted '...constitution-making is more than a display of political goodwill and a photo opportunity.'[2]

These characteristics, difficult to convey on radio and especially television, were not nearly so difficult for newspapers. Newspapers are better able to handle the tough social and economic questions and legal complexities that accompany constitutional change. In Canada, newspapers have held a special place with respect to constitutional reform. In the achievement of Confederation itself, P.B. Waite gave newspapers of the day a 'vital' place in its achievement.[3] As well, because Confederation, the Constitutional Act of 1982, and the Meech Lake Accord have all occurred behind closed doors, allowing little direct public observation or input, the Canadian press has had an added responsibility to inform and comment. For these reasons then, it is not surprising that the Meech Lake accord received significant coverage in Canadian newspapers. It is not surprising as well that the most strident critics of Meech Lake, Pierre Trudeau and Donald Johnston, relied on the press to publicize their complaints.[4]

Initial Reactions to the Accord

What was surprising about the English language newspaper coverage of the 1987 constitutional accord was the extent to which the Meech Lake agreement caught most editors and reporters off guard. Despite the fact that such issues might carry a higher level of importance among print journalists than in other types of media, success was not widely expected or predicted. Coverage in the week preceding the Meech Lake meeting was minimal[5] and many observers doubted the importance of it. The previous failure to resolve the more specific issue of aboriginal self-government encouraged that skepticism.[6] As well, the August 1986 premiers meeting in Edmonton had given that impression, setting Quebec as the principle topic and agreeing to start informal discussions.[7] As a result, many newspapers like the *Globe and Mail* treated the meeting at Meech Lake as preliminary. Its purpose, the *Globe* believed, was to set the ground rules for future discussion that would be more firmly targeted on specific proposals.[8] There were, however, other newspapers more clearly aware that a definite agenda for this meeting had emerged. The *Montreal Gazette*, for example, in its pre-Meech editorial, went through most of the meeting items in detail displaying a strong sense of what was to be important in the upcoming discussions.[9]

This relatively vague sense of Meech Lake's importance had immediate consequences for the manner in which the agreement was first reported by the nation's press. Taken by surprise most newspapers first reacted positively. On the west coast the *Vancouver Sun* commented that 'the language of the Meech Lake Accord is a pretty fine piece of work whoever wrote it.'[10] In western Canada the *Calgary Herald* pronounced that 'fundamental principles of equality have been accepted....'[11] The *Winnipeg Free Press* was more cautious. They had reservations about the possibility of future Senate reform being blocked by the need for unanimous consent. Still, the *Free Press* applauded the clauses concerning immigration and the ability of provinces to opt out of future federal programs in provincial jurisdiction. Even the distinct society clause got their approval. The *Free Press* felt it was 'wordy, convoluted and hedged' yet it was '...likely to do no harm and if it makes Quebec feel more secure, may do some good.'[12]

In Atlantic Canada a positive tone was also the order of the day. The *Halifax-Chronicle Herald* was joyous in its coverage, echoing the 'emotional' experience of reaching accord felt by Nova Scotia's Premier Buchanan.[13] The *Chronicle-Herald* editorial pronounced 'by George and by Jacques, they got it...they must have felt something like Eliza Doolittle finally mastering 'the rain in Spain'.'[14] The fact that Robert Stanfield backed the accord also received attention in their columns.[15] In central Canada, the *Montreal Gazette*, voice of 'English speaking Canada...present in Quebec,' was very favourable, but perhaps somewhat more cautious as well. Like the *Winnipeg Free Press*, the *Gazette* was generally in support, calling the Meech agreement a 'hard-won victory' with 'marvellous points' and 'historic breakthroughs.' There was, however, for the *Gazette*, a 'bitter pill,' an 'ugly aspect' as well – the opting out clause. To the editorial minds of the *Gazette*, this was an opportunity for future separatists to travel the road away from Canada. As such, deletion or repair of the clause was demanded in the days before formal agreement occurred.[16] In Ontario the *Globe and Mail* confirmed that Mulroney had 'won...praise from political opponents as well as supporters.'[17]

The positive first response to the Meech Lake accord came partly from this sudden and unexpected success. But newspaper support also reflected more deeply held beliefs in Canadian society. To a degree, applause for Meech Lake was recognition of agreement achieved in a divided country. Much of the newspaper comment across Canada supported the Meech Lake Accord because it was just that, an accord, because compromises had been hammered out and accepted. In the west, this was the yardstick by which the *Winnipeg Free Press* suggested the agreement be judged. The *Free Press* counselled that 'Canadians should not simply measure each element of the accord against what they consider to be ideal. They must determine whether the accord as a whole represents a compromise which serves the interests of Canada as a whole.'[18] From Calgary came the same emphasis on the Meech Lake agreement as a solution framed for the practical constraints of the Canadian situation. It was, the *Calgary Herald* claimed, '...the best we can get in this nation so long and so seriously divided by language, geography and economic imperatives.'[19] In the *Montreal Gazette* a similar theme prevailed. In a nation molded by responses to practical problems, the solutions had to be judged on their practicality. Agreement between federal and provincial governments on constitutional reform was trying to 'square Canada's eternal circle'[20] and the '...mere fact of a consensus is precious and welcome.'[21]

Regional Aspects of Newspaper Coverage

Following this initial wave of support, newspapers across the country settled into more precise and critical consideration of the Meech Lake agreement. The Meech proposal of perpetual conferences on the economy and constitutional reform was criticized by the *Vancouver Sun* as '...the enshrinement of the inalienable Canadian right to talk forever about ourselves.'[22] As the scrutiny of the Meech Lake agreement intensified, it also became clear that criticisms mirrored the regional priorities of the newspaper's location. This influence on the Canadian press has been the '...most salient characteristic of Canadian journalism' according to George D. Kerr. Although he argues that newspapers are national in their 'technological and institutional linkages,' Kerr contends that their 'essentially parochial nature' has not been destroyed.[23] A clear example of this influence occurred in the *Halifax Chronicle-Herald*. After three days on the paper's front page, the Meech Lake agreement was displaced by stories about toxic gas emissions at a local hospital, the fate of the Hawker Siddeley rail car plant, a locally missing person, the decline of the number of Nova Scotia farms, the possible investment of a Colorado mining company, and an international story, Irangate.[24]

In western Canadian newspapers the favourite theme was the increased power of the provinces. In this respect the underlying objective was one of attaining 'regional justice' in Confederation, an idea that Paul Rutherford found basic to the attitudes of western newspapers in the late 19th century.[25]

Western newspapers were specifically concerned with the question of equality of provincial influence in the Senate. A *Calgary Herald* editorial on the eve of the conference attested to its importance. Although acknowledging that this was the Quebec round of negotiations, the editorial criticized Joe Clark for suggesting that Quebec's demands and Senate reform could be easily disconnected. To the *Herald* these issues might start from different directions but their destinations were similar and it was in Clark's best interests to remember this point.[26] For the *Vancouver Sun* provincial input into the choice of Senators meant that it would '...cease to be a green pasture for Ottawa hacks and cronies.'[27] Other papers, however, pursued the more serious question of whether unanimous consent had derailed Senate reform forever.[28] The *Calgary Herald* entertained this thought with coverage of MP David Kilgour's criticisms of Conservative Senate leader Lowell Murray. Kilgour accused Murray of being '...in charge of a deal to keep him and his colleagues on the gravy train for 30 years.'[29]

Kilgour's criticisms of the Meech agreement also contained another reservation: the question of haste. More thought should be devoted to the question of Senate reform, Kilgour thought, as 'constitutions are not supposed to be done like a McDonald's hamburger.'[30] This apprehension concerning the speed of the agreement was found throughout western Canada.[31] Even the *Winnipeg Free Press* which gave strong support to many aspects of the Meech Lake Accord expressed frustration at the fast paced approval agenda. That speed made the document '...about as inspiring as the owner's manual for a washing machine.'[32] Another editorial outburst by the consistently supportive *Free Press* lamented that 'Anyone who tries to write a constitution at five o'clock in the morning ought to have his head examined. Any country which has to live with a constitution that has been patched together in a 24-hour marathon session has every reason to be worried.'[33]

In the Atlantic provinces the same shift occurred from blanket approval to specific criticisms and concern for the approval process. Although the *Halifax Chronicle-Herald* always worried that 'too much tossing of the Meech Lake salad may spoil the constitutional dinner party,'[34] it advised further reflection before adoption. One specific source of doubt for the *Chronicle-Herald* was the future of the fishery. Transferring fisheries control from Ottawa to the provinces was not viewed as an easy task. Disagreements between the fishermen of each province were predicted. The *Herald* pointed out that Nova Scotian fishermen presently worked in waters that would be considered under Newfoundland's control in any future arrangement. Reminding readers of former Primer Minister Trudeau's observation that 'fish swim,' the *Chronicle* felt provincial jurisdiction was doomed to unsolvable complications.[35]

Also of concern to the *Chronicle-Herald* was the opting out clause. Caution here came from the fiscal inability of smaller provinces to explore alternatives to federal initiatives. Smaller provinces would have fewer resources to accomplish the same task of reevaluation and the creation of provincial versions. Thus the *Chronicle* covered the objections to the opting out clause voiced by Nova Scotia Conservative MP Pat Nowlan and also Manitoba Premier Howard Pawley.[36]

In western Canada the opting out clause was of most concern to the *Winnipeg Free Press*, but it was more preoccupied with its defense than with its weaknesses. For the *Free Press* the opting out clause meant that negotiations would have to occur between Ottawa and the provinces. Institutionalizing negotiations promised better federal-provincial relations in the future, a new cooperative spirit.[37] The *Free Press* also took aim at Premier Pawley for what appeared to be his waning support of the clause after Meech Lake. The *Free Press* claimed that Pawley '…tends to return from federal provincial conferences like a man coming out of a trance.'[38] The *Press* lampooned Pawley's reconsideration of the opting out clause by imagining Pawley asking himself if that had been '…me agreeing with all those Tory and Liberal and Social Credit premiers about how the constitution should be amended? Did I really go on national television to tell the country what a splendid job the prime minister had done?'[39] The *Free Press* reassured Pawley that it had, in fact, been him, but he could relax, the opting out clause did not need further refinement.

Cautiously viewed in Halifax, strongly supported in Winnipeg, the opting out clause was subjected to serious doubts by the *Montreal Gazette*. From that paper's perspective the opting out clause was deficient in one important respect. It allowed the provinces too much leeway. In Quebec that meant more power for a future separatist government.[40] In addition to that concern, the *Gazette* also hammered at another major flaw in the Meech agreement: weak protections for linguistic minorities. To the *Gazette* this issue was of prime concern. Would the agreement abandon linguistic minorities in other parts of the country? Would the distinct society clause mean Quebec was a French only province? These questions appeared repeatedly in the *Gazette*'s news and editorial columns.[41]

For the *Globe and Mail* the central issue was Quebec. Unlike most of the other English language newspapers in the country, the *Globe* focussed most heavily on meeting Quebec's demands and its satisfaction with the agreement. One indication of that emphasis in their coverage came just before the Meech Lake conference in an editorial critical of Alberta premier Don Getty. Getty's suggestion that Senate reform also be discussed at Meech was labelled as 'crass' by the *Globe and Mail*. The conference was to be about Quebec and focussed on this issue alone. *Globe and Mail* coverage showed little appreciation of the idea that Quebec's position in the constitution affected everyone's position, and that this would ultimately be reflected in the Senate.[42]

Following Meech Lake, the *Globe and Mail* maintained a strong focus on Quebec. So strong was their support for the agreement and for Quebec's concerns that it even threatened to have the reverse affect. Daniel Latouche, a Quebec political scientist, wondered 'How can any agreement supported by the (Toronto) *Globe and Mail* and the Crediste government of British Columbia be any good for Quebec?'[43] The *Globe and Mail* was undaunted by such fears. The reality behind this *Globe* position was simply that no Ontario government would move on other constitutional reform without Quebec's cooperation. The risk of proceeding without Quebec, alienating French speaking Canadians throughout the country, and especially in Ontario, was not worth the political damage an Ontario government would suffer. As a result, the *Globe and Mail*'s editorial offerings presented a calm assessment of the distinct society clause. Fears of 'special status' were 'overblown.'[44] The recognition of Quebec as a distinct society was nothing more than the restatement of 'a germane historical truth.'[45] The *Globe*'s contentment with the distinct society clause was exemplified by an editorial comparing the Meech Lake agreement to Beethoven's Brandenburg Concertos – not a comparison that pops quickly to mind. The editorial mused that 'Oh, there are questions about Quebec's legal status as a distinct society, but other provisions in the Constitution would appear to hold their own.'[46]

Through its editorials and through extensive coverage of the hearings before the Quebec Legislative Assembly on the accord, the *Globe* stuck to Quebec's demands as the most crucial issue. Variety in *Globe* coverage came mainly from influential columnist, Jeffrey Simpson.[47] He viewed the removal of Senate appointments from Prime Ministerial hands as a significant loss of flexibility for that office. Gone would be a way of freeing House of Commons seats for byelections, gone would be the chance to signal minorities of their importance by way of Senate appointments, and gone would be the opportunity to cause problems for other parties by elevating their shining stars to the higher chamber.[48] In his summation of Meech Lake's significance, Simpson was even more perceptive:

> The consequences are a pleased Prime Minister, a compliant Quebec, delighted provinces, federal opposition parties scared stiff of losing support in Quebec by opposing the deal, and in all probability a more difficult federation to manage in the years ahead.[49]

From the opening round of praise and then through subsequent criticisms of specific elements of the Accord, newspaper coverage molded itself to the priorities important to its readership. Although that served the interests of local patrons, such coverage was unbalanced and this meant that some equally important issues were ignored. Quebec should have received more attention in the west and the Atlantic provinces. Senate and other reforms deserved more treatment in Ontario. And overall, concerns about the Yukon and the Northwest Territories deserved more attention everywhere in the country than they received.[50] For the most part Canada's newspapers were as closed to northern concerns as had been the doors of the Meech Lake cabins to the representatives of those regions. That neglect by the rest of the country was tersely noted in the *Whitehorse Star* with the observation that 'While premiers patted themselves on the back Wednesday and said it was a great day for Canada, Yukoners mourned.'[51] Ironically, while most newspapers argued that Meech Lake reflected a growing sympathy for regionalism in Canada, they daily demonstrated the reverse with their sparse coverage of the North.

Personalities as Editorial Focus

What was also surprising about newspaper treatment of Meech Lake was the extent to which coverage focussed on the personalities of those involved. Disproportionate coverage was given to conflicts among political leaders and the effects of Meech Lake on their political prospects. Across the country the most consistently covered episode was John Turner's difficulties in maintaining control over the Liberal Party. Highlighting that struggle was the resignation of Don Johnston from Turner's shadow cabinet. Johnston's withdrawal and his negative comments about the Meech Lake Accord drew extensive newspaper coverage[52] due in part to his influence in the Liberal Party and his previous ties to Trudeau, and partly from the colourful and nasty comments Johnston received from his own party members. By his fellow Liberal MPs from Quebec, Johnston was labelled as a 'Westmount Rhodesian' by André Ouellet,[53] a representative of 'English speaking Quebec...of the 19th century' by Raymond Garneau,[54] and as someone with the '...perception of a sales lady at Eaton's 10 years ago...' by Jean Lapierre.[55]

Although most newspapers simply carried reports of these comments, two newspapers came to Johnston's defense. The *Montreal Gazette*, understandably, voice of English speaking Quebec, was one of those defenders. The *Gazette* blasted these 'kneejerk' insults hurled at Johnston by the 'bully-boy' followers of Turner.[56] The *Winnipeg Free Press* described Ouellet's comments as 'bigotry and moral terrorism.[57]

"Courtesy of The Chronicle-Herald, Halifax"

Other discontent in the Liberal Party also received significant attention. For John Turner, acceptance of the Meech Lake Accord did not become, as the *Halifax Chronicle-Herald* first thought, '...a debate mostly with himself.'[58] Instead Turner faced significant opposition in his party which was soon compounded by dissent over free trade. Newspapers focussed extensively on these problems of party unity facing Turner and the various incidents became a consistent thread throughout Meech Lake coverage. There was, for example, the firing of David Berger, the science and technology critic in the shadow cabinet, and flareups from the likes of Lloyd Axworthy, Charles Caccia, John Nunziata.[59]

Not immune from leadership questions and personality clashes was the New Democratic Party. For Ed Broadbent, however, coverage was much milder. The issue of most significance was the question of opposition to the accord by Quebec provincial party leader Jean-Paul Harney. Broadbent escaped press scrutiny with calm acceptance of the disagreement.[60] Also emerging unscathed from press interest in

leadership problems was Premier Bourassa. Most comments concerning Bourassa pictured him as a reasonable politician pursuing reasonable goals.[61] With the exception of some cartoons which depicted him
placing the interests of Quebec ahead of national interests, Bourassa
remained untouched.

Someone who sought the attention of the press and who received
enormous attention during the period from Meech Lake to Langevin
was Pierre Elliot Trudeau. Although pressed for reaction from the moment the Meech Lake meetings ended, Trudeau avoided public comment[62] until the end of May. At this time the former Prime Minister
felt compelled to present his assessment and to do it in a way that
would galvanize others into action. With the publication of his article
in the *Toronto Star* and *La Presse* on May 26th, as a precursor to radio
and television interviews,[63] Trudeau grabbed the attention of Canada's editors and reporters, and enticed them into a binge of personality analysis.

The analysis Trudeau received, however, was rarely positive. In the
Globe and Mail, Trudeau's intervention was labelled as '...predictable,
pugnacious and... sad...' and viewed as '...an ultimately baroque display of personal pique.'[64] The *Winnipeg Free Press* viewed Trudeau's
intervention as '...one-third valid criticism, one-third gross exaggeration and one-third vicious nonsense...'[65] Furthermore, the *Free Press*
added, Trudeau's use of words such as 'weakling, impotence and eu-
nuch' would give a future psycho-biographer '...fertile ground for in-
vestigation.'[66] In Vancouver, the *Sun* described Trudeau's comments
as '...biting, sharp, sarcastic, acerbic.'[67] But the editorial page of the
Calgary Herald expressed the most blistering attack on Trudeau and his
resurrected vision of country with a strong central focus. According
to the *Herald*, Trudeau '...could never see beyond his own autocratic
nose.' He had treated the west as '...an ungrateful colony...' and as
a result the '...seeds of western separatism were sown...'[68] In the news
columns of the *Herald* the impression of Trudeau was also a very negative one, presenting a collection of critical comments from across the
country. Trudeau was an out of date bully, insincere, foolish, mischie-
vous, someone obsessed with central authority, thriving on confrontation and division, and who constantly shot from the hip.[69]

Clearly the intervention into the Meech debate by Trudeau refocussed
much of the newspaper coverage into older molds. The result was an
even stronger concern with personality and leadership questions perhaps more appropriately kept at the margins of Meech Lake discussion. In contrast to the press, Prime Minister Mulroney was subdued
in his reactions to Trudeau. Mulroney merely treated his campaign as
'low level comedy'[70] and suggested that it was more of a problem for
John Turner and the unity of the Liberal Party. Mulroney did note the

fickleness of Trudeau's previous opinions by pointing out that Trudeau once criticized Lester Pearson but later came to think of him as 'the greatest thing since bottled beer.'[71] The underlying theme was that such outbursts should be expected and dismissed.

Over the course of five weeks from the late night announcement of agreement at Meech Lake to the formal signing in the early morning hours at the Langevin Block, newspapers faced the task of reporting and analyzing a major political event in Canada's history. Caught off guard by the success of the first meeting, newspapers adjusted their coverage to assume a more critical stand. Many papers focussed on issues relevant to their regions or issues involving political personalities. Western papers stressed provincial power gains through the Senate or the opting out clause, or old enemies like Trudeau. Added to these concerns in the Atlantic provinces were specific issues like the fisheries. In Montreal, the *Gazette* featured the problems of English speaking Quebec while in Toronto the *Globe and Mail* turned the spotlight on satisfying Quebec's demands. These differing concentrations were a sign of the very problem the Meech Lake accord tried to solve: the country's conflicting regional orientations. Such coverage, although useful and needed by each region, meant that other questions of substance, like the discontent in the North, were pushed far from the center of constitutional debate.

Notes

1 *The Globe and Mail*, 2 May 1987, p. A1; 4 May 1987, p. A1; 9 May 1987, p. A1; 12 May 1987, p. A1; 1 June 1987, p. A1.

2 *The Chronicle-Herald*, 29 May 1987.

3 P.B. Waite, *The Life and Times of Confederation 1864-1867* (Toronto: University of Toronto Press 1962), 17. See also Paul Rutherford, *A Victorian Authority: The Daily Press in Late Nineteenth-Century Canada* (Toronto: University of Toronto Press 1982) for a thorough discussion of the importance of newspapers in 19th century Canada.

4 Ibid., 20 May and 29 May, 1987.

5 *The Vancouver Sun*, 2 May 1987; *Calgary Herald*, 18 April 1987; *The Chronicle-Herald*, 29 April 1987.

6 *The Chronicle-Herald*, 29 April 1987.

7 *Calgary Herald*, 18 April 1987.

8 *The Globe and Mail*, 28 April 1987.

9 *The Gazette*, 30 April 1987.

10 *The Vancouver Sun*, 2 May 1987.

11 *Calgary Herald*, 2 May 1987.

12 *Winnipeg Free Press* 2 May 1987.

13 *The Chronicle-Herald*, 2 May 1987.

14 Ibid., 4 May 1987.

15 Ibid., 4 May 1987.

16 *The Gazette*, 2 May 1987.

17 *The Globe and Mail*, 2 May 1987.

18 *Winnipeg Free Press*, 25 May 1987.

19 *Calgary Herald*, 4 June 1987.

20 *The Gazette*, 2 June 1987.

21 Ibid., 2 May 1987.

22 *The Vancouver Sun*, 2 May 1987.

23 George D. Kerr, 'The Canadian Daily Newspaper: National Elements in a Local Medium,' *Canadian Review of Studies in Nationalism* (Canada) 7, No 1 (1980), 54, 56. For other studies which explore these regional influences on Canadian newspapers see Walter C. Soderlund, Ronald H. Wagenberg, E. Donald Briggs, and Ralph C. Nelson, 'Regional and Linguistic Agenda-Setting in Canada: A Study of Newspaper Coverage of Issues Affecting Political Integration in 1976,' *Canadian Journal of Political Science* 13, No 2 (1980), 347-356 and Herbert G. Kariel and Lynn A. Rosenvall, 'Cultural Affinity Displayed in Canadian Daily Newspapers,' *Journalism Quarterly* 60, No 3 (1983), 431-436.

24 *The Chronicle-Herald*, 6 May 1987.

25 Paul Rutherford, 'The Western Press and Regionalism, 1870-96,' *Canadian Historical Review* 52, No 3 (1971), 303.

26 *Calgary Herald*, 28 April 1987.

27 *The Vancouver Sun*, 11 May 1987.

28 *Calgary Herald*, 1 May and 23 May 1987.

29 *Calgary Herald*, 23 May 1987. The fate of Senate reform was a principle concern in other feature articles and editorial columns in the *Herald*: 2 June, 13 May and 23 May 1987.

30 Ibid., 23 May 1987.

31 Ibid., 31 May, 13 May, 14 May and 1 June; and Winnipeg Free Press, 26 May and 5 June 1987.

32 Winnipeg Free Press, 7 June 1987.

33 Ibid., 4 June 1987.

34 *The Chronicle-Herald*, 1 June 1987.

35 Ibid., 29 April and 19 May 1987.

36 Ibid., 21 May, 23 May, 25 May, 26 May and 29 May 1987.

37 *Winnipeg Free Press*, 2 May, 7 May, 25 May, 26 May, 30 May 1987.

38 Ibid., 7 May 1987.

39 Ibid., 7 May 1987.

40 *The Gazette*, 21 May 1987.

41 Ibid., 2 May and 4 June 1987.

42 *The Globe and Mail*, 30 April 1987.

43 *Calgary Herald*, 26 May 1987.

44 *The Globe and Mail*, 28 April 1987.

45 Ibid., 27 May 1987.

46 Ibid., 7 May 1987.

47 Ibid., 29 April, 2 May, 5 May, 6 May, 7 May, 8 May, 9 May, 12 May and 2 June 1987.

48 Ibid., 5 May 1987.

49 Ibid., 2 June 1987.

50 *The Vancouver Sun*, 15 May 1987; *The Chronicle-Herald*, 28 May 1987; *Winnipeg Free Press* 26 May and 7 June 1987; *Calgary Herald*, 28 May 1987.

51 *The Globe and Mail*, 5 June 1987.

52 *Calgary Herald*, 10 May and 12 May 1987; *The Globe and Mail*, 9 May, 11 May, 12 May, 13 May; *The Chronicle-Herald*, 11 May, 12 May, 15 May, 20 May 1987.

53 *Calgary Herald*, 12 May 1987.

54 *The Chronicle-Herald*, 12 May 1987.

55 *Calgary Herald*, 13 May 1987.

56 *The Gazette*, 13 May 1987.

57 *Winnipeg Free Press*, 14 May 1987.

58 *The Chronicle-Herald*, 6 May 1987.

59 *Calgary Herald*, 27 May 1987; *The Chronicle-Herald*, 16 May 1987.

60 Ibid., 19 May 1987.

61 *The Globe and Mail*, 2 May; *Calgary Herald*, 6 May 1987; *The Gazette*, 30 April, 21 May 1987; *The Vancouver Sun*, 27 May 1987.

62 *Calgary Herald*, 2 May 1987; *The Chronicle-Herald*, 25 May 1987.

63 Ibid., 29 May 1987.

64 *The Globe and Mail*, 28 May 1987.

65 *Winnipeg Free Press,* 4 June 1987.

66 Ibid., 4 June 1987.

67 *The Vancouver Sun,* 28 May 1987.

68 *Calgary Herald,* 28 May 1987.

69 Ibid., 28 May 1987.

70 *The Chronicle-Herald,* 30 May 1987.

71 Ibid., 30 May 1987.

The
Road
Ahead

Canadians were frozen out of the process leading to the Meech Lake Accord. Our voices were never heard. Yet we will be haunted by the ghost of Meech Lake for many years after the Fathers of De-Confederation have passed from the scene. Deborah Coyne.[1]

Canada is already probably the most decentralized federation in the world. The Accord would make it more decentralized still. Canada has already an extraordinarily rigid constitution. The Accord would make it more rigid still. Eugene Forsey.[2]

As a person who makes a living practising constitutional law, I should be elated over the Meech Lake/Langevin Accord. It will provide me with a lifetime of employment because the Accord is infiltrated with ambiguities and platitudes...I am confident that I could effectively argue either side of any legal dispute emanating from the Accord. However, I am not full of adulation because I recognize that the Accord attempts to hold Canada together through a mechanism which will eventually tear the country apart.' Timothy Danson.[3]

THE ROAD AHEAD

The Meech Lake Accord emerged from a constitutional process stretching back to the 1960s. More specifically, it stemmed from the refusal of the Parti Québécois government and National Assembly of Quebec to sign the Constitution Act of 1982. Although the Act became the law of the land nonetheless, Quebec's refusal to sign opened up a wound within the Canadian body politic that Prime Minister Brian Mulroney and Premier Robert Bourassa were determined to close, and it is clear that their objective of bringing Quebec back into the Canadian constitutional family enjoyed broad governmental and public support. This support came from a desire to correct the 'betrayal' of 1981/82,[4] from the electoral ambitions of both federal and provincial political parties in Quebec, and from a near consensus that the Constitution Act would not be fully legitimate until Quebec's signature had been obtained.

Thus it is not surprising that the Meech Lake Accord initially met with a very positive reception. Endorsed by all eleven First Ministers and by the leaders of the two opposition parties in the House of Commons, ratification seemed only a formality. Here it should be stressed, however, that the Accord went beyond addressing the constitutional objectives of Quebec and tidying up loose ends left by the Constitution Act. Once ratified, the Accord would alter not only the constitutional superstructure of the Canadian federal state but also the underlying definition of the Canadian political community upon which that superstructure rests; Quebec would be constitutionally recognized as a distinct society, and outside Quebec provincial divisions within the national political community would receive additional constitutional emphasis. As a consequence the Accord began to attract criticism and controversy across at least four interrelated fronts as two of the premiers who had initially endorsed the Accord went down to electoral defeat before their legislatures had passed the Accord, and as the ratification process became more and more protracted.

The first front was opened up by 'Charter Canadians' — women, linguistic minorities, visible minorities, natives, and ethnic communities, among others — who had been successful in getting their rights embedded in the 1982 Charter of Rights and Freedoms, and who were determined that their rights would not be subordinated by any future constitutional change. For example, Professor Beverley Baines, speaking on behalf of the Canadian Advisory Council on the Status of Women, argued that '. . . the Meech Lake Accord creates a hierarchy of equality rights that puts women's Charter-based equality rights in jeopardy.'[5] Women's organizations and the representatives of many other 'Charter' Canadians, who had emerged in fighting trim from the 1981/82 constitutional negotiations, were simply not prepared to accept such a hierarchy which might subordinate their own rights.

The second front was opened up by an important handful of groups who felt that their interests had not been adequately addressed by the Constitution Act, and who saw the Accord as further compounding their constitutional weakness. Aboriginal organizations, which had just come out of a series of First Ministers' Constitutional Conferences with a heightened political profile but no tangible results, were opposed to the Accord because they had not been at the negotiating table and because the Accord failed to mention much less address Aboriginal constitutional concerns.[6] Residents of the Yukon and Northwest Territories were concerned that the Accord's requirement of unanimous consent for the creation of new provinces would cripple their eventual pursuit of provincehood; they were also angry that Territorians had not been included in the negotiations leading up to the Accord, and that the Accord's provisions for provincial involvement in the appointment of Senators and Supreme Court justices did not incorporate the North.[7] This group of constitutional 'outs' also included many supporters of Senate reform in western Canada who feared that the Accord's provision for ongoing constitutional talks on Senate reform was not sufficient, that the Accord's changes to the amending formula posed a serious obstacle to Senate reform, and that it would be too late to address Senate reform once Quebec's constitutional objectives had already been achieved.

The third front came from those who opposed the provincialist thrust of the Accord, who argued that the Accord would make it very difficult for future federal governments to pursue broad national objectives in social and economic policy. Individuals and groups fighting along this front included those who defended a strong central government on nationalist and/or emotional grounds, including in many cases those who opposed the Free Trade Agreement with the United States. Also involved were groups who defended a strong central government on instrumental grounds, particularly the 'Charter' Canadians discussed above who felt that Ottawa had been largely responsible for the Charter in the first place, and that a strong central government would be essential to the Charter's political defence in the future. It is along this front that we witness much of the commentary on the nature of Canadian society, commentary that will remain of interest to students of national and provincial identities in Canada regardless of the Accord's ultimate fate.

The fourth and clearly interrelated front was opened up by those who opposed the Accord on procedural grounds, who felt that it demonstrated the excesses of an executive federalism system in which eleven men, meeting in private, could reconstruct the country's constitutional foundations. Such critics of the Accord, who have played a prominent role in this collection, offer useful insights into the nature of Canadian executive federalism which again will continue to be of interest regardless of the Accord's ultimate fate.

In late 1987 and early 1988, it was clear that opposition to the Accord along any one front would not be sufficient to overcome the governmental support that the Accord enjoyed. However, as the ratification process moved slowly forward, the opponents of the Accord began to coalesce into a more formidable political coalition. While this coalition lacked any formal leverage on the ratification process, it was given two critically important points of access when Frank McKenna's Liberal government was elected in New Brunswick, and when a minority Progressive Conservative government was elected in Manitoba, with Liberal leader Sharon Carstairs holding the balance of power. Both McKenna and Carstairs have been outspoken critics of the Accord, arguing that it fails to provide adequate protection for women, linguistic minorities and Territorians, and that it offers an insufficient guarantee of Senate reform. Given that neither New Brunswick nor Manitoba have yet ratified the Accord, and that the Accord can be killed by the refusal of either province to do so, the opponents of the Accord had been given a major boost.

As we look ahead in the late spring of 1988, the future of the Accord is very much in doubt. While it may well be ratified, there is now a very real possibility that the Accord may be amended or even that it may be defeated altogether. Indeed, the political situation has become so fluid that we would be foolish to offer any predictions. However, although the outcome of the ratification process is not at all clear, we can speculate with greater confidence on some of the implications likely to flow from ratification or rejection.

If the Accord is eventually ratified, the open sore left when Quebec refused to sign the Constitution Act will be closed, although the scar will remain. At the same time, however, the Accord may be stripped of much of its legitimacy, much of its capacity to bind the country together, by the prolonged attack of women's groups, linguistic minorities, ethnic communities, Territorians, Aboriginals and Senate reformers. Partly as a consequence of the Accord's defenders trying to ward off such attacks by promising future constitutional negotiations, and partly due to the Accord's provisions calling for annual constitutional conferences dealing at least with Senate reform and fisheries, the Accord will open up rather than close down the country's constitutional agenda. Constitutional negotiations will continue across a broad front as groups left out struggle to get in, and as groups already in struggle to protect their position in the hierarchy of constitutional rights. Indeed, one might argue that the Constitution will become an alarmingly politicized document as each year it comes up for review and possible modification. It may be seen less as a stable, enduring statement of rules and values than as an ongoing political arena within which the nature of Canadian society is constantly adjusted.

The Accord's defeat, on the other hand, would be a victory for those Canadians who argue that the Constitution in some important sense belongs to the people, that control over constitutional amendments should not rest exclusively in the hands of the eleven First Ministers. If ratification does not happen, we will have experienced a remarkable situation in which the eleven First Ministers, acting in concert and with the support of opposition parties in the House of Commons, were unable to carry the country. Such a development would throw into question not only the legitimacy of the constitutional amending formula but also its practical utility. However, such a development could also be expected to destabilize, and perhaps radically destabilize, the political environment in Quebec. While many Canadians might rejoice in the Accord's defeat, the issue of Quebec's place within the Canadian society and constitution would still not be resolved. Thus even the defeat of the Accord would not bring the constitutional process to a close, or would do so only at extreme risk to national unity.

The debate on the Meech Lake Accord has proven to be both vigorous and acrimonious. It has also proven to be a very important debate in that it goes well beyond the specifics of the Accord to address the underlying character of the Canadian society. The debate brings into play not only alternative constitutional arrangements but also competing visions of the Canadian society. Regardless of the Accord's ultimate fate, the debate has given Canadians the opportunity to reflect upon the fundamental nature of our country, to discuss our collective past and future. Hopefully this collection will assist that ongoing discussion.

Notes

1 Faculty of Law, University of Toronto. Minutes of Proceedings and Evidence of the Special Joint Committee on the 1987 Constitutional Accord, August 27, 1987, 14:9.

2 Minutes of Proceedings and Evidence of the Special Joint Committee on the 1987 Constitutional Accord, August 4, 1987, 2A:98.

3 Constitutional lawyer. Minutes of Proceedings and Evidence of the Special Joint Committee on the 1987 Constitutional Accord, August 12, 1987, 6A:11.

4 This description of Quebec's formal exclusion from the Constitution Act has been applied by D.V. Smiley, one of Canada's foremost federal scholars. See D.V. Smiley, 'A Dangerous Deed: The Constitution Act, 1982,' in Keith Banting and Richard Simeon, eds., *And No One Cheered: Federalism, Democracy & The Constitution Act*, (Toronto: Methuen 1983), 74-95.

5 Beverley Baines (Faculty of Law, Queen's), 'Women's Equality Rights and the Meech Lake Accord,' a presentation to the Joint House-Senate Hearings on the Meech Lake Accord on behalf of the Canadian Advisory Council on the Status of Women, August 25, 1987 (revised September 4), 47.

6 Donald Ryan, president of the Gitksan-Wet'suwet'en Tribal Council in north-western British Columbia, argued that the provincial appointment of Supreme Court justices called for by the Accord would result in a Court increasingly less sympathetic to Indian legal action against the provinces. *Globe and Mail*, January 5, 1988, p. A1.

7 The March 23, 1988, Throne Speech of the Yukon Government stated that 'as the Meech Lake Accord so clearly showed, we cannot count on other, southern forces to protect our interests. Indeed, we must be prepared for the possibility that our interest may be sacrificed to others.' *Globe and Mail*, March 24, 1988, p. A9.

Appendix

The Constitution Amendment, 1987

Following is the text of the Constitutional Accord approved by the Prime Minister and all provincial Premiers on June 3, 1987, which provided the basis for submitting a resolution to Parliament and the provincial legislatures, seeking approval of the *Constitution Amendment, 1987*.

1987 CONSTITUTIONAL ACCORD

WHEREAS first ministers, assembled in Ottawa, have arrived at a unanimous accord on constitutional amendments that would bring about the full and active participation of Quebec in Canada's constitutional evolution, would recognize the principle of equality of all the provinces, would provide new arrangements to foster greater harmony and cooperation between the Government of Canada and the governments of the provinces and would require that annual first ministers' conferences on the state of the Canadian economy and such other matters as may be appropriate be convened and that annual constitutional conferences composed of first ministers be convened commencing not later than December 31, 1988;

AND WHEREAS first ministers have also reached unanimous agreement on certain additional commitments in relation to some of those amendments;

NOW THEREFORE the Prime Minister of Canada and the first ministers of the provinces commit themselves and the governments they represent to the following:

1. The Prime Minister of Canada will lay or cause to be laid before the Senate and House of Commons, and the first ministers of the provinces will lay or cause to be laid before their legislative assemblies, as soon as possible, a resolution, in the form appended hereto, to authorize a proclamation to be issued by the Governor General under the Great Seal of Canada to amend the Constitution of Canada.

2. The Government of Canada will, as soon as possible, conclude an agreement with the Government of Quebec that would

(a) incorporate the principles of the Cullen-Couture agreement on the selection abroad and in Canada of independent immigrants, visitors for medical treatment, students and temporary workers, and on the selection of refugees abroad and economic criteria for family reunification and assisted relatives,

(b) guarantee that Quebec will receive a number of immigrants, including refugees, within the annual total established by the federal government for all of Canada proportionate to its share of the population of Canada, with the right to exceed that figure by five per cent for demographic reasons, and

(c) provide an undertaking by Canada to withdraw services (except citizenship services) for the reception and integration (including linguistic and cultural) of all foreign nationals wishing to settle in Quebec where services are to be provided by Quebec, with such withdrawal to be accompanied by reasonable compensation,

and the Government of Canada and the Government of Quebec will take the necessary steps to give the agreement the force of law under the proposed amendment relating to such agreements.

3. Nothing in this Accord should be construed as preventing the negotiation of similar agreements with other provinces relating to immigration and the temporary admission of aliens.

4. Until the proposed amendment relating to appointments to the Senate comes into force, any person summoned to fill a vacancy in the Senate shall be chosen from among persons whose names have been submitted by the government of the province to which the vacancy relates and must be acceptable to the Queen's Privy Council for Canada.

MOTION FOR A RESOLUTION TO AUTHORIZE AN AMENDMENT TO THE CONSTITUTION OF CANADA

WHEREAS the *Constitution Act, 1982* came into force on April 17, 1982, following an agreement between Canada and all the provinces except Quebec;

AND WHEREAS the Government of Quebec has established a set of five proposals for constitutional change and has stated that amendments to give effect to those proposals would enable Quebec to resume a full role in the constitutional councils of Canada;

AND WHEREAS the amendment proposed in the schedule hereto sets out the basis on which Quebec's five constitutional proposals may be met;

AND WHEREAS the amendment proposed in the schedule hereto also recognizes the principle of the equality of all the provinces, provides new arrangements to foster greater harmony and cooperation between the Government of Canada and the governments of the provinces and requires that conferences be convened to consider important constitutional, economic and other issues;

AND WHEREAS certain portions of the amendment proposed in the schedule hereto relate to matters referred to in section 41 of the *Constitution Act, 1982*;

AND WHEREAS section 41 of the *Constitution Act, 1982* provides that an amendment to the Constitution of Canada may be made by proclamation issued by the Governor General under the Great Seal of Canada where so authorized by resolutions of the Senate and the House of Commons and of the legislative assembly of each province;

NOW THEREFORE the (Senate) (House of Commons) (legislative assembly) resolves that an amendment to the Constitution of Canada be authorized to be made by proclamation issued by Her Excellency the Governor General under the Great Seal of Canada in accordance with the schedule hereto.

SCHEDULE

CONSTITUTION AMENDMENT, 1987
Constitution Act, 1867

1. The *Constitution Act, 1867* is amended by adding thereto, immediately after section 1 thereof, the following section:

Interpretation

2.(1) The Constitution of Canada shall be interpreted in a manner consistent with
(a) the recognition that the existence of French-speaking Canadians, centred in Quebec but also present elsewhere in Canada, and English-speaking Canadians, concentrated outside Quebec but also present in Quebec, constitutes a fundamental characteristic of Canada; and
(b) the recognition that Quebec constitutes within Canada a distinct society.

Role of Parliament and legislatures

(2) The role of the Parliament of Canada and the provincial legislatures to preserve the fundamental characteristic of Canada referred to in paragraph (1)(a) is affirmed.

Role of legislature and Government of Quebec

(3) The role of the legislature and Government of Quebec to preserve and promote the distinct identity of Quebec referred to in paragraph (1)(b) is affirmed.

Rights of legislatures and governments preserved

(4) Nothing in this section derogates from the powers, rights or privileges of Parliament or the Government of Canada, or of the legislatures or governments of the provinces, including any powers, rights or privileges relating to language.

2. The said Act is further amended by adding thereto, immediately after section 24 thereof, the following section:

Names to be submitted

25.(1) Where a vacancy occurs in the Senate, the government of the province to which the vacancy relates may, in relation to that vacancy, submit to the Queen's Privy Council for Canada the names of persons who may be summoned to the Senate.

Choice of Senators from names submitted

(2) Until an amendment to the Constitution of Canada is made in relation to the Senate pursuant to section 41 of the *Constitution Act, 1982*, the person summoned to fill a vacancy in the Senate shall be chosen from among persons whose names have been submitted under subsection (1) by the government of the province to which the vacancy relates and must be acceptable to the Queen's Privy Council for Canada.

3. The said Act is further amended by adding thereto, immediately after section 94 thereof, the following heading and sections:

Agreements on Immigration and Aliens

Commitment to negotiate

95A. The Government of Canada shall, at the request of the government of any province, negotiate with the government of that province for the purpose of concluding an agreement relating to immigration or the temporary admission of aliens into that province that is appropriate to the needs and circumstances of that province.

Agreements

95B. (1) Any agreement concluded between Canada and a province in relation to immigration or the temporary admission of aliens into that province has the force of law from the time it is declared to do so in accordance with subsection 95C(1) and shall from that time have effect notwithstanding class 25 of section 91 or section 95.

Limitation

(2) An agreement that has the force of law under subsection (1) shall have effect only so long and so far as it is not repugnant to any provision of an Act of the Parliament of Canada that sets national standards and objectives relating to immigration or aliens, including any provision that establishes general classes of immigrants or relates to levels of immigration for Canada or that prescribes classes of individuals who are inadmissible into Canada.

Application of Charter

(3) The *Canadian Charter of Rights and Freedoms* applies in respect of any agreement that has the force of law under subsection (1) and in respect of anything done by the Parliament or Government of Canada, or the legislature or government of a province, pursuant to any such agreement.

Proclamation relating to agreements

95C. (1) A declaration that an agreement referred to in subsection 95B(1) has the force of law may be made by proclamation issued by the Governor General under the Great Seal of Canada only where so authorized by resolutions of the Senate and House of Commons and of the legislative assembly of the province that is a party to the agreement.

Amendment of agreements

(2) An amendment to an agreement referred to in subsection 95B(1) may be made by proclamation issued by the Governor General under the Great Seal of Canada only where so authorized

(a) by resolutions of the Senate and House of Commons and of the legislative assembly of the province that is a party to the agreement; or

(b) in such other manner as is set out in the agreement.

Application of section 46 to 48 of Constitution Act, 1982.

95D. Sections 46 to 48 of the *Constitution Act, 1982* apply, with such modifications as the circumstances require, in respect of any declaration made pursuant to subsection 95C(1), any amendment to an agreement made pursuant to subsection 95C(2) or any amendment made pursuant to section 95E.

Amendments to section 95A to 95D or this section

95E. An amendment to sections 95A to 95D or this section may be made in accordance with the procedure set out in subsection 38(1) of the *Constitution Act, 1982*, but only if the amendment is authorized by resolutions of the legislative assemblies of all the provinces that are, at the time of the amendment, parties to an agreement that has the force of law under subsection 95B(1).

4. The said Act is further amended by adding thereto, immediately preceding section 96 thereof, the following heading:

General

5. The said Act is further amended by adding thereto, immediately preceding section 101 thereof, the following heading:

Courts Established by the Parliament of Canada

6. The said Act is further amended by adding thereto, immediately after section 101 thereof, the following heading and sections:

Supreme Court of Canada

Supreme Court continued

101A.(1) The court existing under the name of the Supreme Court of Canada is hereby continued as the general court of appeal for Canada, and as an additional court for the better administration of the laws of Canada, and shall continue to be a superior court of record.

Constitution of court

(2) The Supreme Court of Canada shall consist of a chief justice to be called the Chief Justice of Canada and eight other judges, who shall be appointed by the Governor General in Council by letters patent under the Great Seal.

Who may be appointed judges

101B(1) Any person may be appointed a judge of the Supreme Court of Canada who, after having been admitted to the bar of any province or territory, has, for a total of at least ten years, been a judge of any court in Canada or a member of the bar of any province or territory.

Three judges from Quebec

(2) At least three judges of the Supreme Court of Canada shall be appointed from among persons who, after having been admitted to the bar of Quebec, have, for a total of at least ten years, been judges of any court of Quebec or of any court established by the Parliament of Canada, or members of the bar of Quebec.

Names may be submitted

101C.(1) Where a vacancy occurs in the Supreme Court of Canada, the government of each province may, in relation to that vacancy, submit to the Minister of Justice of Canada the names of any of the persons who have been admitted to the bar of that province and are qualified under section 101B for appointment to that court.

Appointment from names submitted

(2) Where an appointment is made to the Supreme Court of Canada, the Governor General in Council shall, except where the Chief Justice is appointed from among members of the Court, appoint a person whose name has been submitted under subsection (1) and who is acceptable to the Queen's Privy Council for Canada.

Appointment from Quebec

(3) Where an appointment is made in accordance with subsection (2) of any of the three judges necessary to meet the requirement set out in subsection 101B(2), the Governor General in Council shall appoint a person whose name has been submitted by the Government of Quebec.

Appointment from other provinces

(4) Where an appointment is made in accordance with subsection (2) otherwise than as required under subsection (3), the Governor General in Council shall appoint a person whose name has been submitted by the government of a province other than Quebec.

Tenure, salaries, etc., of judges

101D. Sections 99 and 100 apply in respect of the judges of the Supreme Court of Canada.

Relationship to section 101

101E.(1) Sections 101A to 101D shall not be construed as abrogating or derogating from the powers of the Parliament of Canada to make laws under section 101 except to the extent that such laws are inconsistent with those sections.

References to the Supreme Court of Canada

(2) For greater certainty, section 101A shall not be construed as abrogating or derogating from the powers of the Parliament of Canada to make laws relating to the reference of questions of law or fact, or any other matters, to the Supreme Court of Canada.

7. The said Act is further amended by adding thereto, immediately after section 106 thereof, the following section:

Shared-cost program

106A.(1) The Government of Canada shall provide reasonable compensation to the government of a province that chooses not to participate in a national shared-cost program that is established by the Government of Canada after the coming into force of this section in an area of exclusive provincial jurisdiction, if the province carries on a program or initiative that is compatible with the national objectives.

Legislative power
not extended

(2) Nothing in this section extends the legislative powers of the Parliament of Canada or of the legislatures of the provinces.

8. The said Act is further amended by adding thereto the following heading and sections:

XII-CONFERENCES ON THE ECONOMY AND OTHER MATTERS

Conferences on the
economy and other
matters

148. A conference composed of the Prime Minister of Canada and the first ministers of the provinces shall be convened by the Prime Minister of Canada at least once each year to discuss the state of the Canadian economy and such other matters as may be appropriate.

XIII-REFERENCES

Reference includes
amendments

149. A reference to this Act shall be deemed to include a reference to any amendments thereto.

Constitution Act, 1982

9. Sections 40 to 42 of the Constitution Act, 1982 are repealed and the following substituted therefor:

Compensation

40. Where an amendment is made under subsection 38(1) that transfers legislative powers from provincial legislatures to Parliament, Canada shall provide reasonable compensation to any province to which the amendment does not apply.

Amendment by
unanimous consent

41. An amendment to the Constitution of Canada in relation to the following matters may be made by proclamation issued by the Governor General under the Great

Seal of Canada only where authorized by resolutions of the Senate and House of Commons and of the legislative assembly of each province:
(a) the office of the Queen, the Governor General and the Lieutenant Governor of a province;
(b) the powers of the Senate and the method of selecting Senators;
(c) the number of members by which a province is entitled to be represented in the Senate and the residence qualifications of Senators;
(d) the right of a province to a number of members in the House of Commons not less than the number of Senators by which the province was entitled to be represented on April 17, 1982;
(e) the principle of proportionate representation of the provinces in the House of Commons prescribed by the Constitution of Canada;
(f) subject to section 43, the use of the English or the French language;
(g) the Supreme Court of Canada;
(h) the extension of existing provinces into the territories;
(i) notwithstanding any other law or practice, the establishment of new provinces; and
(j) an amendment to this Part.

10. Section 44 of the said Act is repealed and the following substituted therefor;

Amendments by Parliament

44. Subject to section 41, Parliament may exclusively make laws amending the Constitution of Canada in relation to the executive government of Canada or the Senate and House of Commons.

11. Subsection 46(1) of the said Act is repealed and the following substituted therefor:

Initiation of amendment procedures

46.(1) The procedures for amendment under sections 38, 41 and 43 may be initiated either by the Senate or the House of Commons or by the legislative assembly of a province.

12. Subsection 47(1) of the said Act is repealed and the following substituted therefor:

Amendments without Senate resolution

47.(1) An amendment to the Constitution of Canada made by proclamation under section 38, 41 or 43 may be made without a resolution of the Senate authorizing the issue of the proclamation if, within one hundred and eighty days after the adoption by the House of Commons of a resolution authorizing its issue, the Senate has not adopted such a resolution and if, at any time after the expiration of that period, the House of Commons again adopts the resolution.

13. Part VI of the said Act is repealed and the following substituted therefor:

PART VI
CONSTITUTIONAL CONFERENCES

Constitutional
conference

50.(1) A constitutional conference composed of the Prime Minister of Canada and the first ministers of the provinces shall be convened by the Prime Minister of Canada at least once each year, commencing in 1988.

Agenda

(2) The conferences convened under subsection (1) shall have included on their agenda the following matters:
(a)Senate reform, including the role and functions of the Senate, its powers, the method of selecting Senators and representation in the Senate;
(b)roles and responsibilities in relation to fisheries; and
(c)such other matters as are agreed upon.

14. Subsection 52(2) of the said Act is amended by striking out the word 'and' at the end of paragraph (b) thereof, by adding the word 'and' at the end of paragraph (c) thereof and by adding thereto the following paragraph:
(d) any other amendment to the Constitution of Canada.

15.Section 61 of the said Act is repealed and the following substituted therefor:

References

61. A reference to the *Constitution Act 1982*, or a reference to the *Constitution Acts 1867 to 1982*, shall be deemed to include a reference to any amendments thereto.

General

16. Nothing in section 2 of the *Constitution Act, 1867* affects section 25 or 27 of the *Canadian Charter of Rights and Freedoms*, section 35 of the *Constitution Act, 1982* or class 24 of section 91 of the *Constitution Act, 1867*.

CITATION

Citation

17. This amendment may be cited as the *Constitution Amendment, 1987*.

Biographies of Contributors

ELLY ALBOIM is Ottawa Bureau Chief for CBC Television News. Educated at McGill and Columbia School of Journalism, he has covered all of the major national political stories for the past decade. Mr. Alboim teaches broadcasting at Carleton and Concordia Universities.

DOREEN BARRIE is a Political Science Ph.D. student at the University of Calgary, working on comparisons between the Australian and Canadian federal states.

DAVID BERCUSON is Professor of History at the University of Calgary. He has appeared widely in academic and popular publications and has written books in fields as diverse as Western Canadian regionalism and the history of the Arab-Israeli conflict.

MALCOLM BROWN is Professor of Economics at the University of Calgary. Educated at Dalhousie, Queen's and Cornell, he has published a number of important monographs on fiscal federalism.

KAREN TAYLOR-BROWNE is a native Albertan who was educated at the Universities of Grenoble, Ottawa and Reading. She has taught at the University of Calgary and is currently completing her doctorate in linguistics.

ALAN CAIRNS is Professor of Political Science at the University of British Columbia and was Research Director for the Macdonald Royal Commission on the Economic Union and Development Prospects for Canada. A past President of the Canadian Political Science Association, Professor Cairns is the author of a number of seminal works in Canadian political science.

DAVID ELTON is President of the Canada West Foundation and Professor of Political Science at the University of Lethbridge. He is a leading authority on constitutional politics.

GEORGES ERASMUS has been the National Chief of the Assembly of First Nations since 1985. A Dene leader who was actively involved in the Mackenzie Valley Pipeline Inquiry, he was the AFN Spokesperson at the First Ministers' Conferences on Aboriginal Rights throughout the 1980s.

LORRY FELSKE teaches Canadian Studies at the University of Calgary. Trained in history at the University of Toronto, his special interest is the development of the Crowsnest Pass region in Alberta.

GERALD FRIESEN is Professor of History at St. Paul's College, University of Manitoba. He specializes in Canadian prairie and cultural history and is the author of the award winning *The Canadian Prairies: A History* (1984). He has also served as an advisor to the former NDP government in Manitoba.

ROGER GIBBINS is Professor and Head of the Political Science Department at the University of Calgary. He is the author of *Prairie Politics and Society, Regionalism* and *Conflict and Unity: An Introduction to Canadian Political Life*.

WILLIAM F. GOLD is a columnist for the *Calgary Herald*, and former Editor of the *Herald*. He has worked as a journalist all across Canada for the past thirty years.

OREST KRUHLAK teaches political science at the University of British Columbia. He has worked in the office of the Commissioner of Official languages, was Director of the multiculturalism program and Regional Director of the Pacific region for the Department of the Secretary of State.

GUY LAFOREST was educated at Laval and McGill Universities, was a postdoctoral fellow at the University of Calgary, and is currently teaching political science at Laval University. A political philosopher, he has done extensive research on developments in Quebec and French-Canadian intellectual history.

KATHLEEN MAHONEY is an Associate Professor of Law at the University of Calgary. Educated at the University of British Columbia, Cambridge and Strasbourg, she was called to the British Columbia Bar in 1977. She has published widely in journals and books, and is the author (with Sheilah Martin) of a book entitled *Equality and Judicial Neutrality*.

PETER McCORMICK is Professor of Political Science at the University of Lethbridge. He has written extensively on Senate reform and judicial politics, and has been one of the principal advocates of constitutional reform in Western Canada.

HOWARD PALMER is Professor of History at the University of Calgary. He is a former Research Director of the Multiculturalism program, Department of the Secretary of State and editor of *Canadian Ethnic Studies*. He has written several books on Canadian ethnicity and immigration and Alberta history, the most recent being *Peoples of Alberta* (with Tamara Palmer).

ANTHONY PAREL is a Professor of Political Science at the University of Calgary. Educated at Harvard, he has published extensively in political philosophy. He is President of the Humanities Association of Canada and Chairman, Conference for the Study of Political Thought.

CLAUDE ROCAN is Intergovernmental Affairs Officer with the Government of Saskatchewan. He holds a Ph.D. in Political Science from York University, and between 1978 and 1984 he was the co-ordinator of the Louis Riel Project.

DAVID TARAS is Director of the Canadian Studies programme at the University of Calgary. A former Ontario Legislative Intern, he was Associate Research Director of the Canadian Institute of International Affairs. He is editor (with Leslie Pal) of *Prime Ministers and Premiers,* published by Prentice-Hall in 1988 and several other works.

DALE THOMSON is Professor of Political Science at McGill University. He is the biographer of Alexander Mackenzie, Louis St. Laurent and most recently of Jean Lesage. He was Secretary to Prime Minister Louis St. Laurent from 1953 to 1958.

THE RT. HON. PIERRE ELLIOTT TRUDEAU served as Prime Minister of Canada from the spring of 1968 to the spring of 1984, with the exception of nine months in 1979/80.